The Inventive Mind
in Science

The Inventive Mind in Science

Creative Thinking Activities

Christine Ebert

Edward S. Ebert II

Illustrated by Patty Mathews

1998
Teacher Ideas Press
A Division of
Libraries Unlimited, Inc.
Englewood, Colorado

TEACHER IDEAS PRESS
A Division of
Libraries Unlimited, Inc.
P.O. Box 6633
Englewood, CO 80155-6633
1-800-237-6124
www.lu.com/tip

Production Editor: Kevin W. Perizzolo
Copy Editor: Curtis D. Holmes
Proofreader: Susie Sigman
Typesetter: Kay Minnis

Library of Congress Cataloging-in-Publication Data

Ebert, Christine, 1946-
    The inventive mind in science : creative thinking activities /
Christine Ebert, Edward S. Ebert II ; illustrated by Patty Mathews.
    xii, 241 p. 22x28 cm.
    Includes bibliographical references and index.
    ISBN 1-56308-387-6
    1. Science--Study and teaching--United States. 2. Creative
thinking--Study and teaching--United States. 3. Inventions--United
States. 4. Interdisciplinary approach in education--United States.
I. Ebert, Edward S., 1953-   II. Title.
LB1585.3,E24   1998
370.15'2--dc21   97-43554
                                                           CIP

Contents

PART III

Taking Inventing Activities Across the Disciplines

Preface

Within the framework of a general model of information processing, creative thinking can be thought of as a central part of cognitive processing. Rather than being the talent of a gifted few, creative thinking is an attribute of *everyone's* cognitive processing. The authors define that attribute as a search for patterns, perspectives, and relationships between a stimulus and what an individual already knows. The educational implication is that creative thinking is a *natural ability*, which can be fostered by instructional experiences. Inventing provides an appropriate experience for fostering creative problem-solving ability because of its concrete, manipulative nature. Especially when combined with the science curriculum, opportunities exist for merging academic content with meaningful creative-thinking activity.

The Inventive Mind in Science: Creative Thinking Activities is organized into three parts. Part I emphasizes the theoretical background of the creative thinking concept. We discuss the relationship between creative thinking, problem solving, science, and technology. Part II focuses on three levels of inventing, with each focusing on different educational objectives. Part III discusses the integration of science-based inventing activities with other subject areas. Chapter Seven examines the stepwise development of technology in terms of a Janus perspective. Chapter Nine refers to the patenting process, including its social context, and how to set up a classroom version of that process.

We have several target audiences for this book. The emphasis on creative thinking and its classroom application is appropriate for **staff development** programs. The application to the science curriculum makes the book valuable to **elementary and middle school teachers of science**. Since the book is not dependent on a particular curriculum, it would also fit very well with the experiences that **programs for the gifted and talented** seek to provide. The range of inventing activities and extension activities makes these materials suitable for **teachers who wish to integrate the various subject areas** under a common theme. And finally, the theoretical background and activities designed along a constructivist philosophy make this book a valuable resource for **preservice teacher education programs**.

Introduction

We are surrounded; they are everywhere. In fact, we are virtually inundated with them. Take a look around, inventions are all over the place! Inventing, whether products or ideas, represents human capability at its best. The creative aspect of our thinking underlies science, problem solving, and technological progress. There is nothing secret here; it is not reserved for people with some special talent. We are *all* creative thinkers. With this book you and your students can develop and enhance creative abilities, become a part of the exciting and creative world of inventing in the classroom, and use a creative problem-solving theme to teach across the curricula.

By and large, the grade school maxim has been that there are two ways new things come into being: invention or discovery. Everything falls into one of these categories. For the most part, that is about as far as it goes. Sometimes examples of roles in the process might be suggested, for instance that scientists and explorers deal with discoveries, while engineers invent. Actually, the connection between discovery and invention is much closer than the traditional example suggests. It is possible to suggest an explanation of how we think, that does not separate the processes of discovering or searching and inventing. These processes are the way that people, your students as well, *naturally* go about the business of thinking.

Discovery and invention are not the particular jobs of certain occupations. In fact, Paul Winchell, the famous puppeteer, holds one of the first patents issued for an artificial heart. Do we consider him a scientist, an inventor, or a puppeteer? Thomas Edison, a person widely associated with the term inventor, created much of the technology that facilitated the use of his inventions as well. Should he be classified as a scientist or engineer? More to the point, there might be an attribute of our thinking ability that is common to all of the activities and roles mentioned. That common attribute is creative thinking.

Science curricula provide the classroom teacher at any grade level with an excellent opportunity to teach content and develop creative problem-solving ability through discovery and invention. While discovery *is* the activity in which scientists are engaged, inventing is also a logical, if not natural, extension of scientific investigation. The inventive process makes any discovery valuable in a practical sense. And practical value is the foundry in which progress is forged.

Linking investigative and inventive approaches in education allows students to apply their practical knowledge in an inventive way to solve problems. Nearly sixty years ago, John Dewey offered educators the idea that *genuine thinking* begins with a problematic situation, and that creative intelligence is fostered *by solving authentic problems.*

This book provides guidelines for integrating the investigative and inventing approaches within science and across the disciplines. Inventing provides students with real problems to solve. They can *see* and *feel* an answer, a product, take shape while being absorbed in the process of applying their knowledge to solve problems.

Here are some of the topics that you will encounter: a) creative and inventive thinking as they relate to cognitive processing, b) classroom activities to aid the development of creative and inventive thinking, c) inventing in the science curriculum, d) three levels of inventing, e) instructional units devoted to inventing and units that integrate the curricula, and f) the use of invention festivals as an alternative, or adjunct to the traditional science fair.

Think of *The Inventive Mind in Science: Creative Thinking Activities* as a *development book* that addresses creative thinking in theory and practice. Let's create!

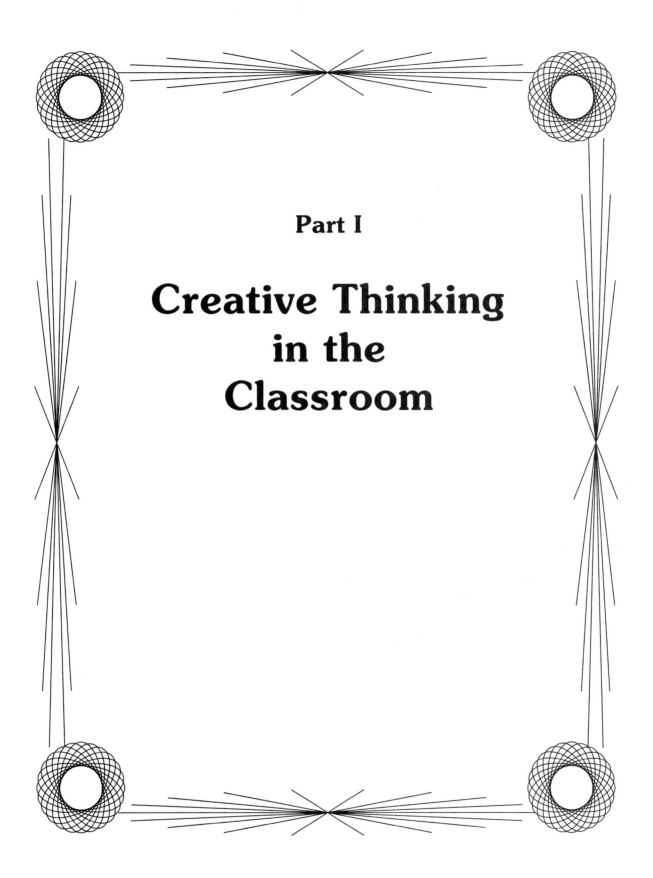

Part I

Creative Thinking in the Classroom

Chapter One

The Creative Person Lurking Within

In this chapter you will find:

>*That we are all creative thinkers;*
>
>*A model that explains how creative thinking is part of our thinking process;*
>
>*The relationship between creative thinking, problem solving, and inventing, and the Inventor's Journal!*

Don't touch that dial! As is the case with many teachers, time is limited. So you might be tempted to skip over this section on creative thinking and go straight to the classroom activities of Part II. You may even have skipped the Introduction! Consider this first. Suppose you were on a field trip to the old quarry with your sixth-grade class and one of the students fell and broke his leg. Another student says "I can set the leg, I learned how when I got my First Aid Certificate!" Having no other options you let her proceed. Chances are that when you get back to civilization you'll still take the injured student to a physician. Why? Because the physician understands more about how to set a broken bone. She knows what other factors enter in to treating such an injury. She understands the how and why of medical care. We call such an understanding, *knowledge*, as opposed to simple *information*. And at our best, knowledge is what we use to guide our endeavors. So let's enter this adventure from the beginning. Let's explore the potential of the creative person lurking within, and then use that knowledge to help develop similar abilities in our students!

We Are All Creative Thinkers

Are you a creative thinker? Many teachers are, of course. Yet most people do not consider themselves to be creative. Or at best, they might admit that they can be creative when they have to be. Other than that, creative thinking is what artists do. It is not something that one uses in everyday life, at least not in adult life. After all, children are creative, right? And they do use their creativity in everyday life. However, as they grow older they tend to lose that creative orientation.

Does it seem strange to you that the wide-eyed, imaginative thinking of childhood is something that we outgrow? Can you think of a time when you came up with a new idea, or imagined a dream vacation? Was it an enjoyable experience? Why should this be the province of children and a few artists? As we grow older and think those deep thoughts that older people think why shouldn't we simply change *what* we think about rather than the *way* we think?

Perhaps the way we think does not change as we grow older. Rather, we simply inhibit the use of our natural cognitive ability. It would seem that rather than "growing out" of our creative habits, we subjugate them to a more efficient way of dealing with our daily conventions. We don't lose our creativity, we simply don't use it.

We limit our potential by limiting our thinking. For example, if at birth we were to shackle the ankles of children to limit the length of steps they could take, their ability to walk would be inhibited by retarding their physical development. The muscles and tendons would still be there, but they would not have developed to their

THE DOCTOR SAID IF I HAD THE WHEEL HE'D PLASTER IT IN!

potential. The same is true of thinking. Inhibiting our ability to think creatively doesn't remove our creative potential, but it does retard its development. Yet, our creative ability must serve some useful purpose. Let's consider the thinking of children and adults.

Play-Dough to Plato

Suppose it's the first day of school and you walk into your classroom ready to greet new students. There they are, sitting at their desks eager for the adventure of school to begin. You scan the front row, and notice the name tags that moms have pinned to their children's clothing. There's little Plato, young Marie Curie, a fidgety Socrates, Albert Einstein, and so on. You feel just a bit intimidated. After all, these are to become some of the greatest minds the world has known. What can *you* tell *them*?

The point is, even the world's greatest thinkers were once children. How do you suppose the world's most profound thinkers, past and present, differ from the children that actually will come to your classroom? Granted as adults, da Vinci, Augustine, Marx, and Edison (to name just a few) spent considerable time deliberating on matters much too sophisticated for children, but did their thinking *processes* differ from others? Were they somehow able to understand because they possessed a special ability? Might it be the case that some people use the same talents that we all possess, but to a greater degree?

Let's settle on Plato for just awhile. As the distinguished philosopher and teacher engaged his students in conversation, it must have been necessary for him to perceive what went on around him. That is, he must have heard what people said, sensed the world of which he was a part, observed the environment in which he lived. And from these perceptions he found patterns and relationships. He found recurring concepts which he could use to bring order and understanding to his experiences. He combined these patterns

in ways that would explain what he observed. He may also have used these patterns and relationships to explain why things happened as they did, and then used that understanding to philosophize about how societies might best accomplish the purpose of life. He deliberated carefully over whether his explanations constituted suitable accounts, and ultimately expressed his ideas in his writings, as well as his teachings. He thought carefully, deeply, critically, and creatively.

Does this differ in terms of *process* from what children do? Let's consider how the child who sits with a lump of modeling clay in his or her hands processes information regarding the clay. The child sees color, feels texture, smells aroma, and is aware that the clay is malleable. The youngster bends and twists and squeezes the clay, and is aware of his or her ability to exert an influence on its shape. The child finds patterns and relationships between the attributes of the clay and the ability to manipulate the clay. With tiny fingers it is molded into some pattern that springs from the child's mind—perhaps a ball, a pancake, or a crude representation of a person. As the pattern emerges, the youngster constantly evaluates it. Does it meet the criteria for representing his or her own idea of a ball, a pancake, or a person?

The child has perceived, identified relationships, determined what could be done with the clay, and ultimately transformed an idea into a physical, though perhaps rudimentary, clay reality. If it satisfies the child, it is perhaps presented to a teacher or parent. Otherwise, in a moment, it is likely squashed back into a lump. Yet in terms of cognitive processing, it can be seen that the processes of thinking demonstrated by the child and Plato differ only in terms of the extent of knowledge possessed by the individual, the amount of practice manipulating perceptions and prior experience to resolve a problem, and the ability to translate ideas into communicable realities. These, however, are only differences in the degree of sophistication between the thinking of children and adults.

It could even be argued that the thinking of children is just as sophisticated as that of adults in that each works with the available knowledge base born of experience. In either case the cognitive *process* employed by the child and the adult does not differ. And that is good news for all age groups!

Children too, observe the world around them. Actually, they are very intent observers from the moment of birth (and perhaps even before birth). The children entering your classroom have spent years making observations and forming explanations of the world around them. And this is not an activity that mom or dad had to teach them. Observing by means of the five senses, identifying patterns and relationships, and inventing (that is, combining discrete pieces of information to form new understanding), are the natural processes of the brain. The child working with modeling clay and the philosopher pondering the ultimate Good are invoking the same thinking processes while dealing with different levels of sophistication and degrees of abstraction. Plato too, you know, started out as a child.

The Psychology of Creative Thinking

The Cognitive Spiral Model

In terms of cognitive processing, the events described above can be expressed by a model consisting of five discrete components, or modes of thought. The five modes are: Perceptual Thought, Creative Thought, Inventive Thought, Metacognitive Thought, and Performance Thought. We refer to this model of how people think as the Cognitive Spiral Model (Ebert, 1994). Try to conceptualize these five types of thought in a model that looks like a loosely coiled ribbon as shown on the next page.

Picture these five modes of thought as occurring in sequence along a spiralling path. The same five components recur over and again, but never return to the exact spot from

which they began: a spiral, not a circle. According to this model, processing always occurs with the five modes of thought in the same sequence.

Perceptual Thought

For any matter that Plato may have considered, there had to be some sort of stimulus. Perhaps it was witnessing the inequities of Athenian government, or the difficult ethical questions of a trial, or stepping on a sharp pebble, but nonetheless, something visual, auditory, tactile, aromatic, or even cognitive (that is, an idea simply coming to mind) must initiate the processing. With physical stimuli, it must be translated into the neurological language of the brain (a cognitive perception, that is, ideas, are already in the neurological language of the brain). In terms of the Cognitive Spiral Model, the detection of stimuli and translation into neuro-chemical impulses is referred to as Perceptual Thought.

Creative Thought

Next in the sequence is Creative Thought. This is an exciting step in our thinking and may well be what makes humans unique in terms of our cognitive abilities. The Cognitive Spiral Model of cognitive processing includes creative thinking as an *integral* and *necessary* component of all problem solving, performance yielding thought. In this context, creative thinking is defined as the cognitive search for patterns, relationships, and perspectives between a perception and the knowledge base possessed by the individual. That means when we think creatively we are searching for patterns and relationships. We look for different perspectives. We see the multiple shades of green when looking at a forest; we recognize that birds keep coming to the feeder if we put out a certain type of seed; we look for the multiple possibilities. The job of creative thinking is to entertain all that might be.

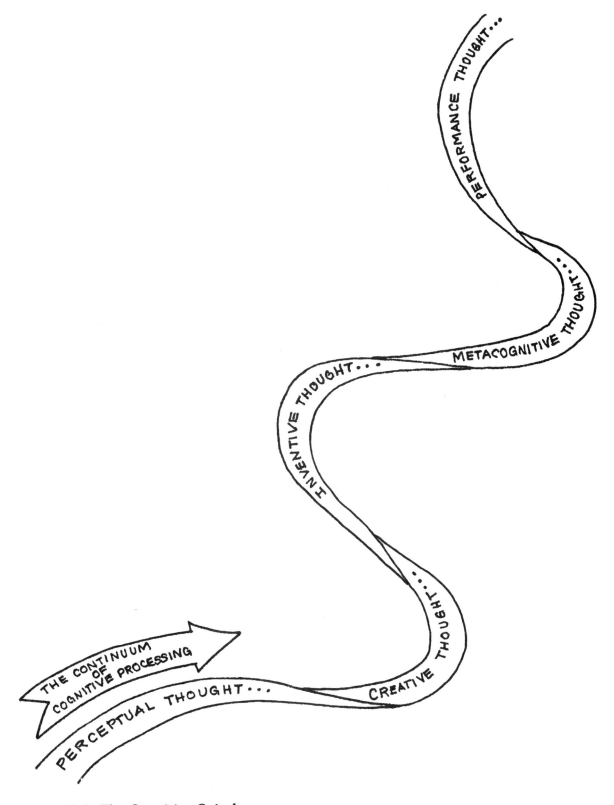

Figure 1.1. The Cognitive Spiral.

This creative component is precisely what traditional education often ignores, and even inhibits, in favor of a focus on particular facts and skills that can be easily tested. Yet creative ability is responsible for new solutions to new problems, development of inventions, and in essence, for progress. Even so, each student comes to the classroom equipped to engage in this type of thinking. It is creative thinking that DeVito (1989) suggests may be "the missing link in the learning hierarchy."

So what goes on in this creative thinking mode? The mind takes the perception and looks for patterns and relationships that match up with what the individual already knows. Long-term memory is searched for prior experiences that are similar to the new experience. Mednick (1962) discusses it in terms of making a list. At the top of the list is the strongest association between the stimulus and prior experience. The list then continues with associations of decreasing strength. For instance, suppose a bell sounds in the house. The sound is perceived, and in creative thought it is determined that it could be the telephone (strongest association), or it could be an alarm clock (less likely but still a possibility), or it could be a news flash on the radio (starting to get a bit far-fetched, but not outside the realm of reason). Notice that a judgment is not being made as to the actual identity of the stimulus; we'll discuss that in subsequent steps of the spiral. Of key importance is that the mind does not have to be trained to do this, it is what the mind does.

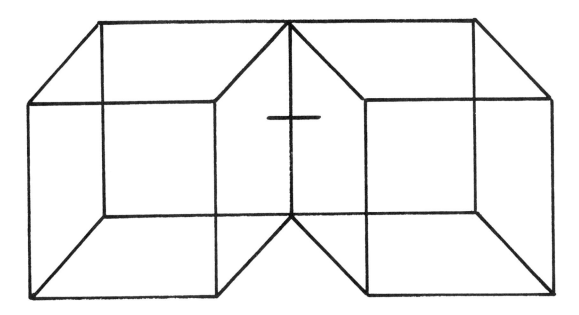

Figure 1.2. The Necker Cube.

Saying that the mind naturally searches for patterns, relationships, and perspectives is one thing. Believing it is another. Let's demonstrate. Take a look at Figure 1.2 above. Focus your eyes on the crossbar in the middle of the drawing and then relax. Continue looking at the figure.

What happened to your perception of the figure as you watched the crossbar? Did the orientation of the figure seem to change? For many people, the figure will appear to shift as they focus on the center. Why is that? We would suggest that it is the brain, in its creative thinking mode, searching for another perspective. You did not have to instruct yourself to find another perspective. *Given the opportunity*, it is what the brain does. Remember, the creative mode of thought does not make judgments about what it finds. Evaluation is the task of Metacognitive Thought. And so, having found one possible match between the stimulus and what you already know, the brain is quite happy to look for more possibilities. Unfortunately, our tendency is to settle for that first association nearly every time. Think of all the possibilities that pass us by!

Here's a second example. A popular art form these days are stereograms, 3-D pictures based on the work in the 1960s of Dr. Bella Julesz (*Magic Eye*, 1994). Also called random-dot drawings, at first glance there does not appear to be an image present, just a bunch of dots. However, give your mind a chance and, amazingly, a pattern emerges from the dots. Figure 1.3, page 10, is one example. Can you read what it says? (*Invent*)

As you might expect, the directions for finding the image are to *relax*, try to focus on a point beyond the picture (for some it works best to cross their eyes and try to focus on a point in front of the picture), and *not* to look for certain patterns or images. The creative aspect of your thinking will naturally look for patterns. We simply need to provide the opportunity to look.

R

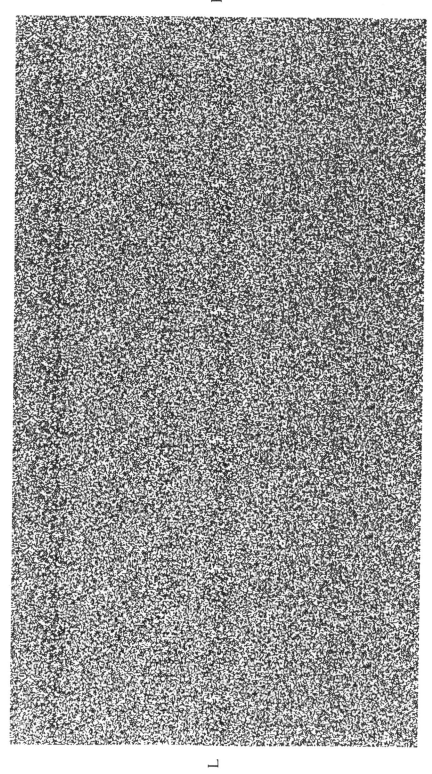

Top

L

Figure 1.3. Our Own Stereogram.

The philosopher Alfred North Whitehead (1967) suggests that reality is the *process* through which we grasp aspects of the pattern of the universe. In other words, our experiences are pieces of a greater pattern. Slowly we combine those bits and pieces of the pattern to extend our understanding of the world and universe around us. From a philosophical perspective, if the universe has a pattern and we are a part of the universe, is it any wonder that our brain naturally seeks patterns, relationships, and perspectives?

So what makes one person more "creative" than another? Perhaps it is simply a matter of how many items on the list one is willing to entertain. Society is very complex and we do not always have the luxury of considering the many possibilities that creative thinking may generate. In fact, most educational institutions very methodically train students to develop one strong association at the top of the list and not bother with other possibilities. Timed tests, multiple choice, fill in the blank, and even the improper use of questioning tend to narrow creative thinking. Students become the repositories of factual information.

There may have been a time when it was necessary for an individual to memorize tremendous amounts of information. Raconteurs and elders were once the primary sources for disseminating the lore of the community to the younger generation. Teachers, of course, increasingly came to share this responsibility, particularly before written materials became so widely available to students. In the information age, however, that requirement has lost much of its importance. And in the *age of problem solving*, information will be the tool, not the product.

Solving problems is not a matter of knowing information, but rather a matter of combining information. Inventions, theoretical advancements, and ideas do not come from the strongest and most time efficient associations, but from looking at the whole list and considering different perspectives. As a teacher, you can help foster a child's ability to see other possibilities without forsaking subject content.

Inventive Thought

As was mentioned previously, creative thinking does not make judgments about patterns, it just identifies possibilities. Therefore, there must be more to cognitive processing than perceptual and creative thought. Following Creative Thought is Inventive Thought. Think of creative thinking as providing the materials with which to work, and inventive thinking as the attempt to build something with those materials. It is during Inventive Thought that the information is assembled into some kind of product.

We refer to this combining of information in a new way as inventing, since it is *always* a unique experience. One might suggest that many things, such as the ringing of the phone mentioned earlier, are so familiar that when the stimulus of the sound is combined with prior experience of that sound, it is not something new. What must be considered is that the brain detects a stimulus, not a ringing phone. That stimulus must be translated into neuro-chemical impulses and subsequently be analyzed. If that stimulus has a strong association with the ringing of the phone, the association is now even stronger than before, and is therefore different (by being stronger) than it ever was before. Of course, if it turns out that the stimulus actually represented a news flash coming on the radio, the association with the telephone will lose a bit of its strength and thus still be different the next time a similar stimulus is encountered. These distinctions may seem subtle, but then the particular example is designed around a very familiar experience.

Suppose instead that you were in a foreign country and were unable to understand the language. Suddenly someone jumps up in a restaurant and starts yelling, people start screaming and racing for the doors. Is there a fire? Is the food poisoned? Did new menu prices suddenly go into effect?

You would probably consider quite a few possibilities as you try to make sense of what is happening and determine what to do. In familiar situations we tend to consider and accept only one association for the sake of efficiency, not because it is the only possibility.

Metacognitive Thought

From Inventive Thought the individual has a possible solution to the problem at hand. Everything to this point may have happened in fractions of seconds and as Costa (1985) suggests, at an unconscious level. It is likely that at this point cognitive processing begins to become a conscious activity, and now Metacognitive Thought takes over.

Metacognition has been discussed a lot the past few years, and is loosely defined as "thinking about thinking." In the Cognitive Spiral Model, it is more precisely defined as the evaluative aspect of cognitive processing. The product assembled in Inventive Thought is analyzed against whatever internal or external criteria may have been assigned to the problem. The question is: Does this cognitive product solve the problem? Metacognitive Thought represents the imposition of criteria. Unlike the divergent nature of creative thought, the process now becomes one of converging on one particular response. This sort of exercise characterizes what often occurs in the classroom and is popularly referred to as critical thinking. Computations in mathematics provide an excellent example of problems that are heavily criteria laden, and designed to allow only one acceptable answer. Metacognitive Thought makes the critical decision of whether or not our cognitive invention does the trick. That decision will affect what happens in the next stage.

Performance Thought

Having evaluated the product, Performance Thought is where the results of cognitive processing find their expression. If the solution was deemed acceptable, the processes of Performance Thought may store it away in memory or cause it to be translated and expressed in a variety of means, for instance spoken or written. If the product was not an acceptable solution, processing starts again. Notice how the process spirals rather than cycles because now there is some additional information telling us that the first solution was not acceptable. We have not returned to the beginning, but rather found a new starting point. If you can think of a time when you kept going back to the same answer even though you knew that it would not work, then you can appreciate the advantage of a thinking spiral rather than a thinking cycle. Why you kept going back to the same answer is a topic for Chapter Two.

And that's it! Five discrete steps in a spiralling continuum of cognitive processing. How often do people go through this spiral? Likely it is not only impossible to say, but impossible to count. And it is conceivable in view of the phenomenal sophistication of the human brain that many spirals occur simultaneously. For teachers, the responsibility is clearly to foster the development of *each* of these modes of thought, rather than provide activities over the course of twelve or more years which inhibit any part of the process. Of course, it is the intent of this book to help you meet this challenge. For now, here's a quick list of the five modes of thinking along with a general educational objective for each.

Perceptual Thought

- *Provide opportunities to make observations and to avoid the tendency to "look past" familiar situations.*

Creative Thought

- *Provide nonjudgmental opportunities to seek out different perspectives, to find patterns, to recognize relationships.*

Inventive Thought

- *Allow opportunities to combine information in new ways by providing tasks which allow for more than one acceptable answer.*

Metacognitive Thought

- *Apply criteria in order to evaluate answers rather than to limit thinking that leads to answers.*

Performance Thought

- *Provide students the opportunity to express their solutions in ways which value thinking.*

Creative Thinking as an Intrinsically Rewarding Experience

It is still the case, however, that some people demonstrate remarkable talents. Einstein, Curie, Edison, and many others were extraordinary individuals, and we cannot simply ignore sophisticated abilities, whether those talents are intellectual, musical, and so on. But neither do we have reason to assume that these were, or are, super-human individuals with powers far beyond those of mortal men, so to speak. After all, it has been nearly 2,500 years since Plato lived and still there is no country established according to his plan in *The Republic*; Socrates was put to death by the Athenians; and Albert Einstein routinely had difficulties with school. There is an obvious, though perplexing, incongruity here that bears further consideration.

Could it be that the drive to see things in new ways, to combine what is known with what could be was so *intrinsically* rewarding that Socrates chose to accept death rather than quietly run away when those who condemned him to die were willing to look the other way? Would Edison have considered the first 500 attempts to construct a lightbulb filament failures, or as steps leading to the solution? We tolerate these traits in a few

people, usually referring to them as "gifted," but it may be the case that they are merely demonstrating an ability that we all possess. Perhaps such people show the rest of us what we are capable of. Perhaps it is a matter of intrinsic motivation that is not yet understood; creative thinking as the "endorphins" of cognitive processing. There are many possible explanations, but none preclude the possibility that creative genius resides within us all. By virtue of the process of thinking as suggested here, *we are all creative thinkers*.

With a bit more emphasis on the *creative* aspect of cognitive processing, your students can gain access to the science behind the facts, and enjoy the chance to put pieces together in new and untried ways. If nothing else, they will have the opportunity to wrestle with relationships and exercise their abilities to find multiple solutions to a problem.

Creative Thinking and Problem Solving

Let's take a break at this point, and engage in some mind-on (instead of "hands-on") creative thinking. We've defined creative thinking as the cognitive search for patterns, relationships, and perspectives between a stimulus (what you're perceiving) and what you already know. This next section will give you a chance to experience just what that means.

Exercising the Definition of Creative Thinking

You've probably noticed the cadré of characters that has been accompanying us so far. They will be showing up throughout the book. Take a moment now to look them over and name each of them. On the next page you'll find them posing specifically for you to complete this activity. So go ahead, give each of them a name and write a brief explanation for the names you chose. If you want to copy the page as an activity sheet, write the names and your reasons on a separate sheet.

Naming the Inventing Crew

Looking for patterns and relationships.

Here is a group picture of some students eager to expand their creative horizons. Working from left to right, give each one of them a name. After providing a name be sure to include a brief explanation of *why* you chose that name.

Name: _____

Why: _____

_____

_____

Name: _____

Why: _____

_____

_____

Name: _____

Why: _____

_____

_____

Name: _____

Why: _____

_____

_____

Name: _____

Why: _____

All right, let's consider that brief activity. Chances are good that you chose names based on children you have known that looked somewhat like the characters (of course, the range of experience would include your own childhood as well). There is not necessarily an accurate match of characteristics, but something about the drawings in the book reminded you of someone from your own experience. And it's very likely that once you settled on a pattern and matched that with a child from your own experience, you supplied not only a name, but an entire personality as well! All of this results from a cognitive search concerning what you see on the page and the experiences that you bring to the activity.

It may be the case that for one or more of the drawings you saw a combination of children you have known. So perhaps you chose one of those names, but you still see the character as a combination of those personalities. Or you may have taken an opportunity to use your favorite name and assign it to a character who can have all the personality traits that you want to accompany that name. Again, you have identified patterns between what you see and what you know.

There is also the possibility that you didn't choose names based on patterns, but rather on relationships. Do you see a tall person and immediately assign the nickname "Stretch"? Do you see a child in a baseball cap and use the name "Sporty"? If this were the case, we're still talking about the same dimension of thinking as in the previous two possibilities, although this time the focus is on relationships. That dimension is creative thinking, the cognitive search for patterns, relationships, and perspectives between what you know and what you are perceiving.

But wait! What if you did not base your choices on any of the scenarios discussed? What if you simply chose names "out of thin air" without searching for patterns or relationships at all? If this is representative of the approach you took, then by choosing one name, you eliminated many other names.

And that implies some criteria of "fit." The "search" was accomplished at phenomenal speed. As we mentioned in the previous section, it is likely that most of our creative thinking occurs on a preconscious level. The mind still did its search.

This brings up an important point. If the cognitive search of creative thinking occurs on a preconscious level, then how can we teach people how to do the search? We emphasize that we cannot *teach* them how to search. We suggest, however, that the creative search *is what the mind does.* Our intention as teachers is to provide our students with opportunities to exercise that ability to *facilitate their development* as problem solvers.

Let's take a physical example. When running a race, it is important that the runner be able to control breathing. The track coach can explain how to relax and breath deeper, but cannot teach the runner *how* to breath. That ability is part of what specific organs of the body are designed to do. We can improve, or inhibit, our ability to breath effectively through proper physical exercise. Similarly, we can improve, or inhibit, an individual's ability to think creatively through proper "cognitive exercise."

The third aspect of creative thinking not yet addressed is the search for perspectives. Finding a new perspective on a problem essentially changes the rules of the previous perspective. It opens a new range of possibilities in terms of patterns and relationships. As an exercise in switching perspectives, turn to the activity on page 16. Take a moment to write down another set of names for the children. This time, give each of the characters nicknames, or if you used nicknames the first time, give them proper names. Make the attempt, however, to provide names that focus on different dimensions of the character than those that you considered the first time. And, as before, write down a brief explanation of why you chose each name.

The Inventing Crew Revisited

Switching perspectives.

Here is another view of the same students. Based on this different perspective, give each a nickname, or if you used nicknames the first time, give proper names. Write a brief explanation of how this second picture influences your thinking about each character.

Nickname: _____

Why: _____

_____

_____

Nickname: _____

Why: _____

_____

_____

Nickname: _____

Why: _____

_____

_____

Nickname: _____

Why: _____

_____

_____

Nickname: _____

Why: _____

_____

The Problem-Solving Connection

Perhaps you've noticed that the term problem solving, as well as the reference to *problem solvers*, keeps showing up. As you will recall, the Cognitive Spiral Model represents an explanation of how we process information, or more succinctly, of how we think. *Problem solving* is a term that we can use interchangeably with *thinking*, if we consider thinking as a goal directed process. As Mayer puts it, "In other words, thinking is what happens when a person solves a problem, that is, produces behavior that moves the individual from the given state to the goal state—or at least tries to achieve this change" (1983, p. 7). To think is to solve a problem; and creative thinking is a necessary step in that process.

We tend to take our thinking so much for granted that it is difficult to consider all thinking as problem solving. However, consider the steps in the spiral model. We perceive a situation; we search for patterns between what has happened and what we know; we construct a possible response to the situation; we evaluate our response; and then we express that response in some way. Could that sound any more like solving a problem? After all, although we have five senses, the impulses that the brain receives are all the same type. The brain does not "hear" a whistle, "smell" the scent of a flower, or "see" a bird perched on a feeder. A sound, a smell, a sight, all must be converted into electrochemical impulses. The brain considers those impulses as problems that must be identified, analyzed, and resolved. The brain, therefore, may be considered as a natural problem-solving entity.

That the brain naturally seeks to solve problems is a pretty exciting idea! Rather than learning how to solve problems, we need to concentrate on the fullest development of those abilities that we are born with. Part of the process of facilitating such development is to practice seeking and manipulating information about a problem. With the current phenomenal access to information, a person may feel that any problem can be resolved.

Equally amazing is that we do not need to consciously attend to the problem constantly for the brain to continue searching for patterns and relationships along the way to a solution. No doubt you have experienced trying to solve a problem and, unable to make any progress, decided to stop working on it. Later, perhaps while driving down the street or walking the dog, the answer just popped into your head. Your mind continued to seek out patterns and relationships and provided you with an acceptable answer. It's often said that Albert Einstein's favorite method of getting through a difficult problem was to take a nap and let his mind work things through without distractions. Consider this, if you are unable to see a parade because the people standing in front of you are blocking the view, do you blame your vision or the obstacles to your vision? The situation is similar with problem solving ability. Often, it is the distractions, not our ability to think, that obscures a solution.

You were solving problems when you chose names for the characters in this book. We placed the emphasis of the activity on the creative aspect of thinking by not providing any criteria. You were not limited by rules saying that the names had to be gender-specific, or based upon particular ethnicities. However, you used each of the modes of thought in the spiral to arrive at a final choice. You solved a problem.

The educational implications are considerable. First, since we are natural problem solvers, one purpose of organized education should be to facilitate the development of that ability. And second, since creative thinking is the aspect of cognitive processing that allows us to find the patterns, relationships, and perspectives that lead to constructing solutions, our curricula should be designed to provide opportunities to engage in such activities. Our students need practice with *manipulating* information to solve problems. We use creative thinking to solve familiar problems, but more importantly we *require* creative thinking in order to solve new and unusual problems that demand new and unusual solutions.

Problem Solving and Inventing

The final step in building a foundation for *The Inventive Mind in Science: Creative Thinking Activities* is to discuss the relationship between problem solving and inventing. To begin, we must break down a few barriers to thinking.

We tend to think of inventions as machines. There is no problem with that. It is a matter of combining previously existing ideas to form something new. The problem is that when someone hears the word "invention," the notion that comes to mind is Thomas Edison working on the lightbulb, or someone putting together a better mousetrap. Since most people don't consider themselves to be inventors, such a notion prevents them from picturing themselves in an activity that involves inventing something. However, when we combine previously existing *ideas* to form a new one, that too is an invention. Newton's Laws of Motion, Einstein's Theory of Relativity, or Piaget's Stage Theory of Cognitive Development all represent invention. In each case information was combined in a new way to understand physical or psychological phenomena. In other words, when we think, we invent ideas.

Of course most of us don't put ourselves in the category with Newton, Einstein, or Piaget. Nevertheless, their inventions *were* ideas. Their ideas were new combinations (or perspectives) of existing information that yielded new information. The same is true for the rest of us. The spiraling nature of the thinking model meets the criteria of "newness" even when we only solve a familiar problem. After all, each encounter with a particular situation expands and changes our knowledge base. From the perspective of the brain, we never solve exactly the same problem with exactly the same information twice.

Admittedly, not all of us will come up with cognitive inventions that *change* the world, but the ability to *affect* the world through our thinking and work (as teachers do in particular) is an invaluable use of our natural abilities. And, who knows? Maybe practice renewing your own creative and inventive abilities, or developing the abilities of your students, will lead to an insight the rest of us have never considered before. Talk about exciting!

Where does all of this leave us? Conceptualizing inventing as a component in the process of problem solving represents an ideal situation for education. As educators, our emphasis is on developing problem-solving ability in ourselves and our students to meet the demanding needs of our society. Inventing, in the typical sense, provides the *vehicle* through which we provide students with concrete problem-solving opportunities. That is, we can provide goal-directed, hands-on classroom activities that can integrate subject areas (Chapter Seven will discuss the integration of subject areas in detail). Even better, when the activity is completed, students have some product to show for their efforts.

At the same time, inventing-based activities address the cognitive aspect of inventing, as well as the other four modes of thought represented in the model of cognitive processing. Inventing (remember to keep the broad conceptualization of "inventing" in mind) as an instructional tool provides the means by which we can address the concrete *and* abstract nature of problem solving. When your students construct inventions for class, whether or not the inventions perform as intended, you will be able to determine whether your students understand the concepts you have been presenting. This is important to understand.

A physical invention with marketing potential is not the aim of our efforts with inventing in the classroom. Our emphasis is on the *process* rather than the *product*. Using inventing as an instructional approach provides you with a concrete vehicle that

mirrors the cognitive process of problem solving. Through inventing-based activities your students can have hands-on experience with the concepts you wish to present. Along the way they will also have the opportunity to work with those concepts in a meaningful and "deep thinking" manner.

The Inventor's Journal

An important exercise when developing creative thinking and problem-solving ability is to provide the opportunity to reflect on experiences and progress. While more will be said about the Inventor's Journal in Part II, it is important to introduce it in the first chapter. We encourage you to keep your own journal as you read through this book and work on the activities. The Appendix has pages that you can duplicate for use as a cover, and for the inside of the journal. You can make four or five copies of the inner pages, a copy of the cover page, and put them together to form a booklet. Of course, this represents *one* way of putting together the journal. See how it works for you and then make modifications that best fit your teaching situation.

As you will notice, journal entries are divided into two types: "Inventive Ideas" and "Inventor's Sketch Pad." As you read through this book and complete the activities, jot down something in your journal for *each* of these sections. Perhaps something that was presented here will really hit home. Perhaps you will disagree with what has been offered. Write them down for future consideration! Sketch ideas also; words aren't always sufficient.

It is also important that you write down questions. Questions drive the construction of knowledge and initiate the problem-solving spiral we've been discussing throughout this chapter. So discipline yourself, and your students, to consider what you have read or experienced so that you can write at least one question that comes to mind.

And certainly, use your journal to draw pictures! You will be surprised by how much your students can demonstrate their understanding through pictures. In our experience, inventing allows students with poor verbal skills the opportunity to express what they have learned. Students with good verbal skills are able to take their thinking even further. Remember, in your journal the drawings need not make sense to anybody but you. So go ahead! Sketch out that better idea!

Chapter Two

Did You See That?

In this chapter you will find:

> *Stumbling blocks to creative thinking;*

> *How to get around those blocks;*

> *How to focus on switching perspectives, and seeking patterns and relationships!*

Having established that creative thinking and problem solving are cognitive abilities that we all possess, you may be asking, "So why don't we use them to get more problems solved?" It is a good question, and one that can have many answers. Our focus is on the notion of *conceptual blocks*. Adams (1979) defines conceptual blocks as ". . . mental walls that block the problem-solver from correctly perceiving a problem or conceiving its solution" (p. 11). Heard any of these before?

> We've always done things this way.
>
> Because the computer says so.
>
> This will be on the test.
>
> Nobody asked you to think. Just do your job.
>
> It is impossible to run a mile in less than four minutes.
>
> This ship is unsinkable.

Conceptual blocks represent mindsets that prevent people from questioning events or parameters. Subsequently, people will fail to entertain alternative explanations or solutions. And, in cases such as the Titanic, the arrogance of one conceptual block may influence design decisions that otherwise would have been routine, like including enough lifeboats for everybody on an ocean-going vessel.

Creative thinking, and consequently problem solving, are often curtailed by conceptual blocks because they foster a reluctance to search for multiple patterns, perspectives, and relationships. It would be like assuming that the view through a crack in the venetian blinds represents all there is

to see. The good news is that overcoming conceptual blocks leads right into considering alternative perspectives.

Recognizing Conceptual Blocks

Obstacles to our thinking abound in everyday life. In some instances the obstacles provide a measure of efficiency, even safety. The soldier who hears a bullet whistle by, for example, is better off hitting the ground immediately than standing around entertaining various explanations for the sound. However, when particular mindsets interfere with our ability to meet problems and resolve them we must question their usefulness. Let's take a look at three types of conceptual blocks.

My Information Must Be Correct

Here's a story. See whether it is at all familiar to you.

"Hello. I was given a message to call this number."

"What's your Social Security number?"

"Well, would you mind telling me who you are? All I had was a message to call this number."

"I can tell you if you give me your Social Security number."

"123-45-6789."

"This is in regard to your delinquent student loan."

"Delinquent! I only graduated in December. This is March. I haven't even heard from you folks yet. And my first payment shouldn't be until six months after graduation."

"That's incorrect, sir. According to the computer you graduated last May. Your first payment was due last November."

"Well that's funny, because I'm sitting here looking at a diploma that says I graduated in December. In fact, I received a student loan for the classes I took last summer. How could I have graduated in May and then gotten a loan in June? Does your computer show that?"

"Uh, let me see. Yes it's on here. But it still indicates that you graduated in May. I need to know how you plan to clear up the delinquency. Do you know the amount?"

Yes, indeed, this a true story. Sadly there was absolutely no way of convincing the representative that the error was in *their* files. As long as the "computer said so" there was no room for question. Eventually it was resolved through a supervisor. It is understandable that when people are given information with which to work they expect that the information is correct. However, it would seem reasonable that when faced with an obvious discrepancy or contradiction people would be able to recognize the possibility of an error and initiate an inquiry. Unfortunately, it is usually left to the consumer to demand appropriate action.

That the "computer says so" or "according to my information" are likely some of the most often encountered examples of people being limited by a conceptual block. Refusing to accept the *possibility* of errors in information is a common example of what we are talking about. By no means, however, is it the only source of obstacles to better thinking.

Stereotyping

Stereotyping, and the resultant prejudice and bigotry that it can breed, represents a category of conceptual blocks that we encounter routinely. Here's a riddle that might demonstrate the idea. A man and his son are driving in a car. There's a terrible accident, and the father is killed instantly. The boy is rushed to the emergency room of the local hospital. The doctor hurries in and, upon seeing the boy, exclaims "I can't operate on him! He's my son!"

How could this be? The answer to the riddle will be provided later in the chapter so you can keep working on it for awhile if you need to consider it a bit more. If you have already come up with a suitable answer, good job! But for now, let's discuss the conceptual blocks at work.

Conceptual blocks that arise from stereotyping are essentially a social phenomenon. We do learn them, but not necessarily as the result of planned formal instruction. We learn them from observing the social interactions that occur around us. We observe what is acceptable and unacceptable in terms of behaviors and perspectives.

Politics provides many examples of stereotyped conceptual blocks. One of the most prevalent at the moment may well be the notion of a woman as president. There are no compelling reasons why a woman could not serve as President of the United States. Yet it would *seem* unlikely that we will *see* a female candidate make a successful bid for the presidency in the near future. Chances are increasingly viable for such an event, yet for many the conceptual block of a woman president, or that the president must be a man, is still a formidable obstacle.

Habits

A third category of conceptual blocks is habit. Chances are good that at some time you've been told "we've always done it that way." Much of our behavior is habitual. Habits serve to facilitate the accomplishment of routine activities. And that's not always bad. However, our zeal to find habitual ways of accomplishing more of our activities results in the inhibition of our creative thinking. Essentially, our natural inclination to search for other possibilities is repressed in favor of behaviors that do not require thinking—they've been "prethought." It's often called being in a rut. So, when you hear someone say that things must be done a particular way "because they've always done it that way," you'll know that the little twinge you feel is your creative thinking ability saying "Hold on, Buster!"

Of course, we do not always find ourselves in situations where we can challenge other's conceptual blocks. But that does not mean we are obligated to impose the same block on *our* thinking. Often there is a good reason for doing things as they've always been done. The uninhibited thinker will seek out that reason, in a non-confrontational manner, before insisting on change. However, "because we've always done it this way" is not a viable *reason*, it is a conceptual block arising out of habit that accomplishes a routine task but inhibits thinking.

In each of the cases mentioned above, our thinking becomes a matter of applying heuristics, rules, that reduce our cognitive activity to something like "thinking by the numbers." James Adams (1979) sees the effect of

conceptual blocks on our problem solving in this way: "The typical response to a problem seems to be to try to get rid of it by finding an answer—often taking the first answer that occurs and pursuing it because of one's reluctance to spend the time and mental effort needed to conjure up a richer storehouse of alternatives from which to choose." (p. 7)

Finding an answer is certainly not cause for alarm. The problem is when we believe that there is only one possible answer. Do you know what problems you are going to face tomorrow? Next year? If not, you likely do not know what solutions you will need either. You should expect that new problems will need *new* solutions.

With regard to your students, it is widely considered that the jobs they will occupy in the next century are yet to be invented. Even so, they will be in your classroom waiting for an education. What, then, should a formal education provide? Instruction should demonstrate *how* to go about finding new answers to new problems. We should avoid the trap of giving children answers to remember, rather than problems to solve. The conceptual block that says school is a place for ensuring that children memorize bits and pieces of information is perhaps one of the chief obstacles that must be overcome. There is no question that there is information that must be provided to students, but school is most appropriately the place where we should be learning to solve problems. And part of that learning involves being given opportunities to practice the abilities we seek to develop.

The next activity, Speedbumps and Potholes That Slow Down My Thinking, provides you with an opportunity to identify just a few of the conceptual blocks that might be restraining your thinking. Take a moment to list three conceptual blocks for each of the categories listed. You need not try to overcome or resolve the block. Just identify some things like whose job is it to cook, to fix the car, or to perform particular tasks at work, just to name a few possibilities. The next section of the chapter may help you address those obstacles.

Speedbumps and Potholes That Slow Down My Thinking

Recognizing conceptual blocks.

Conceptual blocks are ways of thinking that slow down the creative process. Obstacles such as these occur so often that we sometimes do not realize how much effect they have. In the spaces below, try to identify three conceptual blocks for each of the categories. If you think you cannot do this, you have just run into a conceptual block!

My Information Must Be Correct — *These are the conceptual blocks that occur when we fail to question the source of our information or resolve discrepancies.*

1. _____

2. _____

3. _____

Habits — *These obstacles occur when we do things the same way so often that we fail to see the need for change.*

1. _____

2. _____

3. _____

Stereotyping — *Perhaps the worst of the conceptual blocks because there is often no real support for thinking in this way. Examples are things such as girls should be quiet, and boys should be aggressive.*

1. _____

2. _____

3. _____

Thinking Around Conceptual Blocks

Have you ever had the opportunity to lie down outside and watch the cloud formations change? Finding faces and images in the clouds without the anxiety about finding the "correct" face or the "required" image leads to a relaxed and enjoyable feeling as the creative mind is allowed to seek out patterns. The suggestions of images from a friend allow the chance to change perspectives. And the continuous motion of the clouds provides new configurations to consider at a challenging rate of speed.

The good news is that overcoming conceptual blocks leads right into the search for alternative perspectives, patterns, and relationships. In other words, it opens the door for creative thinking. So this would be a good opportunity to spend some time in activities that address creative thinking as we've defined it. By all means take a look outside, and if time and conditions permit, watch the clouds for awhile! Otherwise, we'll provide some activities that will be nearly as good, and can be done in any weather. Since a search typically moves from a general situation to increasingly specific situations, first will be the most general facet of creative thinking: switching perspectives. After that we'll shift to an emphasis on pattern and relationship seeking.

Switching Perspectives

Switching perspectives involves the consideration of a situation from a decidedly different vantage point. It is *decidedly* different since a perspective necessarily carries a lot of baggage with it, and it must be decided that other baggage should be searched as well. That is, when you consider a stimulus your perception drives the search for patterns and relationships from a particular vantage point. As you'll recall, our earlier discussion about the searching that goes on in creative thinking indicated that the mind looks for associations. Rather than taking a stimulus and then searching *every* experience and idea that you have, the search proceeds based upon the strongest association perceived. From there, given the opportunity, the search will yield associations that are not quite as strong. Eventually, this leads to the possibility of associations that one might never have considered before. Still, there is a basic direction to the search. The "baggage" of a particular perspective refers to types of associations that the mind is most likely to consider as a result of the direction taken for the search. For instance, suppose you go to the grocery store for some milk. Typically, items like milk are at the back of the store, or on a side opposite from the front door. You will take a particular direction in order to reach the dairy case, and along the way will see the items that are on the shelves you pass (and as we all know, that's no accident). However, the fact that you chose one particular route does not negate the existence of all of the other items in the store that could have been seen if you'd taken another route. What you *did see*, was a function of the route you followed. You saw items from the perspective of that particular path to the low-fat milk.

That a cognitive search must begin from *some* perspective is easy enough to accept. Any activity, cognitive or otherwise, must begin from a set of circumstances. What must be recognized is that as a result of the circumstances, the search necessarily proceeds in a manner that accesses some information and fails to access other information. The current perspective only searches the baggage that shows up along its path. In order to consider a new range of possibilities a *decision* must be made to switch to another perspective with a different set of baggage. The initial set of circumstances is not necessarily the only, *or the best*, set of circumstances from which to work. Just to remain consistent with our

spiral model of cognitive processing, let's mention that the decision to switch perspectives is made in Metacognitive Thought and is expressed in Performance Thought by sending our thinking through another spiral. That, of course, will lead to Creative Thought once again.

Consider this example of what we've been presenting. Suppose you are driving down the highway and decide to stop for some lunch. Your travelling companion takes out a handy little trip computer and enters in the highway number, direction of travel, the mile marker, and pushes the "restaurant" button. The particular perspective of the computer programming is such that it might list several different restaurants 30 miles down the road, but not the one that you just passed a mile back. The perspective programmed into the computer was one that accessed a great deal of information about the direction in which you are travelling. It

failed to access the answer that was actually closest to your location because its perspective did not include the direction *from which* you'd travelled.

Would it have been impossible to find out about the restaurant just a mile behind you? Certainly not. Your navigator could have entered in the same information on the computer, with the exception of reversing your direction, and then found that lunch was waiting just five minutes away. It would, however, have required the *decision* to consider an alternate perspective.

We've already completed one activity that asked you to switch perspectives. In Chapter One you named each of the characters appearing in the book, and were later asked to name them again. Did *seeing* them from the back have any effect on the new names you chose?

New perspectives necessarily involve new information. When you view a stimulus from a different angle, you actually view a new stimulus. For example, if you are sitting on a couch and looking at a picture on the wall in front of you, a particular stimulus is perceived. If you then lie down on the couch and view the same picture sideways, you perceive a different stimulus. In terms of Gestalt psychology, you rectify the incoming information to better match your past experience. You tell yourself that it is *you* that is sideways, not the room. But this activity *is* different from the first instance. As a classroom example you might want to try the following activity. Rather than merely pointing out to your students that Michelangelo painted the Sistine Chapel while lying on his back, tape some paper to the bottom of a table and let your students experience the different perspective of drawing "up" instead of "down."

The exercises from *Drawing on the Right Side of the Brain* (Edwards, 1979) illustrate this situation very dramatically. Subjects copy a picture that is rotated 180 degrees. Rather than focusing on the image in the picture, the subjects focus on the discrete lines and curves that they see. The results are nothing short of remarkable! The drawings below illustrate the point. The pictures on the left were done by students (college students) when they were asked to draw a man. The pictures on the right were done by the same students when they drew from a copy of Picasso's Stravinsky that was rotated 180 degrees. Every change of perspective offers a new stimulus to the magnificent problem-solving mechanism of the mind!

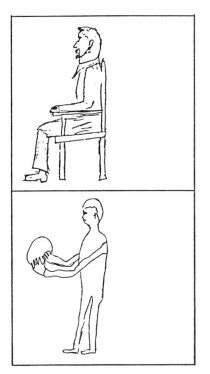

Figure 2.1. "Draw-a-Person." (From Betty Edwards, *Drawing on the Right Side of the Brain*. Copyright 1979. Reprinted with permission.)

Let's try a few perspective switching activities and see what we find. This activity is adapted from one by Alan McCormack called "Holes." Typically we see the items that border the holes, and the holes are, of course, holes. For example, the drawing below on the left is a doughnut. The drawing on the right is the "hole."

In the activity on page 30, the holes are provided. Can you determine what items these holes are from?

The Holes activity is one that you could use with your students just as it is presented here. You also could come up with your own page of holes, perhaps items in and around the classroom. Best of all would be to allow your students to do the activity from the book, and then let them find the examples in and around the classroom in order to compile their own page of holes.

Droodles (see p. 31) provide another interesting exercise with perspective switching. In this case there is no particular answer that is correct. You may see something that is perfectly clear to you while someone else sees another picture that is just as clear to them. What do you see in the pictures? Having found one picture, try switching perspectives in order to find a completely different picture.

Turning Holes Inside Out

Seeing things from a different perspective.

Each of the pictures below represent the "holes" in a common object. Try to identify each one. In the final two spaces draw the holes from some other objects. For instance, would you have recognized the holes in a cassette tape?

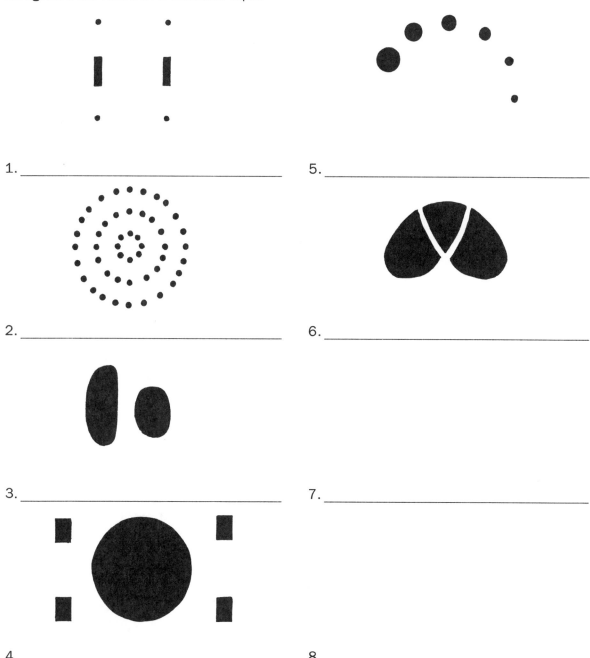

1. _____   5. _____

2. _____   6. _____

3. _____   7. _____

4. _____   8. _____

Droodles

Thinking of more than one possible solution.

Droodles are not pictures of anything in particular. That means that there are *many* possible answers for a single droodle. Try to list at least three possibilities for each of the drawings below.

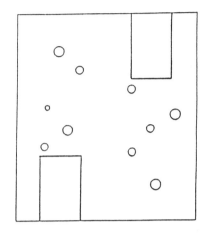

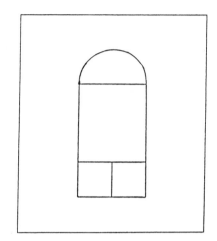

1. _____
2. _____
3. _____

1. _____
2. _____
3. _____

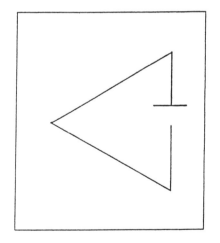

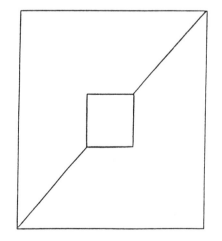

1. _____
2. _____
3. _____

1. _____
2. _____
3. _____

From *The Inventive Mind in Science: Creative Thinking Activities.* © 1998 Teacher Ideas Press. (800) 237-6124.

Switching perspectives is not a strange or difficult activity for your mind to accomplish. Do you remember the Necker Cube from Chapter One? Simply giving yourself some time to focus on the drawing allowed your mind to naturally seek a different perspective. You weren't told what to do, or what to look for, you simply allowed your mind the opportunity to do what it does best. Unfortunately, when a particular problem stumps us, we tend to keep on trying the same approaches. In our highly routinized and heavily scheduled lives we often must remind ourselves to take advantage of our perspective switching ability. By deciding to consider the situation from a different perspective, an entirely new array of possibilities is opened up.

The "What Does My Garden Look Like?" activity on the following page will give you another opportunity to practice seeing the world from different views. The art work need not be destined for the Louvre, just concentrate on the change of perspective. And enjoy!

Seeking Patterns and Relationships

We consider patterns, relationships, and perspectives to be quite distinct. The previous section illustrated that a perspective represents a particular collection of patterns and relationships, and subsequently guides the search for less obvious patterns and relationships. Patterns and relationships, therefore, are the stuff of which perspectives are made. And repeated relationships are the components from which patterns are constructed.

For instance, your *perspective* on good citizenship is characterized by the *patterns* of behavior which you believe constitute appropriate social interaction. In science, searching for and identifying the myriad patterns in

nature is what keeps the discipline vibrant and exciting. Technology is driven by finding the relationships between the patterns in nature and the application of those patterns to meeting needs. By developing our ability to recognize patterns and relationships, and keeping in mind our ability to consider different perspectives (with their different patterns and relationships) we dramatically broaden the range of information in a problem-solving situation.

Relationships

A relationship is the most basic unit of information that a creative search can identify because only two elements are necessary to a relationship. For instance, that you are your mother's child represents a relationship between you and one other person. As such, it does not provide us with enough information to *predict* your relationship to anybody else. But it does provide enough information to make *inferences*. Do you notice those basic science process skills starting to creep in? We might infer that you are your mother's husband's child as well, though that might not be the case for a wide range of reasons. However, as a statement that goes beyond the evidence to explain our observations, the inference is plausible.

A relationship establishes that there is something common between two elements. For example, when you named the characters, you made observations of the drawings. If you determined that one of the characters looks like a young girl, and so named her "Mary," you used the relationship between gender and names that are typically applied to that gender. If one of the characters appears Asian to you, and as a consequence you selected the name Li, you have identified a relationship between the observation and a particular category of names.

What Does My Garden Look Like?

Taking "someone else's" perspective.

The picture on this page is a people's-eye view of a small garden. But what if you were an infant crawling in the yard on a sunny day? or a cat? or an ant? What if you were a bird flying over the garden or sitting in a tree? What would the garden look like from one of those perspectives? Draw your own version of how the garden might appear.

The visual puzzles below are examples of finding relationships. By determining the relationship of the words on the page, a common phrase is found. We consider this to be an exercise with *relationships* because the solution for one puzzle does not necessarily provide a pattern for solving the next.

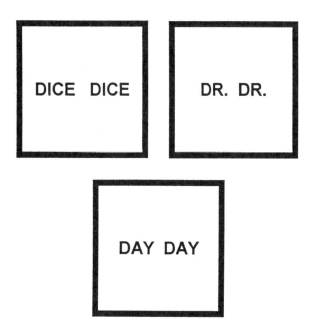

Did you solve them? The one on the top left is "paradise" (pair-of-dice), the one on the top right is "paradox" (pair-of-docs), and the one on the bottom is "day by day" (one day is "by" the other day), though if you determined that it was "day after day," that would be quite acceptable as well. In each case you had to find a *relationship* that could explain the placement of the words in terms of a common phrase. This was a bit sneaky in that we established a pattern with the first two puzzles. That pattern, however, did not carry over to the third puzzle. If you tried using the pattern, "pair-of" with the third one, you probably got sort of frustrated. If you really fought to make the pattern fit, you might want to reread the section on conceptual blocks and switching perspectives! The next activity (p. 35) provides a whole page of puzzles to exercise relationship seeking!

It is important to be able to discern relationships before they become parts of a pattern, just as it is important to know which side of the road to drive on before joining rush hour traffic. Understanding of the parts always contributes to a greater understanding of the whole. This leads us to another exercise for developing the ability to recognize relationships—analogies. Typically exercises with analogies are presented with one word pair followed by the first word of a second pair. The first pair of words establishes the relationship. The second set expresses the same relationship when the appropriate word is provided. For instance, night is to day as dark is to _____. In order to provide the appropriate response, you must first identify the relationship expressed in the first word pair. In this case, we might say that "light" is the word to fill in the blank since the relationship in the first word pair is that of opposites.

Using analogies provides good practice at finding relationships. However, providing the first word of the second pair tends to border on the use of patterns as well. This is not something to be avoided. In fact, we will discuss using one to find the other after the section on Patterns. You'll notice that the Analogies Activity Page (p. 36) has some examples with the format that we've used so far, and then goes to "open ended" analogies. For these just the first word pair is provided. You (or your students) can then provide both terms for the second pair based on the relationship identified.

It is not always the case that there is only one relationship represented by a word pair, and we certainly don't want to inhibit the thinking of someone who has found a relationship we had not intended. For instance, Red is to Green as . . . could be followed by Stop is to Go (traffic signals), Blue is to Orange (primary and secondary colors), or Port is to Starboard (position of red and green running lights on a boat).

Visual Puzzles

Identifying relationships.

Each puzzle represents a different familiar phrase.

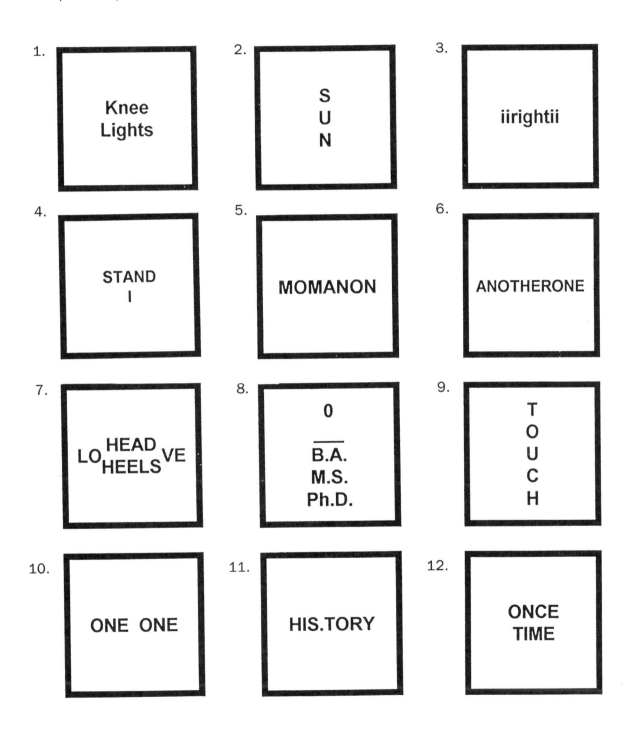

1. Knee
   Lights

2. S
   U
   N

3. iirightii

4. STAND
   I

5. MOMANON

6. ANOTHERONE

7. LO HEAD VE
   HEELS

8. 0
   ――
   B.A.
   M.S.
   Ph.D.

9. T
   O
   U
   C
   H

10. ONE ONE

11. HIS.TORY

12. ONCE
    TIME

Analogies Are to Relationships as . . .

Finding relationships in comparisons and contrasts.

The first ten analogies offer a word pair and the first word of a second pair. Though there is a particularly appropriate word for each blank, there is not necessarily just one correct response. It is the relationship that counts. The last five analogies are open-ended; you supply both terms for the second word pair.

1. **Hot** is to **cold** as **melted** is to _____ .

2. **Run** is to **walk** as **fast** is to _____ .

3. **Success** is to **work** as **good health** is to _____ .

4. **Laughter** is to **happiness** as **crying** is to _____ .

5. **Wet** is to **dry** as **rain** is to _____ .

6. **Left** is to **right** as **North** is to _____ .

7. **Gifts** are to **birthdays** as a **gold watch** is to _____ .

8. **Cats** are to **birds** as **birds** are to _____ .

9. **Teaching** is to **knowledge** as **preaching** is to _____ .

10. **Short** is to **tall** as **tents** are to _____ .

11. **Right** is to **wrong** as _____ is to _____.

12. **Sweet** is to **sour** as _____ is to _____ .

13. **Wood** is to **tree** as _____ is to _____ .

14. **Writing** is to **words** as _____ is to _____ .

15. **Age** is to **wisdom** as _____ is to _____ .

Now that we're rolling with these activities, let's try one more variety. The puzzles below and on the next activity page (p. 38) will combine numbers and words. Each represents a common phrase or item with which you are no doubt familiar. The prompt provides the number and then the initials of what the number represents. For instance:

88 K. on a P. would be
　　88 Keys on a Piano

52 C. in a D. would be
　　52 Cards in a Deck

Here are a couple without the answers to get you ready for the full list on the Activity page:

99 B. of B. on the W. would be
　　?

29 D. in F. in a L.Y. would be
　　?

Do you smile when you find an answer? Is finding a relationship an enjoyable and rewarding experience? Sure it is, like going for a walk after you've been sitting in a car for hundreds of miles—it feels good to use those muscles as they were meant to be used. Allowing your mind to engage in its creative search, not to mention finding a suitable solution, is necessarily an *intrinsically rewarding* experience!

Number/Word Puzzles

Looking for relationships.

You should be familiar with each of the items on this list, though it might take some creative thinking to recognize them!

99 B. of B. on the W.	29 D. in F. in a L. Y.
8 S. on a S. S.	101 D.
32 D. F., T. at which W. F.	11 P. on a F. T.
13 D. in a B.'s D.	3 P. for a F. G.
4 T. on a C.	2 T. on a B.
5 D. in a Z. C.	5 F. on O. H.
31 V. of B. R. I. C.	3 C.'s S.—N., P., and S. M.
100 S. in the U. S. S.	3 N. in an A. C.
57 H. V.	20,000 L. under the S.
3 B. M., S. H. T. R.	30 D. H. S., A., J. and N.
26 L. in the A.	5 V. and S. Y.

Patterns

When a relationship is repeated a pattern is formed. Once a pattern has formed, we can predict the next element in a given sequence. The prediction may not always turn out to be correct, as we know so well from weather forecasts. However, that does not invalidate the pattern, it simply calls for adjustment. Either we failed to incorporate all facets of the pattern in our prediction, *or we do not yet know the entire pattern.* Suppose the letters below represented M&Ms. Each letter indicates the color of the M&M. Of course, now you're so good at identifying relationships that you probably didn't need us to tell you that! As presented below, do we have a pattern or a relationship?

Y R B G O

If you said it is not a pattern but it is a relationship, that's just great. If you didn't, consider the following. Except for the fact that each letter represents an M&M, the sequence does not repeat itself at any point. We will agree that it would be correct to say that the next element in the sequence will be an M&M since there is a pattern of one M&M followed by another. However, let's focus on the colors of the M&Ms. If you were to say the next one will be tan because tan has not yet occurred, you are inferring something beyond what has been presented. And that inference represents a characteristic based only on the presence of a relationship. If, on the other hand, you were to say the next one will be brown, because there are typically more browns than any other color, again you would be making an inference. Because there has not been any *repetition* of relationships, as of yet there is no pattern. Suppose instead that we had the following sequence:

Y R B G O Y R

In this case we might well predict that the next M&M will be brown since the yellow and red have repeated. It is true that brown still may not be correct. As mentioned earlier, it is possible that we have yet to see the entire sequence, the entire *relationship*, that could eventually begin to repeat itself. However, in terms of predicting based on a pattern of repeating relationships (often referred to as a "model"), the evidence presented on the page would support selecting a brown M&M.

We can emphasize two points from this example: a) repetition of a relationship is required to form a pattern, and b) repeated relationships are the building blocks of patterns. Do you think that might have implications for understanding things like the nature of the universe or the cost of postage stamps? You bet!

All along we've been using examples that referred to drawings, numbers, and words representing tangible objects. But since we are discussing relationships and patterns with regard to the psychological construct of creative thinking, it is important to include the notion of *ideas* as observable themes. They are observable in the sense that they can be consciously considered. We refer to this as a *cognitive perception*. Thus, just as we can observe patterns of traffic flow at an intersection visually we can also observe patterns in our personal opinions cognitively.

Both the Holes activity and Droodles require the search for a pattern. In each case, switching perspectives is first required, and then it becomes a matter of finding patterns that could account for the drawing on the page. How about the cartoon characters following along in the book? Though you've only seen a few drawings, you have identified patterns of dress, posture, and social interaction among them. What patterns of "personality" have you identified for each? Are those patterns distinct? Very likely they are. There may be some characters you like, and others you do not. And all of this just from a few drawings and phrases. Patterns are powerful stuff!

Here's another sort of pattern finding exercise.

1 2 3 4 5 6 7 8 9 ____

What is the final number in the sequence? And what pattern led to the answer? The intended answer (though that certainly

does not mean the *only* answer) is that the next number is 10, and that the pattern is that each number is increased by a value of 1 over the preceding number. But that was easy. How about this one:

1 2 4 8 ____

What is the final number in this sequence? Yes, 16 is the correct answer. Each number after 1 was double the preceeding value. Try this one:

1 2 4 5 7 ____

Admittedly, this one was a bit tricky. However, there are at least two ways that the intended answer could be found. First, you could have stayed with the calculation pattern that was established through the first two exercises. You may then have found the pattern of adding 1 to the first number, then adding 2 to that, then 1, then 2. In that case, 1 would be added to 7 in order to find the next number—8.

However, there is another pattern. Rather than focusing on the mathematical aspect of the progression, look at the numbers in terms of shape. Do you notice that 1 has no curved lines, 2 is curved, 4 is the next number in order with no curved lines, 5 has a curve, 7 would be the next with no curves, and 8 is curved? Yes, it required a perspective shift. Though, had 8 been included in the sequence and it was the *next* number that had to be determined, the calculation method would not have worked—now *that* would have been sneaky!

Patterns and relationships exist because of our ability to combine discrete bits of information. That ability is constantly at work. Try to experience situations in terms of the patterns and relationships that you perceive. Play some music and listen for its subtle elements. Then listen again to the pattern formed by the combining of those elements. Look at a garden and see the relationship of leaf placement on a stem, and then the distinct pattern of leaves for that particular plant. Take a look at the side of a brick building. Two bricks beside each other form a relationship. The recurring relationship forms the brick pattern of the building. The same type of brick can be used to form many different patterns.

Before closing this chapter, let's consider an exercise that requires finding both patterns and relationships. The game "Queen Anne" is one that requires recognition of a pattern, and then use of the relationship repeated in the pattern to continue. The game goes something like this:

> There are things that Queen Anne likes, and others that she does not.
>
> Queen Anne likes apples, but she does not like oranges.
>
> Queen Anne likes to go swimming, but she does not like walking.

Do you see the pattern? If so, what can you add that Queen Anne likes and does not like? Would the following fit the pattern?

> Queen Anne likes milk but does not like water.

This last phrase does not fit the pattern. Presumably because "Queen" and "Anne" each contain a double letter, the things she likes have double letters and the things she dislikes do not. From the pattern established in the first two lines we can derive the relationship required to continue the pattern in subsequent lines. We could also say:

> Queen Anne likes patterns but not relationships.

So Queen Anne has a bit to learn, what can we say? Perhaps substituting "associations" for "relationships" would do the trick.

When playing this with students, someone can start with phrases like the first two. Then the next person tries to add a phrase. If their phrase does not match the pattern, the student listens again to all who have found the pattern as more examples are added.

Summary

Queen Anne would like summaries, but not conclusions, right? Whether or not you wish to consider the universe as finite or unfolding, our potential for understanding the world around us is a function of our ability to recognize relationships and patterns. When assembled into perspectives they represent our cognitive representation, our knowledge, of all we experience. Patterns are everywhere. We see them in the leaves on plants, in the ripples of a pond when a stone is thrown in. We see patterns in weather systems, and in the movement of planets. As we are a part of the universe, patterns pervade our behavior. Our search for understanding of the world around us, and perhaps of the world within us, is a search for patterns and the relationships that comprise them. And rather than referring to the absence of pattern, chaos is simply a term for patterns we have not yet recognized.

Our ability to think creatively, seeking out patterns, relationships, and perspectives, is tremendously important. The best news is that this is not some special talent reserved for a chosen few. This ability reflects what people do when they think. And as such, facilitating the development of creative thinking should be a primary focus of organized education.

By the way, remember the riddle earlier in the chapter? How could it be that the father died in the accident yet the child was the emergency room doctor's son? There really is no tricky genealogical manipulation going on here, but you might have run into a stereotypical conceptual block. The doctor, you see, is the child's *mother*!

Chapter Three

Creative Problem Solving in the Classroom

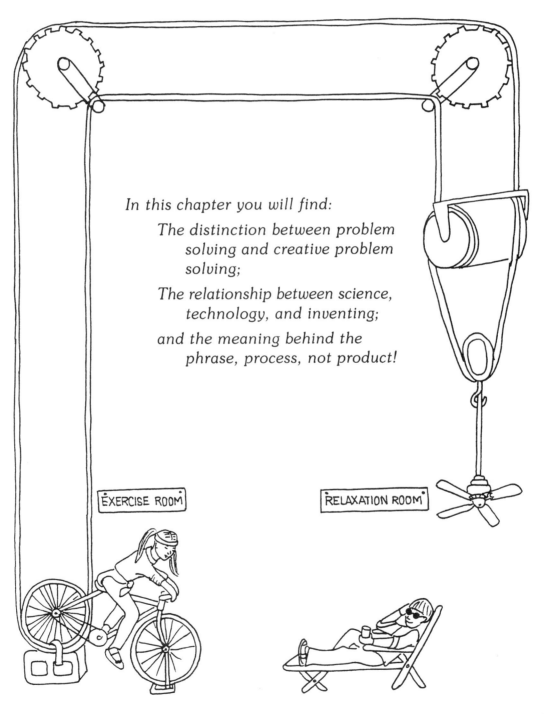

In this chapter you will find:

The distinction between problem solving and creative problem solving;

The relationship between science, technology, and inventing;

and the meaning behind the phrase, process, not product!

EXERCISE ROOM

RELAXATION ROOM

By now we hope that you agree that a) creative thinking pervades our thinking process, b) to think is to solve problems, and c) that to foster this ability in students is a good thing. If we are together on that, we are approaching the need for an instructional vehicle, a technique, to educate our students to be creative problem solvers. First, let's make some final distinctions.

Specifically, in this chapter we wish to complete the foundation by adding pieces which will enable us to move from theory into practice. We'll address problem solving more closely by drawing a distinction between problem solving and *creative* problem solving. We'll point out the match between creative thinking and "doing" science. We will then discuss the mutually beneficial relationship between science and technology. Finally, we will tie together science, technology, and inventing into a practical and creative approach to the teaching of science. Let's get started!

Problem Solving vs. Creative Problem Solving

Why Distinguish Between the Two?

Since we tend to refer to problem solving vs. *creative* problem solving you may suspect a bias for one of these processes. We do, in fact, wish to draw a distinction between the two, and argue for a much greater use of *creative* problem solving. Rest assured that we have no vendetta against problem solving. After all, we very much agree with Dewey that *genuine* thinking begins with a problematic situation.

A focus on creative thinking in problem solving emphasizes a more dynamic approach to solution finding, rather than the mechanistic approach of answer identification. This dynamism can be seen in four thinking abilities which, based on the work of

Guilford (1959), have come to be associated with creative thinking. As we describe each of them, you will see how they reflect our definition of creative thinking as a cognitive search for patterns, perspectives, and relationships. You will also see that they are not the sort of abilities that are bound by rules and rigid limitations.

First to consider is *fluency*. Idea fluency refers to the ability to generate many responses relating to a particular attribute. For instance, if asked to name terms for "boat," fluency would be demonstrated if you responded with a list such as: canoe, ferry, vessel, rowboat, ship, aircraft carrier, submarine, oceanliner, raft, barge. Do you see how they all fall into the same category of "boatness"?

Flexibility refers to the ability to switch from one characteristic to another. So, if asked the classic creative thinking test of listing uses of a brick, you might respond: as a doorstop, as part of a building, as something you put in a toilet tank to take up space so that the toilet uses less water. Unlike the examples for fluency, these show uses of a brick based on at least three of its attributes—weight, enduring strength, and the volume it occupies.

Another of the four abilities is *originality*. In this case the emphasis is on a new application. As educators it is important to remember that what is unoriginal to us may be original to our students. The typical response to a student's original idea tends to be "That's been done before." You can't do much more to stop creative development than to say such a thing to a student. The importance of placing *value* on original thinking cannot be overstated. If every time a runner posted their best time the coach said, "People have run faster than that," we would likely have few people willing to run another race. Originality of thinking refers to the *individual's* thinking, and we need to demonstrate that such thinking is valued.

Finally, we come to *elaboration*. This is the ability to take a thought and provide greater detail—to extend the possibilities. Essentially it is creative thinking set in motion and then following through the possibilities that arise. The brick that is used as a doorstop could be covered with a nicely quilted brick jacket so that it doesn't scratch the floor, or the foot, as it is moved around. And the jackets could be different designs, representing seasons of the year. Or perhaps they could have embroidered family members' names so we know whose turn it is each week to shut and lock the door.

Was it obvious to you that a creative search was the common thread in these thinking abilities? Let's look at the next page for an activity to pursue creative thinking in terms of these four abilities. Rather than use Torrance's (1966) classic multiple uses for a brick, let's come up with uses for an old shoe. As you make your list, review it periodically to see which categories you address more or less frequently. Challenge yourself to come up with some ideas for those underrepresented groups. Keep in mind, no pressure here, list what you can. This activity will give you an idea of how much you (or your students) need to free your creative thinking. And by all means, let's have some humor! There is no need to pretend that each of your answers needs to be plausible or practical. To that end, we've started the list for you. What better use of an old shoe than as a planter for growing . . . shoe trees!

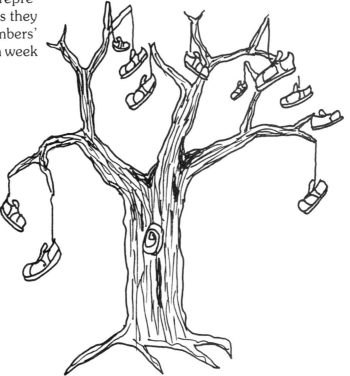

Uses for an Old Shoe

Exercising the thinking abilities of fluency, flexibility, originality, and elaboration.

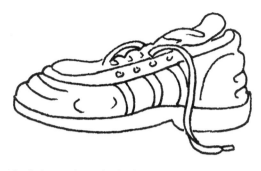

Picture your favorite old shoe; it can be a sneaker, a boot, a slipper, or whatever. In the spaces below, list as many ways that you can think of for putting that shoe to use. *After* compiling a list, look over each entry in terms of fluency, flexibility, originality, and elaboration. Label each to see which categories are your strongest, and which can use more attention.

Fluency—Listing many uses of the *same type*. For instance, using the shoe to *protect* your foot or your hand.

Flexibility—Listing many *categories* of uses. For instance, using it as a planter, a doorstop, a paperweight.

Originality—Listing *new,* uses. For instance, using it as a shoe-shaped lamp shade.

Elaboration—Extending one idea to include *more* information. For instance, using the lamp shade in a shoe store, with different shoe-shades directing customers to categories of shoes.

Category   Use

_____   _____

_____   _____

_____   _____

_____   _____

_____   _____

_____   _____

_____   _____

_____   _____

_____   _____

_____   _____

_____   _____

_____   _____

Finding uses for an old shoe represents a problem. Allowing for a creative approach to that problem provided for an interesting and enjoyable experience. It is also likely that some ideas could be adapted for practical use. And so we come back to the need for distinguishing between problem solving and creative problem solving. Why *should* we distinguish between the two?

Our concern is that problem solving, when it is used in education, seems to have become synonymous with "critical thinking." That is, the emphasis is on the decision-making aspect of a criteria-laden task. Criteria refers to the standards for a judgment. And critical—as in critical thinking—refers to the application of those standards in that judgment process. The problems presented to students tend to come with a set of rules by which the problem is to be solved, heuristics which must be applied, established parameters within which the solution must be found. Typically, the expectation is that there is only one acceptable answer.

Without a doubt this constitutes a good exercise in thinking for the problem designer! But what about the problem solver? The student who fails to find the correct answer is left with the sense of having *failed in their thinking*. The fact is that they have simply failed to think the same way the problem designer thought. A good example was Calandra's (1964) story of a physics student who refused to have his thinking curtailed and narrowed. His point was made on a physics test when in response to a question about measuring the height of a building using a barometer he offered suggestions such as attaching the rope to the barometer and lowering it over the side of the building. The length of the rope from the top of the building to the ground represented the height of the building. Alternatively, one could walk up the steps of the building marking barometer lengths on the wall along the way. The result would be the building's height in barometer lengths. In this story, the student did, in fact, know the answer being sought. However, his point was that it was not necessary to assume that there is only one answer to the problem—or one way to solve it for that matter.

It would be foolish, of course, to argue that mathematics, science, or English should be taught without attention to rules and facts. However, the story above indicates a familiar situation. That is, the notion that education is simply categorized facts and rules that must be imparted to the student. As such the *thinking* behind those facts and rules is left out. Imagine that! Doesn't it seem strange to leave thinking out of an educational curriculum?

You might be wondering, "Wouldn't the student in the story have to think in order to solve the problem the way the teacher wanted it solved? Are you saying we don't think when we solve problems in algebra, or conduct experiments in science?" That is not what we're saying. In the story, it was not the use of "rules" that caused the student's objection. Rather it was the notion that only one rule should be used. Teaching people to apply specific rules under specific circumstances is training, not education in the broad sense. Which leads to the old question, "Is there a difference between training and education?"

One difference is passion. Training involves little passion. A procedure for accomplishing a task in a specific manner is presented and memorized. In its own way, it is very efficient. Education, on the other hand, is passionate for the educator and the student because it involves a mutual effort in the construction of knowledge and personal understanding *that yields ownership*—cognitive ownership. People tend to prize those things in which they have ownership. Establishing cognitive ownership involves all of the modes of thinking that we use when processing information.

Let's return to the concerns about an over-emphasis on critical thinking. Certainly we would not argue against teaching situations which require judgments based on relevant criteria. In fact, as you'll recall, making judgments is part of the Cognitive Spiral Model of cognitive processing. During

Metacognitive Thought a solution is evaluated, or judged, with regard to the particular criteria of the problem. No doubt people need to learn to make decisions by matching a possible solution to the criteria. The difficulty lies in the noticeably absent opportunity to use *creative* thinking.

Excluding the possibility for creative thinking is like building a fence to confine thinking. Fences are not always bad, but fences always confine. Keep in mind that we have emphasized the idea that creative thinking is involved whenever we process information and is not something to be used only occasionally. The opportunity to discover relationships and patterns, or find new perspectives, and try to assemble a response based on those activities is lost. Should it surprise us that students want to scale those fences and not return?

Again, under some circumstances and to some extent a narrow focus is appropriate. However, we question the degree to which these activities *pervade* the curriculum, just as we question the tendency to base instruction and evaluation primarily on the knowledge level of Bloom's famous *Taxonomy of Educational Objectives: Cognitive Domain* (1956).

The taxonomy might be a good place to spend some time in our consideration of thinking. As you'll recall, the taxonomy is indicative of the increasing sophistication of thinking from the knowledge level through evaluation level. Does the ascending order of the taxonomy also reflect the difficulty of thinking? That is, does the mind find it easier to work on the knowledge level than on the synthesis level? Take a look at the activity on the next page. We admit it's a quiz and probably no one warned you there would be quizzes involved. Go ahead and work your way through quiz number one. By the way, the questions have been written for an adult reader, so the following page is blank. Use that to write questions suitable for your students.

Quiz Number One— For Teachers

Read and answer all of the questions below.

1. Who were the three men who manned the first American spacecraft to land on the moon?

2. Gneiss is an example of what kind of rock?

3. What is a female fox called?

4. Who was the first man to fly a powered airplane?

5. What is the square root of 144?

6. What is the meaning of the word laser?

7. What is a six letter word for merry?

    _ _ $\overset{\mathsf{v}}{\_}$ _ _ _

8. Define the following word: light

Quiz Number One

Answer as many of the questions as you can.

1.

2.

3.

4.

5.

6.

7.

8.

That wasn't bad, was it? Just in case you are not sure about the answers to a question or two; Mike Collins was in the Command Module, while Armstrong and Aldrin were strolling on the moon; gneiss is a metamorphic rock; a female fox is called a vixen; Orville was supposed to be second to fly, but malfunctions hampered Wilbur's attempt and so Orville actually flew first; the square root of 144 is 12; LASER is an acronym for Light Amplification by Stimulated Emission of Radiation; jovial would be an acceptable term; and the definition of "light" is entertaining, not requiring deep thought. (You didn't know it had to be *our* definition? Do you suppose your students feel the same way?) Move on to quiz number two (p. 52). Come back here when you've finished.

What did you think of that? Pretty sophisticated stuff, taxonomy-wise. Did you notice that none of the questions were on the knowledge level? Everything required some degree of analysis, synthesis, and/or evaluation. Yet answering these questions probably seemed easier. They may even have made you smile. In all honesty, we have presented this series of quizzes to many teachers, and virtually each time someone says the first quiz was easier because he or she either knew the answer or didn't. Of course, the pressure that we typically put on our students in a testing situation is missing. It is likely that if there were a consequence motivating teachers to come up with the correct response, they would reconsider their perspective. The point is that *the mind does higher level thinking*. We don't have to teach it. It's actually the boring and mundane lower-level thinking that is difficult.

It could be argued that there was a time when it was necessary to memorize many facts and figures—though memorizing them just for memorization practice would still seem to be questionable. Today, however, information is available as it has never been. There likely has never been a better opportunity to bring our creative abilities to bear in concert with vast stores of information to solve problems of all sorts.

It is discovery, by virtue of our own creative and inventive thinking, that gives us "ownership" of solutions. The more engaging activity is the one requiring more facets of our thinking ability, on higher levels, than those which are "prethought" except for one aspect of thinking. As you'll see in Part II, there is an instructional technique which provides a true sense of solution ownership while still demonstrating the concepts the teacher has presented.

What, Then, Is the Distinction?

Let's address this question by comparing several activities. The following list in the activity on page 53, contains some classroom activities in science. Take a few minutes to consider the list in several contexts. First, in the blank space indicate whether you feel the item represents a problem-solving activity, a creative problem-solving activity, or some other activity. When completed, take another look at the list and consider whether the activity is representative of a traditional classroom activity. Finally, go back to the list and consider which activities would engage your students' thinking across all five of the thinking modes we have discussed.

Quiz Number Two

Read and answer all of these questions.

1. What is your favorite TV sitcom this year?

2. What is the best "after school snack" for kids?

3. Which subject was your favorite when you were in elementary school? Why?

4. Suppose you got a new dog for the family and wanted to propose three names that your family could choose for the dog. What three names would you choose?

5. Write a word which rhymes with light.

6. If you were going to travel from New Orleans to Washington, D.C. and you had no limitations affecting your decision, what form of transportation would you use?

7. What color looks best on you?

8. Suppose you were writing a story about a young person who teaches school and that person recently took up a new hobby. What would that hobby be?

Classroom Activities in Science

Listed below are several activities which might occur in the classroom during a science lesson. Identify the examples as being:

C   creative problem-solving activity

P   problem-solving activity

A   other activity

_____ 1. Students are watching a video tape of a space shuttle mission.

_____ 2. Students are conducting an experiment following directions in the science book.

_____ 3. Students are writing answers to questions at the end of the chapter.

_____ 4. Students are conducting a product test using a form the teacher has given.

_____ 5. The teacher has created a game and students are using it to review for a test.

_____ 6. Students are packaging an egg to survive a 10 foot drop with the dimension requirements 20 cm or less on each side.

_____ 7. Students are drawing what they think is inside a mystery box.

_____ 8. Students are labeling a diagram of a plant.

What did you notice? Did it seem to you that items such as 1, 2, 3, and 8 sound very much like what goes on in school, yet do not qualify as something that engages student thinking across all modes of thought? Perhaps you saw that item 5 was an activity that required the teacher to think creatively, but the emphasis for students is still on demonstrating knowledge of content material.

Item 4 comes closer to an activity driven by student thinking. Though the teacher has provided a form (criteria), the student may be allowed to provide items for evaluation. In such a case it may be necessary to *adjust the criteria to match the situation. You wouldn't evaluate paper towels in quite the same way that you would chocolate chip cookies. Right?

Items 6 and 7, which probably didn't strike you as standard fare in the classroom, both place emphasis on the student's approach to the problem. There is room for perspective switching, relationship finding, pattern identification. Notice that creative thinking has not been limited, and critical thinking is not eliminated.

Problem solving, in the context of our discussion, is an activity seeking to identify a solution within given parameters. Rules and criteria with regard to both the approach and the anticipated outcome are established along with the scenario, yielding a well-structured problem. Its strength as an instructional tool is in providing practice with specific procedures and conditions. Its weakness is that problems in everyday life are rarely contrived, typically are ill-structured, and usually call for the application of heuristics in a context *different* from the learning situation. You have likely watched students appropriately apply concepts in a classroom situation who fail to do so in an analogous situation outside of the classroom.

Creative problem solving is an activity that may *question the implied or established parameters of the problem* to find new perspectives and responses. For an example,

let's look to NASA, an organization that lives and dies by its calculating and problem-solving strength.

The space shuttle represents a dramatic perspective change in the design of spacecraft. The problem was to design and build a *reusable* spacecraft. Ultimately, an enterprise whose primary focus was the design of powerful engines found its reusable solution in the notion of powerless flight, the glider, for its return to earth.

That particular switch of perspective was not without costs, as is the case with any decision. Shuttle astronauts have just one shot at landing each time. Without engines there is no option to "go around" and try again. Yet, thousands of sailplane pilots around the world fly under this condition everyday. The concept was not unprecedented, just the application.

In order to reach this solution, the typical rules had to be questioned. Was it really necessary for a craft returning from space to have propulsion? "Well, now that you mention it," someone probably said, "I guess not." Is it necessary for all adhesives to grip with great tenacity to be valuable? Ask the Post-It note people. The creative problem solver sees the rules as just another part of the problem that is open to question. And that particular distinction differs considerably from our traditional notion of how to solve problems. Possibilities first; rules second!

Creative Thinking and "Doing" Science

Defining creative thinking as a search and discussing creative problem solving as an activity questioning parameters of a problem, sounds like scientific thinking as well. Though scientists certainly have a direction in mind as they investigate, they are also consistently going beyond what is known. That is the essence of what they do. Scientists question what is known to understand more about what is not yet known. So, we can see that they search for patterns, perspectives, and relationships, and they question the parameters of current knowledge. It is a *systematic* application of creative problem solving.

We already know that we want students to approach science in terms of "doing" science. That is, we try to design our lessons around the use of the science process skills to make science an *active* learning experience. Inventing, which Bentley and Ebert (1996) include in their list of investigative techniques, offers the opportunity to *apply* science in a practical and observable manner. Applying concepts in a genuine problem-solving scenario provides a concrete demonstration of a student's understanding of science concepts. By allowing students to engage in an inventing-based investigation, we bridge the gap between science and technology. And if the inventing work happens to center on issues and applications that relate to the student's community life, we apply the social aspect as well. It's science, technology, and society genuinely addressed in the classroom.

This brings us back to Dewey. We've mentioned his suggestion that genuine thinking begins with a problematic situation, but he also suggested that creative intelligence flourishes when solving *real* problems. Educators can put students into such situations. We need not ask them to solve the problems of the world (though you probably would not complain if, as your student accepts a Nobel prize, the comment is "And I'd like to thank my teacher for giving me real problems to solve."), but designing a machine to pop a balloon or extinguish a candle in a new way is a challenge your students can tackle. Rather than seeking to match the teacher's answers, the student embarks on the task of bringing something new to the world. Add the notion of student responsibility for engaging all modes of thought and the student's "stake" in the outcome is also increased. Can

this be done in the classroom—in your classroom? Sure it can! And the implications reach beyond the time spent in school.

Creative problem solving as we've presented it closely resembles the problem-solving situations that students will encounter outside of school. Our task is to find an instructional approach to put students in real problem-solving situations that require the application of classroom knowledge. Science, with its inherently creative component, would seem to provide a strong basis from which to work. Such an approach would require a concrete application of scientific knowledge to solve a problem. Inventing allows that process to be observed by the teacher.

Is all of this just a matter of semantics? Thinking is problem solving is creative problem solving? We agree that the mind solves problems. And, since we consider creative thinking to be an integral component of that process, it may not be necessary to provide the moniker, *creative* problem solving.

However, because the notion of "problem solving" has become so context-specific and criteria-laden, we feel it is worthwhile to offer a distinction to put emphasis on the *role of creative thinking* in the cognitive process. Nothing is lost with regard to critical thinking—since criteria is still a part of the process. And criteria can always be added to the decision-making process. Yet by putting greater emphasis on the creative aspect, the student's role in a genuine problem-solving situation significantly increases.

Science, Technology, and Inventing

A Mutually Beneficial Relationship

Where does technology fit into this picture? Metaphorically, it fits as a symbiotic relationship with science. Simply stated, science seeks to understand the world around us, and technology takes scientifically generated knowledge and gives it *practical value* by developing processes and machines that extend capabilities. The information gathered through scientific inquiry provides the "materials" with which the technologist works. The machines and processes developed by technologists extend the capabilities of scientists, who are then able to generate new knowledge. One endeavor facilitates the other. As investigation is the active process of science, *inventing* is the active process of technology.

Can the same person be both scientist and technologist? Certainly, just as a musician can also be a composer. But one does not *have* to be both. And the products of each endeavor often are not the same. The composer's product is something to be performed (by the composer or by someone else). The musician's product is the performance.

Similarly, the product of science is information, which when interpreted in relationship to other information, we call knowledge. Its value, *in terms of pure science*, is academic—sometimes esoteric. The product of technology is a process, an implement, or machine. Its value is a function of its practical application. However, in both examples the work of one bridges the gap between the two. The relationship between them gives value to the work done by each—a positive transfer of related endeavor. In education, providing opportunities for students to experience the world of the scientist and technologist can greatly enhance transfer of learning from the context of information to *using* information to solve problems.

The "-ology" of Technology

Let's spend a moment discussing technology in greater detail. Technology, like creative thinking, is one of those terms that people use with the presumption that everyone understands what it means. What is technology? Or, since we know that the "ology" part means "the study of," what is the study of "tech"?

You might try asking some of your students what technology is. Here are some of the responses which typify what our college students tell us:

Technology is computers.

It's microwave ovens and satellite dishes—electronics.

It's new stuff that makes life easier.

Technology is supposed to make work easier, but sometimes it just means you have more work to do.

Notice that technology is usually thought of as "things" rather than as a process. And usually technology is the *latest* things. Nobody ever tells us that technology is a steam engine, a loom, or an electric toaster. Do these examples constitute an understanding of what technology "is"?

Don't take our word for it. "Technology" is a term that your students and contemporaries have all heard many times. Go ahead and ask some of the folks that you encounter regularly to define technology. Don't set them up, and don't provide a lot of explanation. Simply ask, "What is technology?" In addition to listening for the definition they offer, also pay attention for that pause that often occurs when someone is about to define what they thought was obvious, but turns out to be somewhat evasive. If asking for an outright definition seems to result in people leaving the lunch table when you approach, you might want to use the following questionnaire. Rather than starting off asking for a definition, the form offers examples and asks whether or not the items are representative of "technology."

The question remains "What is the study of 'tech'?" Perhaps it would be helpful to consider technology again in terms of its relationship to science.

Defining science as *a systematic investigation of the world around us*, tends to take a rather general approach. Though scientists typically have a specific agenda in mind to guide their work, it is still fair to say that what is eventually learned may or may not match expectations. And we are all aware that more than one scientific breakthrough has occurred through serendipity (with due respect given to Pasteur's notion that chance favors the prepared mind).

As an example, consider a nature walk on the beach. Though an oversimplification, it would be correct to say that what you find on the beach will be what happens to be there. You can't specify what will be there beyond general categorizations. You go out, you investigate, and whatever you find is whatever you find. Science has an implied acceptance that one is charting new territory. Prediction, expectation, and speculation aside, what's actually there remains to be seen.

Technology, on the other hand, seeks to develop a specific product or process in order to accomplish a function. And it will use specific information to do so. This technique is not investigation with the goal of discovery, but rather the *combining of information* to serve an identified need or purpose. Technology combines the knowledge gained through science in ways that have practical value.

Do you want a definition? We offer this: technology is that field of endeavor which combines discrete bits of information to yield products or processes that *extend our capabilities*. Did any of the people you asked give that answer? If so, you may want to keep that person in mind when you start inventing activities with your students!

Technology extends our capabilities. That distinction emphasizes a particular value to the work of technologists. By definition, all inventing yields something new, yet not all inventing represents technology. The same is true of the active process of science—investigation. We could say that while all science involves investigation, not all investigation is scientific.

For example, perhaps you enjoy sitting at your breakfast table watching the various bird species that come to the feeder. You may even jot down which species you see. Then again, some days you watch, some you don't. Sometimes you write down what you've observed, sometimes you don't. Though you are employing the basic science process skill of observation and the investigative technique of documenting, the *systematic* approach that characterizes scientific inquiry is lacking.

Testing Your Tech-*knowledge*-y

Match the items below with the appropriate terms by placing the corresponding letter(s) on the line below each term.

<u>Terms</u>   <u>Items</u>

1)   Technology   a) computer

                                                        b) hand lens

_____   c) inventing

                                                        d) pencil

2)   Products of Technology   e) space program

                                                        f) book

_____   g) hammer and nails

                                                        h) gravity

                                                        i) CD player

                                                        j) hot air balloon

                                                        k) heat makes things expand

                                                        l) engineering

Similarly, an invention that adds a new perch to a bird feeder, such as that in the drawing below, does involve inventing, but it is not necessarily an example of technology.

The perch made from a coat hanger represents the combination of previously existing materials in a new way—though not one that extends our capabilities. The perch has not increased my *ability* to see more birds. It *has* increased the capacity of the one feeder to accommodate more birds. That might increase my opportunities to see more birds at one time, but my abilities have not been enhanced. If, however, I use a telescope to watch birds from a distance because they won't approach an area occupied by humans, then the telescope has enhanced my ability to observe birds. Without it, I would have been unable or incapable of seeing something the size of a bird from so far away.

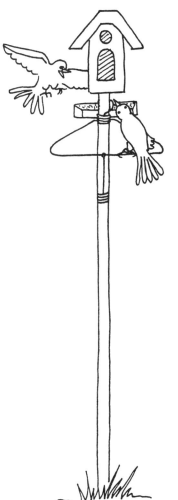

To bring the example closer to home, for many of us reading these words might require one of two things—very long arms, or a pair of eyeglasses. Designing an adjustable pair of sticks that would support a book may be a good inventing activity for students learning the inventing process. Designing a set of lenses that enhance the ability of my eyes to focus on the page is characteristic of inventing through the combination of discrete bits of information (optics and the related processes for preparing lenses) with the goal of enhancing my ability to see. This we call *technology*. Designing the sticks, inventing, represents the first step in eventually moving to the sophisticated application of information that results in a pair of eyeglasses—or the Hubble telescope.

Process, Not Product!

The activity with the bird feeder perch did, however, provide an example of how a common item can be used in an uncommon way. That creative change of perspective puts the focus where we want it—on inventing as a *process*. Our intention in science education is not to turn every student into a scientist, nor is the intention of this book to turn all students into technologists. Rather, our goal is to engage students in the active processes of science and technology, because doing so facilitates the development of their ability to think. It's an added bonus that such an emphasis also enhances understanding of subject content. Here's our motto as we begin to explore the use of inventing as an instructional technique: **Process, not product!**

This emphasis on the inventing process has another advantage. It provides an entry-level experience to the world of technology. That is, it allows students to engage in the process of inventing without the pressure of producing something that meets high tech criteria. Too often the well-intentioned unit on inventing requires that a student develop some practical working invention. The emphasis in such situations is squarely on the product. If the product works, great. But realistically only a handful of projects become working products. This is particularly true when inventing is addressed simply as a unit of instruction, rather than as part of an instructional strategy.

How many students out there failed to make it to the *elite* display at teachers' conventions? How many were unable to think of that great idea or a "need to fill"? Yet the *process of thinking* that all students used—those students who didn't make it to the regional convention display as well—is important. What would happen in science if we walked in and said, "OK class, I want each of you to identify a gap in our scientific knowledge and conduct an investigation to fill the gap." Not a pretty picture. Developing the thinking process is the road to improving the product of human thought. In the classroom it must be the case that the thinking is valued. Yes, it *is* the thought that counts.

Look for yourself. The drawings below are intended to represent student projects. One of the projects relates to physical science, the other is an example of the create-a-creature activity. Whether or not the machine works, and whether the creature lives, you can tell from these inventions whether the students understood the concepts of simple machines and environmental adaptation. Would a student with weak verbal skills have been able to demonstrate understanding as well in written form?

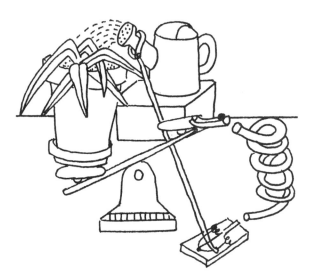

Figure 3.1. A Rube Goldberg Type Drawing.

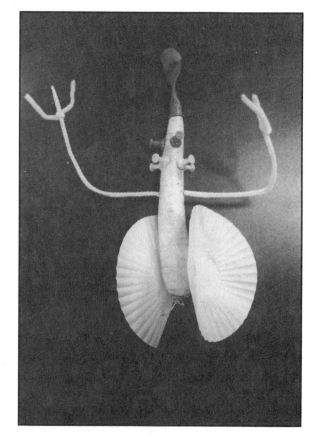

Figure 3.2. Create-a-Creature Masterpieces.

Summary

This chapter ends our discussion of the "what" and "why" of creative thinking and creative problem solving in the classroom. From here we'll move to the all important "how." Let's take a moment to summarize Chapter Three.

Problem solving is what we do when we think. The notion, however, has tended to become so associated with the idea of critical thinking that problem solving in the classroom tends to take the form of prethought exercises that limit, rather than expand, students' thinking. An emphasis on creative problem solving is intended to provide students with the opportunity to engage all the modes of thought in cognitive processing to increase their ownership of the products of their thinking. We have conceptualized creative problem solving as an approach that allows for questioning problem parameters to entertain new perspectives, seek out patterns, and identify relationships.

We have also discussed the symbiotic relationship between science and technology. Though each facilitates the work of the other, it became apparent that the active processes of each have striking similarities and differences. Both are highly creative endeavors that facilitate the work of the other as they eventually improve our lives and understanding. Their primary difference is the products each yields. Science is an enterprise engaged in a systematic, though creative, search for new information and understanding. Technology yields new processes and machines that extend our capabilities. And the processes of both, investigation and invention, provide appropriate experiences for the cognitive levels of our students.

In the search for an instructional technique to facilitate creative problem solving, inventing offers several advantages. First, it provides the context for genuine problem solving. Second, it offers the opportunity for the application of learning from one context to a problem with another one. In this way, positive transfer of learning is enhanced.

An inventing-based approach to creative problem solving also provides students with an introduction to the work of technologists. These experiences can help demystify the world of technology.

Finally, inventing can emphasize the thinking *process* and so remove the anxiety associated with developing a wildly successful product. Whether or not the product works, the teacher will have a concrete representation of the student's understanding of the concepts considered in class. And with an emphasis on the process, rather than the product, a good attitude toward inventing and creative thinking can be fostered, just as we try to foster a good attitude toward scientific investigation.

Let's move to Part II and consider activities in the three levels of inventing that combine the worlds of science and technology!

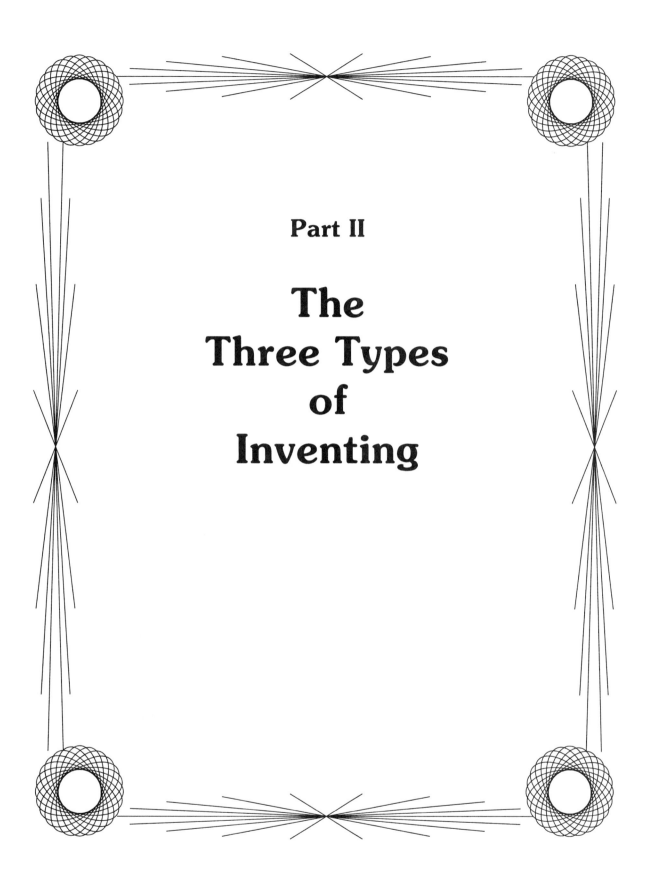

Part II

The Three Types of Inventing

Chapter Four

Discovery Inventing

In this chapter you will find:

The two phases of Discovery Inventing;

Discovery Inventing activities;

and the Invention Investigation Project!

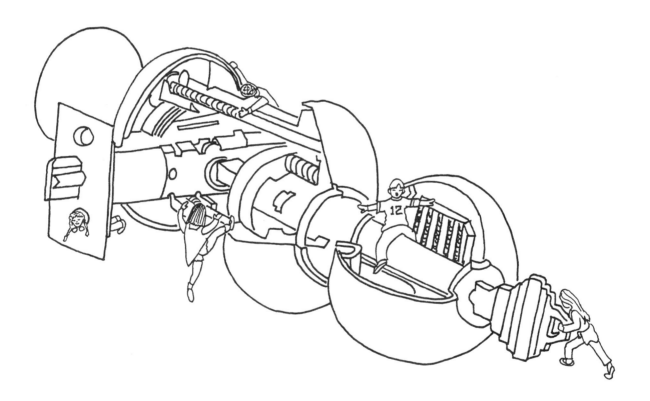

Discovery Inventing is an instructional approach to finding out how things work. Items as simple as a clothespin or a can opener reveal much about simple machines. In this chapter, we'll focus on activities which provide the opportunity to discover the relationships and principles underlying common utensils and tools. The knowledge gained from such activities broadens the knowledge base that students bring to more sophisticated inventing activities. Let's begin with an example of Discovery Inventing in the classroom that capitalizes on a "teachable moment."

The Pencil Sharpener Scenario

It wasn't quite an argument, by no means a fight, but there was a definite commotion over by the pencil sharpener. Greta, Kent, and Diane had gone to sharpen pencils before the math lesson began, and were involved in what appeared to be a very serious discussion. Mr. Toriello went over to see just what was going on.

"What's the big discussion over here?" asked Mr. Toriello. "Is the sharpener devouring pencils again?"

"Greta says that pencil sharpeners have files in them that put the point on a pencil, and I told her that it has a little knife like the sharpener in my school kit," said Kent.

"I think they're both wrong, Mr. Toriello," said Diane. "My father is an architect and he has lots of pencil sharpeners. When one of them broke, I got to see inside. It had a slanty stone in it that the pencil rubs against."

"Who's right?" Greta wanted to know.

As Kent fought to get the cover off of the sharpener, Mr. Toriello was struck with an idea. "Well, it sounds to me like you are all correct."

"Mr. Torielloooooo!" an exasperated Greta chimed, "We can't all be right."

"Let's see about that, Greta. Has everybody gotten their pencils sharpened?" he asked. He told Kent to leave the cover on the sharpener for now, and that they would check inside later on.

Mr. Toriello went to the chalkboard and drew the outline of a huge pencil sharpener. He included the crank, and a picture of an equally large, though noticeably dull pencil poised for re-pointing, but left the "insides" of the sharpener blank.

"Okay, boys and girls, today we are inventors." He stressed the word "inventor" with his voice and smile. "Take out a sheet of paper, and draw what you think is inside the sharpener that makes the point on a pencil when you turn the crank. It can be whatever you think it is, little mice that chew the wood away, or knives that swirl around and whittle a point on the pencil for you. Just draw whatever you think might be underneath that shiny metal cover. I'll work on a drawing too."

The students in the class drew a number of different plans, ranging from the "very possible" to the "wild and wacky." But as the students explained each drawing, Mr. Toriello was careful to point out that if woodpeckers could fit into a sharpener, then that idea could work, and if little rocks like those in the driveway could be ground against the pencil by turning them in a drum—that too would work. There was merit to every idea.

Mr. Toriello told the students that they would continue the great pencil sharpener mystery the next day. That afternoon he asked the custodian for old, broken, or worn-out pencil sharpeners. He located an electric pencil sharpener, a draftsman's pencil sharpener, and a sharpening pad. He also purchased enough children's pencil sharpeners so each student would have one. His plan was to have the students investigate the types of sharpeners and compare the by-products produced by each.

The next morning Mr. Toriello had three clear plastic cups on his desk. The contents of each were obviously different, but still seemed somewhat similar. He began by saying, "Today's topic is the great pencil sharpener mystery, part II."

In addition to the cups, he had a piece of sandpaper, a carpenter's plane, a wood rasp, and a small board. He invited the students to examine the contents of the three cups, and discuss their observations. One cup had a very fine powder that got everybody's fingers black. It had the strong smell of pencils. The second cup had some of the black powder that was seen in the first cup, but also had shreds of wood. They were not like splinters of wood, but were soft. The shreds were skinny and short. The third cup had thin shavings of wood, many of which had a narrow strip of yellow at the edge. They smelled more like wood than the contents of the other two cups. The shavings had little ridges on them that could be felt with fingers. They were not brittle, but could easily be broken into smaller pieces. The students recognized that all three cups contained ground up pencils, but they were ground up by three different machines. Kent recognized the same sort of shavings that he got from his little sharpener. Greta identified the material in cup 2 as the same as what they empty from the classroom sharpener. Diane said that the messy contents of cup 1 were the same as she saw in her father's broken sharpener.

Mr. Toriello provided an opportunity for the students to use each of the tools he had brought from home. As one group used the rasp on a piece of wood, they saved the resulting materials. Similarly, the groups with the sandpaper and the plane saved their materials in plastic cups. Each container of by-products was labeled with the name of the tool: rasp, sandpaper, plane.

Next, they examined the tools and found that the plane had a sharp knife that shaved the wood. The rasp had many teeth that tore the wood into soft shreds, and the sandpaper had a rough surface that made little dust piles of wood on the desk. They then compared filings, shavings, and sawdust with the contents of cups 1, 2, and 3, and found them to be similar. The shavings and sawdust from the board did not get their fingers messy. The class decided that this was because there was no pencil-lead in the board. Mr. Toriello gave each student one of the small sharpeners he had purchased, and also brought out the broken sharpeners he had gotten from the custodian, as well as the sharpening pad from the art teacher. The students examined all of the sharpeners and discussed the similarities between the tools and the sharpeners Mr. Toriello had provided.

Greta exclaimed, "We were all right about the sharpeners, weren't we, Mr. Toriello? Different sharpeners work in different ways."

Mr. Toriello smiled and nodded his head. "Yes. Some sharpeners use a sharp blade to slice the wood. Some use a rough surface like sandpaper to remove little bits of wood at a time. And some use files with tiny teeth that tear away small shreds of wood, though they have the same purpose—to put a sharp point on our pencils for math!"

■ ■ ■

Discovery Inventing refers to early experiences with inventing when the focus is on understanding how things work. This level of inventing is obviously appropriate for younger students given their limited experience with the functioning of simple machines. However, Discovery Inventing exercises are equally important for older students and in-service teachers for accomplishing the same purpose. After all, you have probably used a stapler hundreds of times, but do you know how it works?

Books such as David Macaulay's *The Way Things Work* do a wonderful job of exposing the inner-workings of machines without the cumbersome detail of an "exploded-view" technical drawing. With simple machines there is nothing like the opportunity to see the parts and the way they interact. The Discovery Inventing format enables the teacher to provide students with the opportunity to engage in creative thinking, to apply science process skills, and have *first-hand* experience with the relationship between science and technology. Even better, this investigative approach is driven by natural curiosity and wonder. The motivation for learning is an intrinsic desire to answer the question, "What's inside?" The entire lesson in the pencil sharpener scenario was derived from a question generated by the students. By capitalizing on curiosity, teachers can provide a creative problem-solving opportunity that encourages the search for new patterns, perspectives, and relationships. Such an activity is a *creative* problem-solving opportunity when a minimum of criteria is imposed on possible solutions. For instance, in our scenario the only criteria was that the answer fit inside the pencil sharpener . . . and miniature people would fit this criteria.

The Two Phases of Discovery Inventing

There are two distinct phases to Discovery Inventing lessons. First is the *inventing phase* which forms explanations of how things work. During this phase the emphasis is clearly on the **generation** of ideas. It is in the *discovery phase* that the actual workings of the object or machine are examined.

Whether the explanations from the *inventing phase* match the actual workings of the object is not of great importance. The two phases of Discovery Inventing provide information that can be compared as part of the process of conceptual change and development. Perhaps the student had a proper conception of how the machine works, and that conception will then be reinforced. For the student whose explanation differed, the newly acquired information may serve to appropriately alter the original conception. But, as is evident by Mr. Torriello's acceptance of all possibilities in the scenario, creative thinking is *valued* and *encouraged*, rather than inhibited.

The Invention Phase

During the *invention phase* the value of the creative process is emphasized more than the product or problem solution. As in the scenario, it is not necessary that the students' explanations were practical. In fact, ideas for practical inventions often come from improbable suggestions. The stories of H. G. Wells are a good example. As improbable as his bullet-like spaceship to the moon must have seemed at the time, it provided the *idea* from which others made such travel a reality. As students discuss their explanations, the ideas from one stimulate thinking in another. If we were to impose practical criteria at this point, we would necessarily inhibit consideration of novel patterns and relationships that could provide the spark for still more creative ideas.

Using an Everyday Item to Expand Your Thinking

Here is a chance to practice some of what we have learned. In Chapter Three we listed possible uses of an old shoe, paying particular attention to several categories of responses. This next activity (p. 70) provides a chance for some free-wheeling idea generation. Listing 101 possibilities may be a bit much at this point, so for this exercise, just list 25-and-1 possible uses for a dull pencil. The activity's objective is to provide an opportunity to generate ideas with a minimum of criteria. Remember to consider the pencil from various perspectives: as a writing instrument, a colorful stick, a shock absorber, etc. Considering something as simple as a pencil from the perspective of alternate uses leads to a greater appreciation of individual parts. This awareness will provide the basis for understanding how parts interact as systems. When you get right to it, that's all there is to anything: some sort of parts assembled into some sort of system. Though the activity page has a picture of a suitable pencil, it may be a good idea to have pencils for everybody involved to use.

25-and-1 Pencil Possibilities

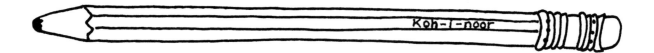

Generating ideas with a minimum amount of criteria imposed.

Take a pencil and look it over. Look it over *very carefully*. Notice the color, shape, size. Look for any writing on the pencil. Check the many parts of the pencil and note the materials from which they are made. Take another look. Now, list 25-and-1 possible uses for the pencil.

1._____	14._____
2._____	15._____
3._____	16._____
4._____	17._____
5._____	18._____
6._____	19._____
7._____	20._____
8._____	21._____
9._____	22._____
10._____	23._____
11._____	24._____
12._____	25._____
13._____	+1._____

In your opinion, what characteristic of the pencil makes it most useful for something *other than* its usual use for writing?

How many of your ideas focused on the pencil as a marking tool? Did you include using it to mark in sand, dirt, or wet cement? How about the lettering on the pencil? Could you make rubbings of the letters in order to spell out a message? What about advertising space? Or even more symbolically, did you notice the phrase "koh-i-noor" on the pencil in the drawing? What does that mean? What about the shape? Did you consider using several pencils as a transport device (after the manner of the ancient Egyptians)?

Did any of your ideas involve taking the pencil apart? If you had, the range of potential uses would have expanded to the characteristics of graphite (slippery), wood (non-conductor of electricity), rubber (flexible), and metal (rigid support though malleable—and, of course, a conductor of electricity).

There are many more than 25-and-1 possibilities ranging from the highly pragmatic to the wild and wacky. Most important for this activity was simply the willingness to seek alternate perspectives, and to entertain a wide spectrum of possibilities. It is likely that once you got past the focus on practicality, you were able to rapidly increase the length of your list. A long list of ideas provides a wealth of information from which to invent solutions.

The Discovery Phase

The activities of the second day in the scenario were concerned with the *discovery phase*. During this phase the lesson emphasizes the use of science process skills while students investigate the properties of the materials provided. They make observations, inferences, and gather information from which to draw conclusions. The information learned during the lesson is useful and can be applied to other situations.

Of great importance, however, is the lesson's order of presentation. By providing the *discovery phase* second, the teacher was able to take an otherwise *convergent* lesson and add a *divergent* orientation. Students may have been less creative and perhaps more confined in their thinking if the workings of the pencil sharpener had been exposed on the first day without speculation. It would have been difficult for imaginative thinking once they had seen how the pencil sharpener operated.

There are many objects in the classroom and around school that are interesting to investigate with the two phase Discovery Inventing format. A stapler, which incorporates springs, guides, and the plate that forms the closed staple could be investigated. Manual typewriters have complex mechanisms which provide excellent examples of transfer of motion. Students can see what happens when a key is pressed and a letter is formed.

Pianos are usually made with large panels that are easily removed for tuning and regulating. Removal of panels makes it easy to discover what happens when keys are played. First, of course, allow students to explain (or draw) what they think might be happening before revealing the actual mechanism.

Music boxes are also fascinating mechanisms to observe. With just a few parts, virtually all of which are visible, students can watch how the raised pins "pluck" the metal fingers of the tone bar. You will likely have some students who have jewelry cases containing the small musical movements which are often visible without dismantling part of the box. By asking around, you may be able to locate some that could be taken apart. Craft stores and woodworker supply stores often sell the units (in a wide variety of tunes) for installing in homemade boxes. If possible, you may want to bring in one of the more sophisticated movements that plays several songs.

We suggest (and this comes from personal childhood experience) that you don't try taking apart a valuable musical movement, clock, or other mechanism. Somehow, it just seems that after putting it back together there's always some pesky part left over. Stay with the "no longer in service" items that clutter up closets and attics. You should have little trouble finding an adequate supply of such items that can be examined.

Of course, in our solid-state, no-moving-parts world there are many items that reveal little when opened. Telephones and computer circuit boards are amazing to look at, but without a sophisticated knowledge of electronics, we can't really discern much about their functioning. However, there are more mechanisms just waiting to be discovered. Soda machines, retractable pens, and old cameras can take your students through mazes of switches, springs, and levers—and on into the optics of lenses and mirrors. Your local photo finishing outlet may gladly give you a few filmless disposable cameras.

Identifying Attributes

An easy start with Discovery Inventing is offered in the Clothespin Attributes activity (p. 73). A wooden clothespin with a metal spring provides a good introduction for examining something to see how it works. Unlike the uses for a pencil activity, the observations made of the clothespin should include the interaction of the parts and the results of that interaction. This means that you might have to encourage students to consider the range of motion possible, the direction of motion, the pressure required, etc. All of these observations will contribute to the student's understanding of how this particular machine works. And the information from this exercise may well be used in subsequent inventing activities. For instance, you and your students might consider how a clothespin might be used as a switch, as a release mechanism, or as a means for supporting some sort of track.

Using Eye Opening Discovery Inventing Activities

The pencil possibilities and clothespin attributes activities provided some warm-up exercises for more involved Discovery Inventing experiences. The next four activities become increasingly sophisticated in terms of use of knowledge and information learned.

Attributes, Components, and Systems

The Attribute Finding activity (p. 74) is an extension of the Clothespin Attribute activity. This activity involves examining several objects, all of which are somewhat more sophisticated than a clothespin. Also, note that this activity calls for identifying systems. A system is a group of components assembled to accomplish a task, which the individual components alone cannot accomplish. The clothespin, for example, is a system. The wooden pieces alone could not hold clothes on a line, nor could the spring, but working together as a system they do the job quite nicely.

This activity, therefore, has two primary objectives. The first is to provide opportunities to see how common items work. The second is to provide an opportunity to understand that most common items are not just collections of components, but are collections of components combined in a system.

We have provided a space on the activity page for filling in the particular items to be explored, but have not listed items, since what might be easily obtained by one person may not be easy for another. Typically, however, this activity would involve eggbeaters (do you think you can still locate one of those?), can openers (particularly the kind with the crank on the side), scissors, and other kitchen items. Another approach is to use workshop tools. Particularly with young students it is wise to avoid sharp tools; however things like pliers, clamps, and even hammers (a hammer is a multi-function tool) work well.

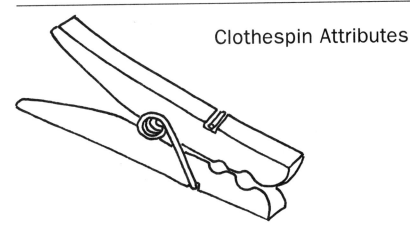

Clothespin Attributes

How might you describe a clothespin to someone who has never seen one? Besides the color and size, what else can you say about it?

1. _____
2. _____
3. _____
4. _____
5. _____
6. _____
7. _____
8. _____
9. _____
10. _____

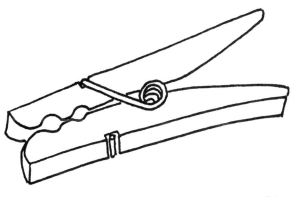

Attribute Finding Activity

Select objects such as an eggbeater, can opener, or scissors and examine them closely.

Objects: _____

_____

_____

Identify the component parts. Observe any possible movement of parts.

Components:

_____	_____	_____
_____	_____	_____
_____	_____	_____
_____	_____	_____
_____	_____	_____
_____	_____	_____
_____	_____	_____
_____	_____	_____

Identify systems within each object. Compare systems among the objects.

Systems:

_____	_____	_____
_____	_____	_____
_____	_____	_____
_____	_____	_____
_____	_____	_____
_____	_____	_____
_____	_____	_____

Exercises with Discovery Inventing

The Pencil Sharpener scenario that began this chapter is an activity that we have used with great success around the world. The activity allows students to answer the question of what is inside the sharpener by using both phases of Discovery Inventing. In addition, students can see how tools used in one context can be used in the specific context of sharpening a pencil. It will, however, require some preparation beyond making copies of the activity pages that follow.

Here's what you will need for this activity:

Tools:

carpenter's plane

wood rasp (A file is not good enough—you will need a rasp. A rasp has really big sharp teeth that will cut shreds of wood from the board.)

sandpaper or artist's sharpening pad (An artist's sharpening pad is just small sheets of sandpaper attached to a wooden stick.)

Materials:

Three containers containing:*

Container 1—shreds of wood from using the regular sharpener

Container 2—shavings of wood from the student's sharpener

Container 3—sawdust from using the sandpaper

A Board—preferably something soft, like pine

Clamps—to hold the board steady while students are planing, rasping, and sandpapering it. (You can try to do without this, but life will be much easier if you ask around and locate one that you can borrow.)

Sharpeners—it would be a nice touch to have those little plastic sharpeners. (Take a look at it, you'll see a small blade much like the blade in the carpenter's plane.)

You can present this lesson much like it happened in the scenario. Begin with the drawing of the pencil sharpener (p. 76). Allow students to explain what they think is inside. Most importantly, do not insist on a practical explanation. As Mr. Toriello did, find merit in all drawings, and *never* say that one drawing is the *correct* answer. The assignment is not to identify what *is* inside, but rather what *could* be inside. Who knows, an idea for a better sharpener (a cleaner one, sharper one, or perhaps a *quieter* one) just may arise from this activity!

After discussing the drawings, allow the students to use the tools to get shavings, shreddings, and sawdust from the board(s). Allow them to compare their products with the contents of the containers you provided. They should be able to see which type of tool is represented by each of the sharpeners you used.

---

*Note: In the scenario Mr. Toriello had containers with these same items, except that they were all cut from pencils. You can certainly do that if you like, just be prepared for the mess that results from having students handling pencil shavings. Alternatively, you could use a small dowel in each of the sharpeners in order to get "clean" shavings.

What Happens Inside the Pencil Sharpener?

Inside this outline of a pencil sharpener, draw what you think might be there that could sharpen pencils.

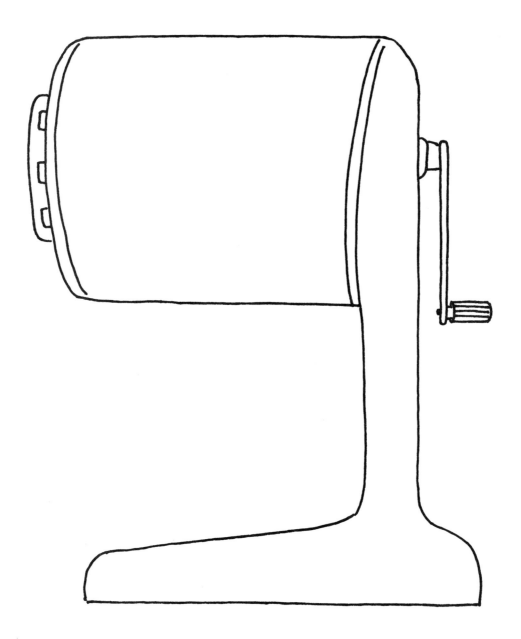

Sharpener By-products
Comparison Form

Examine and describe the wooden by-products made by each of the following tools:

Wood plane:

Rasp:

Sandpaper:

Examine and describe the wooden by-products from each of the pencil sharpeners:

Student (hand held) pencil sharpener:

Artist pencil sharpener (pad):

Wall mounted pencil sharpener (don't look inside just yet):

Compare the by-products of the tools to the by-products of the pencil sharpeners. Which ones are similar? Why?

Now, make a prediction about the internal workings of the wall mounted pencil sharpener. After making your prediction, look inside the pencil sharpener to see how it works.

Finally, if you've got some sharpeners that can be sacrificed for the cause, great. Let the students take things apart. (Be especially careful with those little sharpeners, once the blade is removed from the plastic housing it is a dangerous item.) Though it will be evident that for the artist's pad and the small sharpeners the pencil is moved against the tool, the regular sharpener will be different. There, the pencil is held still while a *system* of gears rotates two files around the pencil.

The next activity will allow your students to consider how a flashlight works, investigate an inexpensive flashlight to find the systems and subsystems it uses, and to take what they've learned to construct their own flashlight. It may sound simple, but chances are good that three out of four of your friends would not be able to describe flashlight operations without thinking about it for awhile!

If you have more than two students in your class, you will probably want to let them work in groups. The exception is drawing the inside of the flashlight during the Inventing Phase. Group work is a wonderful thing, but when it comes to drawing these pictures, we need individual work. This brings us to another reality. Some students (especially adults) balk at this opportunity to draw. We often hear (from adults) "Oh, I'm not creative." Though students are not usually as adamant in their refusal, it will be your responsibility to do two things. First, let them know that it is important, imperative, that they do *some* drawing of their own. But let's face it, there are times when drawings are simply not forthcoming. In such cases we usually ask for either a written explanation (written right on the blank picture) or a verbal explanation of what makes the particular item work. The emphasis is squarely on providing students an opportunity to do, and express, their own thinking.

Second, you must establish an atmosphere that clearly values student thinking. When you discuss the drawings it is very important that you find merit in each idea. Does this mean you have to accept something that is obviously inappropriate for the school setting? Of course not. Simply look for the redeeming aspect in each drawing. It may be the degree of originality, imagination, insight, efficiency, or whatever. Of all the minds in the classroom, yours must be the most open to various perspectives.

Well, with all of that said, let's get back to the activity. In addition to the following activity pages (pp. 79–81), here is what you'll need for this illuminating exercise.

Materials:

Flashlights—Get the inexpensive plastic ones. They often come two or four to a pack. You wouldn't want to rely on them during Hurricane Buster, but they are great for this activity.

Batteries—You will need enough for each flashlight. Avoid the heavy duty alkalines.

Lightbulbs—After taking the flashlights apart, those bulbs could be used. It is nice to have a supply of small bulbs on hand. Be sure the bulbs you buy can be operated by two "D" cells.

And: *Paper Towel Tubes, Wire, Paper Clips, Brass Fasteners, Aluminum Muffin Cups, Aluminum Foil, Duct Tape, Wire Cutters.*

Begin by asking how a flashlight works. Allow each student the opportunity to draw what they think is inside the flashlight that makes it work. After reviewing the drawings, let students move to the second activity page. This page has two parts. Part I asks that students make observations of the flashlight while it is still intact. Part II provides the opportunity to make a list of parts and describe the systems and subsystems that they find. We have put Part II on one separate page so that you can decide whether Part II is feasible for your class setting. Very young students may not be up to the task of identifying subsystems.

Just What Is in a Flashlight
That Makes It Light?

Inside this outline of a flashlight, draw what you think is there that could make it work.

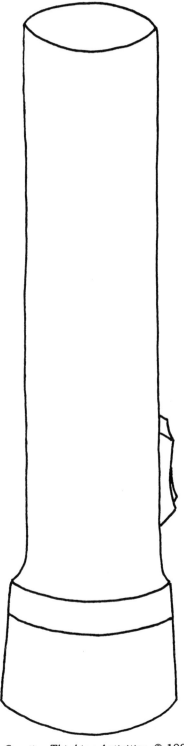

What Makes a Flashlight Light?

PART I

Examine a common flashlight.

What flashlight parts do you notice while looking at the outside of it?

_____   _____

_____   _____

_____   _____

_____   _____

_____   _____

_____   _____

What flashlight parts do you notice while looking at the inside of it?

_____   _____

_____   _____

_____   _____

_____   _____

_____   _____

_____   _____

What Makes a Flashlight Light?

PART II

Now that you have observed the flashlight, inside and out, list the components necessary for a common flashlight according to the systems involved. (Remember, a system is a group of components which work together to accomplish a task that the components alone cannot do, such as the electrical system or the system for focusing the beam of light.)

System: _____

_____   _____

_____   _____

_____   _____

_____   _____

System: _____

_____   _____

_____   _____

_____   _____

_____   _____

System: _____

_____   _____

_____   _____

_____   _____

_____   _____

System: _____

_____   _____

_____   _____

_____   _____

_____   _____

Now that you have shed some light on the functioning of flashlights, allow your students the opportunity to assemble one of their own. The third activity (p. 83) is provided to do a drawing of how their flashlight will work. "Back to the drawing board" is not a bad phrase, and, in fact, is the nature of the beast when it comes to designing things. Encourage your students to make initial drawings and then update their drawings as they find that some things work and some do not. Keep in mind that while the student's goal may be to build a working flashlight, your goal is to provide opportunities that allow students to express their thinking. Thoughts expressed are thoughts that can be discussed, elaborated, and acted upon.

Now for the reality check. Will these flashlights just fall together like the pieces in a child's jigsaw puzzle? No. Will all of the construction requirements become self-evident by just opening up a flashlight? No. Is this an activity requiring powers and abilities far beyond those of mortal men, as they used to say about Superman? No. Can you and your students handle this? Yes. Will your students be proud of the thinking and work that went in to building that fragile paper and muffin cup search light? You bet!

Invention Investigation

Don't worry, we are not talking about doing an investigative exposé of automotive computer diagnostics or CFC-free air conditioning systems. This activity deals with the high-tech world of staplers, sprinklers, or perhaps fishing reels. All of those everyday items provide for a good invention investigation. It is true, however, that the Invention Investigation is an activity that you will likely have to tailor to your particular class situation. Though it can be adapted for younger grade levels, it is best suited to students in middle school and beyond (we typically use this with pre- and post-graduate, preservice teacher education classes) who can take on independent research and project development.

The activity exemplifies all that Discovery Inventing has to offer. As mentioned, the topic invention should be something familiar. The idea is to let your students, independently or in small groups, select an invention to research. The product will be a presentation that explains the purpose of the invention, some background about its development, how it works, and the implications it has (or has had) for society and/or the environment. Skits, demonstrations, models, and examples are components to consider in designing a class presentation. A written version of the presentation is a handy way to integrate the activity with language arts, and discussing the social implications, past and potential, allows teaming the assignment with social studies. However, the focus of the activity is the generation of models to represent the invention. Avoid the poster presentation approach and encourage building models, however rudimentary, or using real examples to demonstrate the machine. Of course, some things are a bit awkward to bring to school. Sailboats, for instance, may be too big for the classroom, but they are not too big for a video camera.

Though the objective for the student is a project to be presented, the objective for the teacher is to provide the student with the opportunity to do independent thinking that leads to understanding. The Invention Investigation Guidelines (p. 85) is designed to give the student evaluation help, while leaving tremendous latitude in the design and presentation of the final project.

Constructing Your Own Flashlight

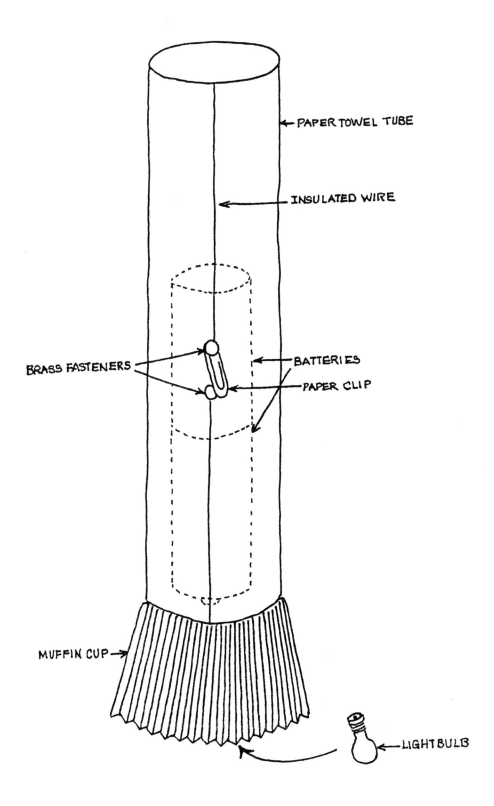

PAPER TOWEL TUBE

INSULATED WIRE

BRASS FASTENERS

BATTERIES

PAPER CLIP

MUFFIN CUP

LIGHT BULB

The following activity page (p. 85) lists the basic components of an Invention Investigation project. Included are spaces to write the names of group members, and to identify the invention to be investigated. It would be nice for you to provide students with a list of inventions to choose from. This also provides a measure of control over what might show up at presentation time. You might compile a list similar to the one below. We selected the items on this list because they included observable objects, either directly or replicated by simple models. The functioning parts of each object demonstrate basic mechanical principles of science, and are appropriate for elementary age students to understand (with the possible exception of the copy machine and computer, which is why the list below is a suggestion rather than an activity page). To broaden the categories and level of sophistication you could include topics such as fasteners for clothing (pins, buttons, zippers, velcro), or time pieces (water clocks, mechanical clocks, electric and quartz clocks). However, avoid putting sophisticated electronics and such things on the list. First, because many electronic devices store electricity and are hazardous even when unplugged. Second, without a thorough knowledge of electronics, there isn't much to see when looking at the circuit boards in such devices. They may look interesting, but it's difficult to see how anything happens.

Some Suggestions for Invention Investigations

- sailboat
- mechanical clock
- lightbulb
- doorknob
- fishing reel
- vacuum cleaner
- record player
- sewing machine
- typewriter
- piano
- icemaker
- elevator
- telescope
- camera
- toilet
- bicycle
- pencil sharpener
- fire extinguisher
- copy machine
- weighing machine
- garage door opener
- lawn sprinkler
- computer
- movie or slide projector

Once your list is compiled, have your students select an item for investigation. Along with the description of the expected presentation, be sure students have a copy of the Invention Investigation Evaluation Form (p. 86). Notice that our form allows for students to self-evaluate the presentation. That little device is intended to provide for reflection on what has been done. Also note that "humor" is listed among the evaluation criteria. Humor is itself a creative exercise, and making it part of the inventing experience emphasizes that creative thinking is valued.

Invention Investigation
Guidelines

Select one of the objects listed and do the following.

1. Explain the task of the object.

2. Describe all the components of the object. Be sure to include a name for each part even if it means that you invent a name for the part.

3. Explain how the parts interact to accomplish the task.

4. Provide information regarding the historical development and related social implications of the object.

Invention Investigation Evaluation Form

Name: _____ Object Investigated: _____

Directions: For each of the following criteria, circle the number that best represents your evaluation of your work. (1 is lowest . . . 5 is highest) On the lines provided, write a brief explanation of your numerical evaluation. You will have a possible total of 30 points and so will I. You will receive 15 points for making the presentation with your group.

1. The parts of the object and their importance were specified. 1 2 3 4 5

_____

_____

2. The explanation for how the object works was informative and clear. 1 2 3 4 5

_____

_____

3. The historical importance or evolution of the object was explained. 1 2 3 4 5

_____

_____

4. The presentation was visually and auditorially attractive. 1 2 3 4 5

_____

_____

5. The presentation had personality, style, and humor. 1 2 3 4 5

_____

_____

6. I was a significant contributor to my group. 1 2 3 4 5

_____

_____

Score: Self-awarded points: _____

Teacher's points: _____

Presentation points: _____

_____ Total

Summary

As an instructional technique, Discovery Inventing is intended to begin the process of demystifying technology by letting students see how things work, while also serving to foster the use of creative thinking vital to technological progress. In fact, all inventions, whether machines or processes, are merely a collection of parts or steps which proceed methodically to a particular end. If we begin with machines that offer an "entry-level" appropriate for students of a given age, understanding the interaction of parts is not so difficult. The flashlight activity in this chapter is a good example. It is important to recognize the difference between a) providing instructions to assemble a flashlight and b) allowing students to discover how to design and construct their own versions of a flashlight. In the first situation someone has already done the thinking necessary to understand how flashlights work and how the parts can be assembled to make one. That defeats the purpose of the activity presented here. Inventing investigation allows students to discover the thinking needed to produce a working object, such as the flashlight. With appropriate guiding experiences, students *can* accomplish such a task.

Discovery Inventing can fit into your overall program of creative thinking in science in several ways. If you are working with very young students, you may want to use it as the format for inventing activities throughout the school year. Alternatively, if working with older students it may be more appropriate as an initial experience with inventing before moving on to Rube Goldberg Inventing and Practical Inventing. In either case, it provides a low-anxiety approach to fostering creative thinking and self-confidence.

Chapter Five

Rube Goldberg Inventing

Designing Appropriately Preposterous Inventing Activities

In this chapter you will find:

The spirit of Rube Goldberg;

How humor can be a part of the plan;

Desktop inventing;

How you and your students can build full-size creative contraptions!

88

Are we making this up? After all, *Rube Goldberg* inventing? But we are not making it up. It is even likely that though the name is not familiar to you, the cartoon probably is. Rube Goldberg was a cartoonist in the first half of this century. His drawings typically depicted a complicated and humorous way of accomplishing a simple task in lettered steps. He received a Pulitzer Prize for his work in 1948. The picture on page 88 is an example. Does it seem more familiar now? Stay with us; this may well be one of the most creative and enjoyable things you've ever done with your students!

A "Rube Goldberg in the Classroom" Scenario

The materials spread around the room did not have the particular look of "science." Tables were covered with ropes and rubber bands, gears and blocks of wood. Elsewhere various lengths of white PVC pipe and handfuls of screws and brads could be seen. The small tool boxes with hammers, tape measures, and sandpaper did not contribute much to a laboratory look either. Most notable of all was the intense concentration punctuated by occasional blips of laughter. One could almost *see* the thinking going on.

All in all, the task was simple—build a machine that could pop a balloon. The balloon could be squashed, squeezed, pounded, or pinched. How a balloon met its deflating fate was, within limits of safety, left to the teams of students. There were just a couple of other considerations. First, the machine should work without assistance. Second, a minimum of three energy sources had to be used. Third, there must be at least ten steps from starting the machine to the popping of the balloon. Finally, points would be awarded for humor. This class of 24 students had six balloon popping design teams engrossed in the task. (By the way, if you think an automatic balloon popper is not a realistic task, just look up Patent No. 4,881,733.)

Though each team obviously had a different approach to popping the balloon, there were similarities. For one thing, everybody was free to take materials from a common "junkbox" in the classroom. One person might look right past the old telephone cord and pick up the slightly deformed slinky. Someone from another group would see the phone cord and snatch it up as if it were the perfect project item. Each group also had a small wooden toolbox with some basic hand tools. Most notable was the white PVC frame that stood in the middle of each group. The frames stood about five feet tall and were four feet long. They looked like white window frames on legs. Apparently each group had a frame on which to build their balloon popper. Tape, bolts, hooks, and hose clamps were used to fasten components to the frame. It was fascinating that with so many similarities, the emerging projects were so different.

All but one of the groups determined that the puncture method was the way to go. Each group, however, was working on a different means for delivering the point of a pin or tack to the balloon's surface. In one group, a thumbtack was mounted beneath a cup suspended from two rubber bands. As the cup filled with sand, the point of the tack slowly approached the balloon. Another preferred to strike quickly, presumably catching the balloon by surprise. They had attached a pin to a stick, and then attached the stick to the strike bar of a mousetrap. When the mousetrap was tripped in another step, the polished pin would swing swiftly to its target. The stick was tethered by a length of string to the PVC frame so that it just reached the balloon and could not fly off into the class. This was by no means a room to be caught in if you were a balloon hoping to live to a right bold age.

The group not using the puncture approach had decided to use a candle to burn the balloon instead. They had rigged a system that would not only burn the balloon, but also douse it with water to extinguish the flame.

The challenge was to figure out how to have their machine light the candle in the first place.

"Those frames really are handy," said Mrs. Larson, the classroom teacher. "Since they are so skinny, we can just push them up against the wall when we are done for the day instead of taking up a lot of table space. And they come completely apart so that at the end of the year they can be stored away in a box until the next year."

"Is popping a balloon a typical topic for science class?" I asked.

"Actually, popping the balloon was just the challenge," she told me. "But we have studied simple machines, types of energy, and simple circuits this year. If you take a look at these machines you'll see evidence of that throughout. In a glance, I can see whether the students really understand the things we've studied."

"But what happens if the machine doesn't work?" I asked in my best devil's advocate voice. "Does everybody on the team fail?"

"The beauty of this is that it really doesn't matter whether the machine actually works," explained Mrs. Larson. "I can see by the way they apply the various principles whether or not they understand the concepts we are studying. Popping the balloon provides a way for them to demonstrate what they know. I'm sure that given enough time to revise and redesign, they could build a smoothly operating machine. Do you think that's very different from the way new products are developed?"

I had to admit that she was right about that. In fact billions of dollars have gone into the design and refinement of all sorts of products from baseballs to space ships. And these kids were doing the same sort of thing and loving it. This is not to say that there was not some heavy duty frustration going on in that room, because it was clear that sometimes things worked and sometimes they didn't. Without a doubt it was exciting to see the enthusiasm and satisfaction in a group

any time some small component or system in the overall machine functioned as it was intended. I would hear "Yes!" or "All right!" or cheers with high fives all around. The eventual product was the goal, but the *process* permeating this classroom was like watching ideas being born!

The Spirit of Rube Goldberg

If you have a fairly new dictionary around, look up "Rube Goldberg." *Webster's* refers to a "Rube Goldberg" as a contrivance or method to accomplish an apparently simple task in an extremely complex way. But, as you can see from the illustration on page 91, Professor Butts' Moth Exterminator is much more complex than the name implies. For instance, this particular invention uses fourteen separate transfers of energy, dropping the flower pot, and ultimately ambushing the moths. Goldberg has used readily available materials—ropes, pulleys, water (OK, and the occasional lamb)—to construct his devices, along with various sources of energy. Although this and his other drawings represented complex ways to do simple things, you can see that there was a considerable element of humor involved in the cartoons, right down to the emergency backup in case the machine did not work. As he suggests in this cartoon, if the moths are a problem, perhaps you should just move away.

This is an ideal mix for an approach to teaching science. Rube Goldberg inventing incorporates science concepts and principles, simple materials, and *creativity and humor* in a dynamic approach to science education. It's an opportunity for students to manipulate materials and ideas, yet it provides the teacher with a concrete demonstration of student understanding—whether the machine actually works. And in case you are wondering whether this is some outdated idea best left to the 1930s and 1940s, think back to that NASA shuttle mission a few years back.

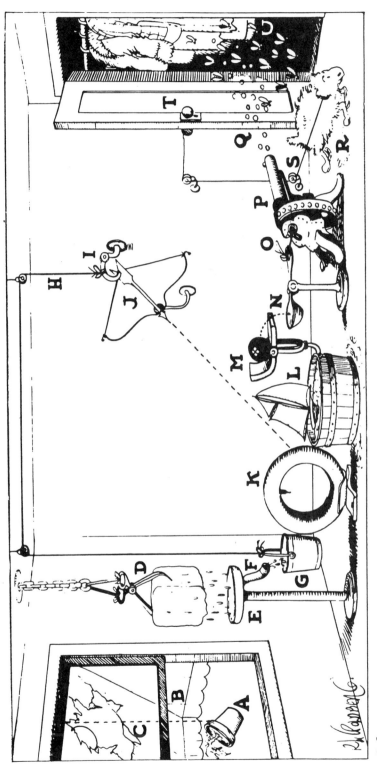

Figure 5.1. Professor Butts' Moth Exterminator.

The NASA astronauts were trying to rescue an ailing satellite. Armed with all sorts of high-tech paraphernalia, they headed for the final frontier. Ultimately they had to fashion a make-shift tool to grab hold of the satellite. Jim Borgman did an editorial cartoon in true Rube Goldberg fashion that summed it up: the spirit of Rube Goldberg is alive and well! If a Rube Goldberg approach is good enough for NASA, how can we possibly keep it from our students? Sure, the astronauts were not necessarily pushing for humor, but the basic elements were there. And not only that, it worked!

Humor as Part of the Design

Why bother with Rube Goldberg inventing rather than just inventing something practical? That's a viable concern. After all, there are a number of national inventing competitions open to school age students. But you must keep in mind our purpose: we want to foster the development of creative thinking through the *process* of science.

Inventing competitions place their emphasis on development of a product. Of all the inventions that students may come up with, only a handful ever make it to the awards banquet or displays at teachers' conventions. And those that get there do so because of their practicality. Our next chapter will address practical inventing. However, the emphasis in such situations is on the product, not the *process*! We believe that if students are able to develop their creative thinking and creative problem-solving abilities, then practical inventing will follow. That is why throughout this book you have read about the emphasis on *process, not product*.

By taking the focus away from practicality, we can reduce the anxiety level typically associated with school work and projects. Rube Goldberg inventing allows the use of decidedly low-tech materials assembled in a manner that invites laughter. If a piece of bubble gum really will stick a component in place just the way it needs to be, then great!

A relaxed and accepting atmosphere is far more conducive to creative problem solving than is the pretense of standing on ceremony—making sure all the margins are even and all the posters are lined up nicely. When the machine being built is intentionally humorous, students can focus attention on solving the problem without constantly monitoring public perception of their progress.

The *Invent! Cards*: Desktop Inventing

If the idea of jumping into Rube Goldberg inventing has you just a bit intimidated, then consider starting with the *Invent! Cards* (Ebert & Ebert, 1989). Even if you are ready to start inventing, the *Invent! Cards* may provide a good warm up. The cards are intended to give desktop practice with the use of ropes, pivots, pulleys, gears, and mousetraps.

In the Appendix you will find several pages of cards that you can copy. Check to see whether your copier can handle card stock. If it can't, and you don't have access to one that can, then paper cards will do—they just won't be quite so durable. Make one copy of each page to form a complete set. Make as many sets as you like for your class (working in groups of two usually works well). Also, if you can, it is worthwhile to have one set of cards copied on transparencies. Cut out the individual cards and use an overhead projector when you want the class to see a card or combination of cards.

Working with the *Invent! Cards* is low cost, neat, and tidy, and though some assembly is required, you don't even need a few household tools. Welcome to the world of desktop inventing! The cards will provide a means for applying the basic science process skills to a study of motion, transfer of energy, and simple machines in a creative way. Using the cards to "invent" machines also serves to illustrate the science and technology link as concepts and principles are applied to accomplish a task. So, let the cards begin!

The next several pages will provide pictures and descriptions of each of the 18 *Invent! Cards.* The number in parentheses at the beginning of the description indicates the frequency of the card in the set. An asterisk (*) following the number indicates there is a mirror-image version of the card. You'll find this very useful as you invent.

(1) The top card. Save it so you can remember the name of the set.

(2) * The 5 lb. weight. This represents a bag containing five pounds of the object of your choice: fudge, feathers, ungraded papers, etc. It's tied to a rope.

(1) The candle. A source of light and/or heat. But since the light isn't of much use here, think of it in terms of burning through a rope or stick to drop a weight, etc.

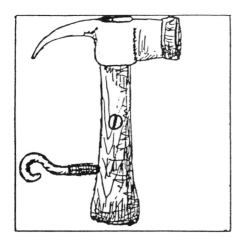

(2) * If I had a hammer, chances are I'd put a screw through the handle so it could pivot, and attach a hook so that it could be pulled by a rope.

(2) * Boot on a stick. Not exactly as tasty as a sausage on a stick, but, when attached to a pivot, it really swings into action.

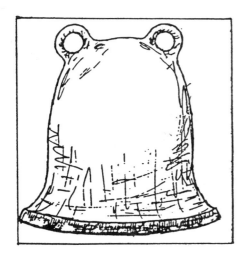

(1) A bell. Notice that there is no clapper. If you want to ring this bell you'll have to drop a weight on it, kick it with a boot, hit it with a hammer, or drop it. You can't just lift it up and wiggle it back and forth. It does come equipped with two handles (would we give you just *any* bell?) so it can be attached to a rope on either side (or both)!

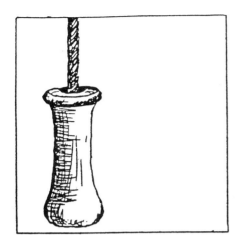

(1) The fob. What do you say about a fob? Attach it to the end of a rope and pull on it.

(2) * The official pre-set and pre-baited mousetrap. Notice that a rope is attached to the bar. When the trap is tripped, the twine is tugged toward the tempting tasty treat. No need to wait for an unsuspecting rodent to arrive; have your invention trip the trap using the weight or hammer, etc.

(1) Gear with crank. The crank can *only* be turned in the direction of the arrow! The rope does not attach to this card, but this does make a good invention actuator when combined with the other gear cards.

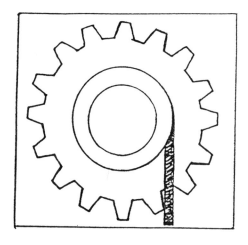

(1) Gear with winch. This gear can turn clockwise or counterclockwise depending on how the Gear with Crank card and Gear Cluster card interacts with it. The good news is that the rope attaches to the winch. The downside is that the winch cannot act alone; it must be driven by the Gear with Crank.

(1) The gear cluster. This handy card enables you to position the other two gear cards in different ways and thereby change the direction of rotation of the winch. All four gears mesh together, so be sure to carefully track which direction each gear in your invention turns. Raising the weight and lowering the weight are two very different tasks. Some might even say they're opposites, so the gears must be set up properly!

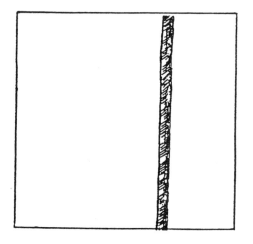

(5) Rope. Use the rope to connect to other rope, to the hook on the hammer, to the ring on the candle holder, and/or to the bell. A rope does not, however, connect to the end of a stick.

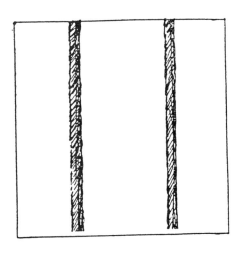

(2) Double rope. Twice as good as the single rope, but both ends must connect to something. No fair letting ropes just end all of a sudden.

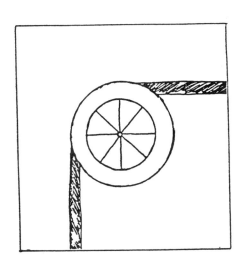

(4) The 90-degree pulley. You decide the direction that the rope travels. Use these cards to get out of tight corners, or to make tight corners.

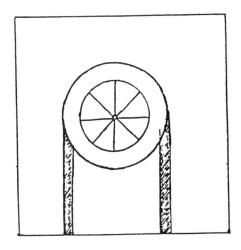

(2) The 180-degree pulley. For reversing the direction of the rope . . . what else can we say?

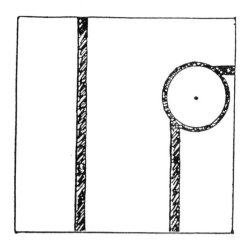

(2) * The double rope with pulley. This is a real handy card. Once again, however, each end of the rope must attach to something—no fair letting them dead-end.

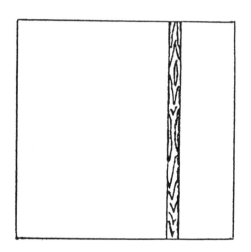

(4) The stick. No, this is not a rope. Our artist took great pains to provide you with these distinctly non-rope-like sticks. They connect directly to other sticks, like the ever popular boot-on-a-stick.

(2) * The pivot bar. Connect a rope to the length of rope on this card and then maybe the boot-on-a-stick to the stick on this card. Give the rope a pull somehow, and suddenly you have a swinging boot. Just think of the possibilities!

Using the Invent! Cards to Illustrate the Basic Science Process Skills

The cards provide you with an effective way to have your students use the basic science process skills while getting started with some desktop inventing. Just using the cards involves the skills, but the next series of activities are intended to address each in a specific way. Well, let's amend that statement. We don't really address "measurement" in any of these activities. Since the different pictures are not all drawn to scale, we decided to leave measurement to your own creative approaches.

Desktop Inventing

Now that your students are familiar with the *Invent! Cards* and have combined a few of them, it's time for some inventive thinking! In the next four activities, students combine cards to perform tasks. Each challenge can be solved many ways, some more obviously than others. Encourage your students' creativity by finding multiple solutions for each challenge. However, to avoid overload, we will tell you that the fewest possible cards for completing the first activity in Loops Are Us is two.

The final activity, In Great Combination, allows students to do free-style inventing. The open-ended challenge fosters the development of creative problem-solving abilities. Of course, these activities, and the five from the previous section, are just a sampling of what you can do with the cards. Be creative—invent your own activities using the *Invent! Cards*.

(Text continues on p. 120.)

What's in a Card?

(Observation/Inference)

Purpose: To identify items on the cards while practicing observation and inference skills.

Have students remove one of the cards from the deck that has a drawing of a bag marked "5 lbs." As a group, have the students make observations and inferences about the cards. List these responses on the board or on some other sheet of paper so they can be referred to again. The "What's in a Card?" activity sheet provides space for discussing three cards.

From student responses, distinguish between observations and inferences. For example, an *observation* would be that the drawing of the bag has the numeral 5 and the letters "lbs." written on it. An *inference* would be that the bag weighs five pounds. Another example would be the observation of roughly parallel lines with diagonal lines between them. The inference is that this design represents a rope. Continue this activity with the different cards so that all of the items and their *inferred* functions have been identified.

What's in a Card?

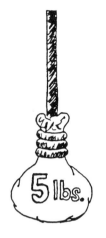

Observations

1. _____

2. _____

3. _____

4. _____

Inferences

1. _____

2. _____

Observations

1. _____

2. _____

3. _____

4. _____

Inferences

1. _____

2. _____

Observations

1. _____

2. _____

3. _____

4. _____

Inferences

1. _____

2. _____

Preferring Inferring

(Inference/Observation)

Purpose: To recognize the potential usefulness of the cards in combination while inferring the motion that is represented.

So far we have used observations and inferences to identify the cards. Now it is time to figure out how they "work." For example, the picture of a hammer has a circle with a line through it (observation) which represents a screw (inference). The screw, were it truly a screw, could act as a pivot point, which means that if one end of the hammer is pushed or pulled to the right, the other end will move to the left (an inference of movement).

Inferences of movement can become much more dynamic when cards are combined. The activity sheet for this lesson has two card combinations, but keep in mind that these are only two examples of the many combinations that can be created.

As you talk with your students about the card combinations, such as the "gear with crank" and the "winch," help them to distinguish between observations, inferences about objects, and inferences about motion. Finally, allow your students the opportunity to explore the possibilities.

Preferring Inferring

Inferences

1. _____

2. _____

3. _____

4. _____

5. _____

Inferences

1. _____

2. _____

3. _____

4. _____

5. _____

A Card by Any Other Name

(Binary: Classification/Communication)

Purpose: To familiarize students with the cards so they will know what is available to use in later lessons and to practice classification skills. Communication skills are enhanced when students explain their classification schemes.

Have students work in pairs, sharing one set of cards. Use one card of each item in the deck, that is, one single rope card (rather than all five), one double rope, one hammer, etc. Set the other cards aside.

Choose one characteristic and have the students separate the cards into two groups based on the presence or absence of that characteristic. You might use characteristics such as parallel lines, circles, ropes, "metal" parts, "wooden" parts, and so forth. This is binary classification.

Have students combine the cards again. This time allow one of the two partners in each group to choose a characteristic; separate the deck accordingly, and then have the other partner determine the characteristic that was used. Continue this binary classification activity several times. Encourage the students to be challenging in their classification schemes, perhaps using two or more characteristics. For example, the cards could be classified as those with wood *and* metal (such as the hammer and mousetrap) vs. those which do not have both wood and metal (such as the bell and the pulleys). Be sure to let the students discuss the classification schemes.

A Card by Any Other Name

Illustrate your classification scheme on the chart below:

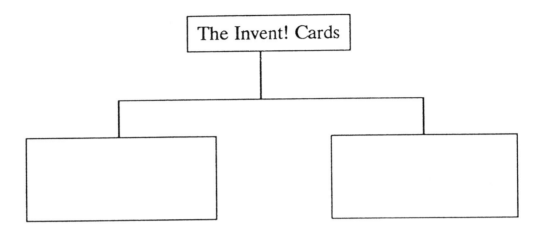

List characteristics which can be used to classify the cards:

1. _____

2. _____

3. _____

4. _____

5. _____

All the World's a Multi-Stage

(Multi-stage Classification/Communication)

Purpose: To extend the lesson on binary classification to hierarchical classification. Communications skills are enhanced when stu - dents draw classification schemes and explain them to others.

Multi-stage classification is a succession of binary classifications. With the cards there are many possible classification schemes depending upon the characteristics identified and the order in which they were selected.

Have students begin the classification activity using the large group of cards, one of each item, and separating them according to an agreed upon characteristic—for example, cards with rope vs. cards with no rope. Then have the students work with one of those two groups (perhaps the cards with rope) and classify those cards into two groups. For instance, the cards with rope could be divided into those cards that *only* have rope, and those that have rope with something else (pulleys, mousetrap, etc.). Continue this process, each time dividing the resulting group into two more sub-groups until all of the cards are in distinct groups. The activity page provides a *sample* format for filling in a classification scheme. Try to help students understand that all classification schemes are not required to fit into this neat symmetrical chart. In fact, to help you, on the back of the activity page is another, much more open-ended format that they may wish to use—like coloring outside the lines.

All the World's a Multi-Stage

Illustrate your classification scheme on the multi-stage classification chart below:

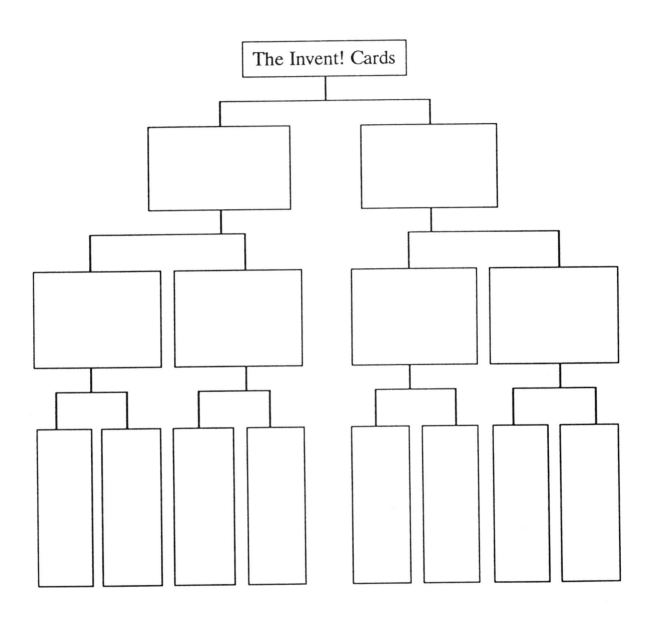

All the World's an Open-Ended
Multi-Stage

This form provides the first category for you. Everything else is your design!

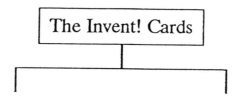

What Would Happen If . . . ?

(Prediction)

Purpose: To identify card combinations, recognize possible interactions among the cards, and predict the outcomes.

Since prediction is a statement or forecast of a future event and is based on a conceptual model, your students can use the cards to make predictions, too. The model they work from is based on the observations and inferences made in "What's in a Card?" and "Preferring Inferring." You can then extend that model by having students combine cards to form simple systems.

No doubt some group of students will put two rope cards together (as below) and say that nothing will happen. And, that *would* be a valid prediction. But for the sake of argument, let's encourage thinking in terms of systems. For example, the two cards on the next page don't do much, but they do represent a system. In fact, that system was (and is) used by thousands of people for . . . sure, for drying clothes!

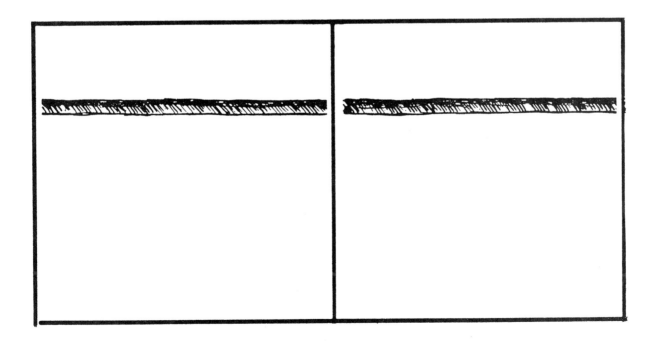

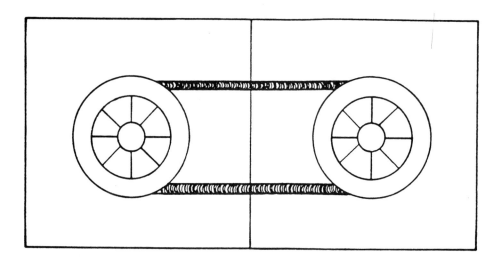

You'll notice that our page is set up to make predictions of increasingly complex systems, beginning with a two-card arrangement and moving to a four-card combination. Students should write down each card used, and then fill in their prediction. Without sharing predictions, allow other students to assemble the same system and make their own predictions. If you made a set of transparencies, you could let groups of students "demonstrate" the systems on the overhead and let the class make their predictions before the particular group explains what they predicted would occur.

What Would Happen If . . . ?

Card 1: _____

Card 2: _____

Predict what would happen: _____

_____

_____

Card 1: _____

Card 2: _____

Card 3: _____

Predict what would happen: _____

_____

_____

Card 1: _____

Card 2: _____

Card 3: _____

Card 4: _____

Predict what would happen: _____

_____

_____

Loops Are Us

Purpose: Combining cards to design inventions and to ensure that students understand relative motion among ropes and pulleys.

Working with one set of cards per pair of students, have students separate the cards that use ropes alone and ropes with pulleys (15 cards). Set other cards aside.

Ask each pair of students to combine the cards so that the rope forms a continuous loop. This task can be accomplished with just two cards (our little secret for now) by placing the two 180-degree pulley cards together as shown below. Encourage students to find different combinations after finding one solution and to use as many cards as possible. Also, be sure to have students place the cards with the sides flat against each other and corners matched up as in the previous illustration. It makes things more challenging.

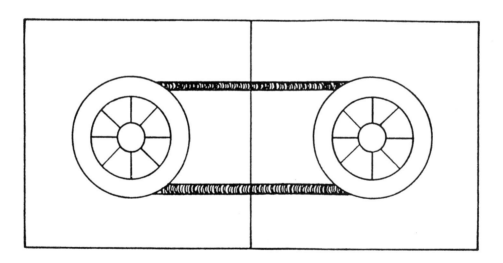

You might want to discuss the ease and/or difficulty in combining the cards. For instance, some students may say that it was easy to select up to six cards to form a loop, but beyond that it was difficult.

Loops Are Us

1. Sketch your solution using the fewest cards that you can:

2. Sketch your solution using the most cards that you can:

3. What is a pulley used for?

4. When would you want or need to use a pulley?

Gearing Up

Purpose: To ensure that students understand relative movement among gears.

Using the 15 cards of ropes and ropes with pulleys, have students add the three gear cards (the gear with crank, the winch, and the gear cluster) and the two weight cards.

Challenge students to combine cards so that turning the crank would *raise* the weight. This can be done with as few as three cards, as shown below.

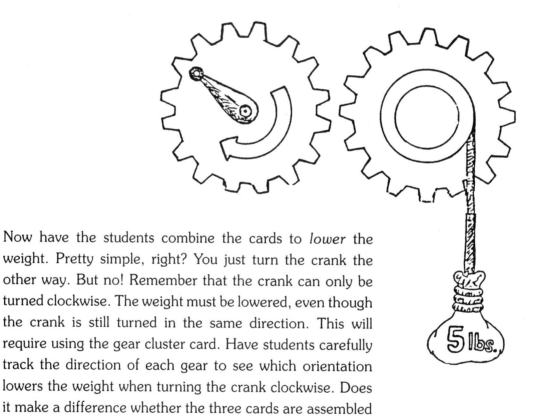

Now have the students combine the cards to *lower* the weight. Pretty simple, right? You just turn the crank the other way. But no! Remember that the crank can only be turned clockwise. The weight must be lowered, even though the crank is still turned in the same direction. This will require using the gear cluster card. Have students carefully track the direction of each gear to see which orientation lowers the weight when turning the crank clockwise. Does it make a difference whether the three cards are assembled in a straight line as opposed to an L shape? Check it out.

Finally, allow your students some time to form additional combinations making use of as many cards as possible.

Gearing Up

Design a machine to **raise** a weight using as *few* cards as possible.

Which cards did you use?

Design a machine to **raise** a weight using as *many* cards as possible.

Which cards did you use?

Design a new machine to **lower** a weight using as *few* cards as possible.

Which cards did you use?

Design a different machine to **lower** a weight using as *many* cards as possible.

Which cards did you use?

Ring That Bell!

Purpose: To allow students to use their knowledge of the inferred inter-actions between the cards to design inventions that accomplish a given task.

Students, working in pairs, should work with the entire set of cards during this activity. Challenge your students to combine cards to accomplish the task of ringing the bell. Note that the drawing of the bell does not show a clapper. This means that the bell cannot ring simply by being lifted. Rather, it must be struck with some object, or dropped.

Students can accomplish this task in numerous ways. Encourage your students to elaborate on their inventions to incorporate as many of the cards as possible. There are many solutions, so encourage students to try *new* combinations that improve on *previous* designs.

Take some time to share the inventions. If possible, display some using your transparency set of cards. Allow students to see and mentally manipulate the inventions of other groups. Also, allow the designers the opportunity to explain how their inventions work.

Ring That Bell!

Which cards in the deck could be used to ring the bell?

Invent a machine to ring the bell using the fewest number of cards.

Sketch your invention:

Invent a machine to ring the bell using the greatest number of cards.

Sketch your invention:

In Great Combination

Purpose: To use inventing as an activity to stimulate creative thinking, while applying science principles and processes.

Students work individually, in pairs, or small groups, and, using the entire set of cards, should select their own challenge. For example, some might want to combine the cards to build an "automatic nailer" or a "mousetrap resetting machine." They also might want to combine the cards of two groups to make a much larger machine.

Allow students to see the inventions of other groups. Provide the opportunity for inventors to explain their designs. Discuss the ramifications of some of their inventions by asking questions such as: How could this be used on a larger scale? Who could benefit from such a machine? You might discuss the feasibility of building some of the inventions, particularly if you intend to pursue the next part of this chapter, which uses real live ropes, pulleys, and whatnot! Encourage the use of as many cards as possible—and the use of humor.

This is also a good opportunity to extend the activity by asking students to consider how machines that they have used might work. For example, pencil sharpeners and vending machines are just collections of simple machines arranged as systems.

In Great Combination

Answer the following questions about your invention:

What does your invention do?

How could it be used in real life?

Who could benefit from your machine?

Make a materials list of the items you would need to build this invention:

The Invention Record

So you say the thought of inventing is really neat, but everytime you put the cards away you lose your invention? What can you do? Begin by numbering the back of the cards. It doesn't matter which card you start with, just be sure that *every* card gets a different number (you could even name each card if you want to think up 36 names). Next, be sure that you have a copy of The Official Invention Record handy (see p. 121). Now, go ahead and record those inventions!

When you have finished inventing, simply write the numbers from the back of each card onto a cell on The Official Invention Record. For instance, if the three cards below were numbered 21, 32, and 13 (reading from left to right), then your Official Invention Record would have a series of cells that looked like this:

You now have a record that shows how to re-assemble the cards to replicate your invention! This example only has three cards, but wait until your invention uses 20 to 30 cards. You might even be able to string together several sets of cards to form one huge invention. Think of all the possibilities! No, better yet, *invent* some of those possibilities!

A couple of final notes about the *Invent! Cards*. In the Appendix you will find a Certificate of Invention that you might want to use with your students during this time. Don't let the cards themselves become limiting. When you or your students realize that "Gee, sure would be nice to have a lightbulb card and a battery card," go ahead and draw some up. The artwork just has to be sufficient to understand what it represents!

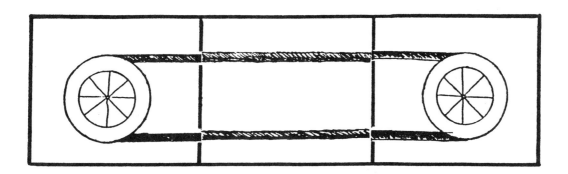

The Official Invention Record

Figure 5.2. Official Invention Record.

Moving Up
to 3-D Inventing

There is nothing quite like watching students using real pulleys and ropes, mousetraps, and aluminum foil to make machines that work (or don't work *yet*) according to their own designs. It is the obvious intensity of thinking that will strike you as an educator. You can virtually *see* the thinking going on.

Such thinking, however, is not without its frustrations. It is your job to help students maintain the perspective that "this is a challenge" in the face of a problem that seems to defy solution. In any case, this is an educational experience that moves, shakes, and even finds some laughter along the way.

Tools of the Trade

There is no getting around the fact that inventing requires some tools. Of course, if it helps your cause when talking to the principal about funds, what you *really* need is science equipment for the inventing unit. Hammers, pliers, and screwdrivers might be considered somewhat non-traditional for stocking your lab, but equipment is equipment. Fortunately, the tools of the trade that we are talking about are familiar, readily available, and inexpensive items.

The Inventor's Tools
for the Classroom

Though not *every* student needs a complete set of tools, it would be a bit difficult to have an entire class share the "class hammer," so check around and try to rustle up the number you actually need. If you plan to have students work in pairs or small groups, one set of tools per group will do. It is likely that you can get parents to loan some items for the duration of the unit. If you go that route, it is a good idea to contact parents yourself, so that mom's prized 16-ounce framing hammer doesn't disappear from the tool rack

one day. Alternatively, this may be a good time for you to work on a grant from your local educational funding agency. The PTA may also be willing to help put together a few sets of tools. Keep in mind that these things are not consumables; once you've got them in hand, you've got them available for a long time. They do represent educational equipment.

Though these items are going to last for some time, you need not purchase from the expensive tool counter. Your local builder/homeowner supply store will have all of these things. One set of tools, brand new, should cost about $11-12. We recommend one of each of the following items for a basic inventor's toolkit:

> 16 ounce claw hammer (a claw hammer is your standard type hammer)
>
> pair of pliers (probably the most expensive item, about $4.00)
>
> medium, flat head screwdriver
>
> medium, Phillips head screwdriver
>
> 6 ft. tape measure
>
> 1 roll of masking tape
>
> sheet of #60 sandpaper
>
> sheet of #100 sandpaper
>
> small bottle of white glue

It is also a good idea to get a small cross-cut saw. These often have names like "short-cut" or "quick-job." Not all groups need to have a saw. One or two for the class should work well.

These are inexpensive tools, basic tools, but they are tools. As such, they come with a degree of danger when not used properly. You probably will encounter very few parents who don't like the idea of their student learning basic skills, such as hammering and sawing, but they don't like having their student hammered or sawed. Don't let this frighten you! Parents also don't like students cut with dissection knives or burned with mild acids either. Simply include safety rules with these activities as you would when using any other potentially harmful materials.

Take another look at that list of tools. Exciting, isn't it? Tools, and knowing how to use them, open up a whole new creative outlet. Tools are willing to build whatever you want to build. As discussed in Chapter Three, they are products of technology that extend our capabilities. With tools and a junk box filled with neat stuff, you open up a world of unexplored possibilities to your students. What a dynamic environment for activities that will be lead *by the student's own thinking.*

An Inventor's Toolbox for You and Your Students

You might think that it would be nice to have some place to corral all of these tools. That's a great idea, and a good place to start teaching your students to use these tools. We need a toolbox.

Any sort of container in which the tools will fit accomplishes the task. A shoebox is good, though they tend to be flimsy with a hammer and pliers flopping around inside. One of those plastic shoeboxes (not the brittle plastic, but the flexible kind in the kitchenware department) is nice. Those containers come in all sizes and shapes and have tight snap-on lids. Of course, the downside is the additional expense. If you've gotten financial support from the principal, the PTA, or a minigrant, then you might want to go this route. Your students can also build toolboxes. True, there will still be expense involved, but building the toolbox can be part of the instructional

event. By building toolboxes, students will learn the basics of working with tools. You will be surprised to find out how many students, whether elementary or in-service teachers, have no idea how to drive a nail or use a saw.

The size and shape of a toolbox is a direct function of the size and shape of materials available for toolbox building. So if you've got a bunch of 1x4 lumber around, chances are you'll have a toolbox with sides that are ¾-inch thick and 3½-inch wide (the actual dimensions of 1x4 lumber . . . don't ask; it's just the way it is in the world of wood). Keep in mind that all we want is something that holds tools.

Let's suppose, however, that a) you already have some woodworking skills and equipment, b) you are related or married to someone who does, or c) you know of an unsuspecting neighbor or parent with the aforementioned skills and equipment who could be persuaded to help you out. Collect as many of the materials listed on the Inventor's Toolbox plan needed for your situation, and take them and this book to the person determined from a, b, or c above. Your request of the local woodworker is that all of your materials be cut according to the following plan. You *do not* want to have the toolboxes built for your students. Just get materials cut into nice little toolbox "kits" that your students can assemble.

With all of your tools in one heavy box, and all of the toolbox pieces in another, head for your classroom and the first construction exercise! Here is the sequence for assembling the kits (refer to the exploded-view drawing to see how the parts relate to each other, p. 124).

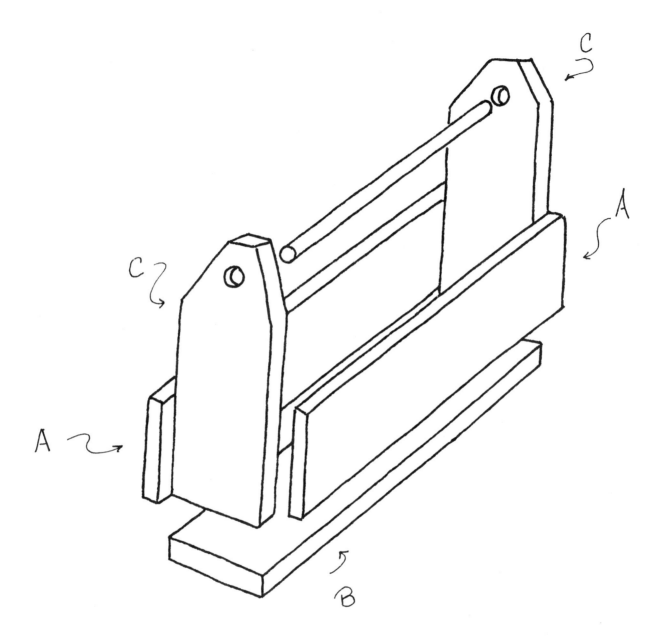

Figure 5.3. The Official *Invent!* Toolbox.

1. Locate the two side pieces (A) and the two end pieces (C).

2. Using 1-inch flathead wire nails, start two nails in each end of the two side pieces (A). Don't nail all the way through, just get the nails started.

3. Stand one of the side pieces (C) on its edge, and put a line of glue along the side where the plywood will be fastened. (Take a look at the drawing).

4. Line up one of the sides with the bottom and side edges of the end piece, and drive the nails.

5. Put a line of glue on the edge of the other end piece (C). Line up the other end of the side you just attached, and nail it down to the end piece. You now have one side piece (A) with an end piece (C) glued and nailed to each end.

6. Flip this unit over so that it is lying on the plywood side. Put a line of glue on each of the end piece edges that are facing up. Nail the second side (A) onto the end pieces.

7. Stand the unit up, with the holes in the end pieces toward the table. The open bottom of the toolbox will be facing up. Run a line of glue around all four sides of the bottom.

8. Line up the bottom plywood piece (B) with the sides and edges of the box and nail it down. Put two nails into each end. Your students can try driving one nail through the bottom plywood and into the side plywood at about halfway between the ends. Depending on your students, this may be kind of tricky. If so, instead of nails use some masking tape to hold the bottom to the sides while the glue dries. Use two pieces of tape on each side, about a third of the way down. (Take another look at the drawing.) And don't forget to remove the masking tape after the glue has dried.

9. Slide the dowel through the holes in the end pieces, and then drive a nail through the top of one end piece and into the dowel.

10. Allow your students to decorate their toolboxes, though by the time they finish building them they will definitely have a sense of ownership!

You might want to let the glue dry overnight before tossing all of those tools in. Once it dries, the toolbox, with its basic complement of tools, will have you and your students ready to invent. Don't forget to display toolboxes on the night of your invention fair!

Junk Is . . . In the Eye of the Beholder

Tools are certainly not enough. Appropriately preposterous inventions require appropriately preposterous materials. It is important to collect raw materials early in the school year and continue stockpiling various objects throughout the inventing process. As students become familiar with objects in the Inventor's Junk Box and identify potential uses for those objects, they will begin to see previously unvalued materials in an entirely different way. Junk becomes valuable stuff! Here is a list of some suggestions for the junk box:

Inventor's Junk Box

string	paper clips
magnets	clothespins
wire	pipe cleaners
yarn	plastic bags
washers	newspapers
toothpicks	pulleys
marbles	brads and nails
glue	steel balls
funnels	fishing line
balloons	PVC
springs	mirrors
feathers	wheels
batteries	lightbulbs
candles	paint brushes
strainers	popsicle sticks
sand	coat hangers
tape	aluminum foil
hooks	packing materials
duct tape	rubberbands
film canisters	aluminum pans

cork and water bottles?

plastic tubing	brass fasteners
nuts and bolts	mousetraps
scraps of lumber	shoestrings
paper towel tubes	dowel rods
discarded toys	panty hose
tea bags	waxed paper
paper plates	empty ribbon spools

You and your students can add whatever articles can be found at home or in the neighborhood. Discarded machines (such as tape recorders, or, if you could imagine it, an old record player!), old appliances, building scraps, doorknobs, garden hose, clocks, bricks, etc., enhance the collection of inventing supplies.

Some materials could be useful, though you might not want to toss them in a box in your classroom. Here is a starting list:

Other Useful Stuff

vinegar	baking soda
oil	salt
wax	modeling clay
food coloring	cornstarch
dishwashing liquid	

Boxes conveniently store the stuff, but your students need to see and manipulate the objects to become familiar with them as raw inventing materials. Occasionally, provide some table space to spread out the "treasures" and allow your students to see the objects without the demands of a task. This provides an incubation opportunity for ideas. Even a show-and-tell exercise of objects added to the box is valuable. The key question about each item is: How could this be used in an invention?

Exploring Alternative Uses: Today a Mousetrap, Tomorrow a Switch

The value of the "inventor's junk" increases according to the number of ways in which the objects can be used. For instance, if we think of the junk list in terms of what they are designed to do, we find several objects that "hold things together." Rubber-bands, string, shoestrings, tape, glue, paper clips, nails, and brass fasteners are designed to hold—albeit in their specific ways and with unique advantages.

However, there are other things on the list, such as pipe cleaners, tea bags, magnets, and even panty hose, which can be used to "hold things together," though they were designed for very different reasons. By looking for objects that can be used in alternative ways, we are expanding the usefulness of our collection.

This is only the beginning when it comes to assessing the real value of the junk. Suppose we examine the attributes of each item of junk. How useful is each item? What can it do?

Let's begin with the film canister. It is a cylindrical plastic container, about 2 inches in height and 1 inch in diameter. As designed, it is useful for holding small objects and could be useful as we organize our supplies of toothpicks, washers, or nails. Without a lid, it could be used to catch falling objects, such as marbles or even water. What if we turn it upside down? The canister could be used to trap a steel ball and hold it in place or, vice-versa, hold a steel ball in place until the appropriate time when the canister is raised and the steel ball rolls out from under it.

Another alternative is to turn the canister on its side. Since it is cylindrical, it will roll nicely. It is capable of rolling down an incline, perhaps with something inside it. Several canisters could function as rollers to move a heavy object, or could be combined to serve as wheels on a vehicle.

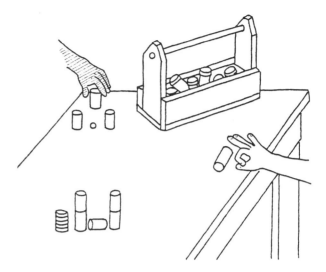

Perhaps the value of other items is becoming easier to see. What about the paper towel tube? We could fasten a string to the tube and then wind the string up or down as we need it. We could pass the string over the tube and let it function as a pulley. The tube could serve as a tunnel through which something solid such as sand could pass. The tube could even be moved in order to direct the flow of that material. If the tube were cut in half, a trough could be made to transport moving objects such as marbles, and be twice as long as the original tube.

What alternatives can you find? Start with pipe cleaners or panty hose. Their functions are obvious and limited. What else could you do with them? Now select other "junk" and generate lists of other uses. Did you think about filling tea bags with sand and using them as weights to counter balance other objects?

What if we were to examine objects in terms of conductivity? The brass fasteners, paper clips, and aluminum foil could be used to conduct electricity. They could serve as switches. If we had a simple circuit, which involved batteries, a lightbulb, a few wires, and a piece of cardboard with 2 brass fasteners inserted about 1 inch apart, we could connect one wire to a fastener and another wire from the lightbulb to the second fastener. A paper clip can fit under the head of one brass fastener so that it could rotate and eventually touch the other fastener—thereby completing the circuit. The movement of the paper clip then could switch the light off and on.

A small piece of aluminum foil could also be used as a switch. Start with a similar setup but instead of using a paper clip, attach one end of the aluminum foil strip to one fastener and place the other end on top of the second fastener. The circuit would be complete and the light should be on. To switch it off, raise the foil just a little bit so that it is no longer touching the fastener. Now the circuit is open but could easily be closed if something dropped on the foil or rolled across it and forced the aluminum foil to again touch the fastener.

Other objects on the list made of a combination of materials (such as metal and wood) make interesting switches, too. The wooden part of a mousetrap, for example, does not conduct electricity and could serve as an insulator, while the metal pieces conduct electricity. With a slight modification, you can make a switch in the spirit of Rube Goldberg inventing. Using screws, attach a small metal plate to the wooden part of the mousetrap that serves as the final resting place for the spring loaded wire loop . . . and perhaps an unfortunate mouse. Attach one wire of a simple circuit to the wire loop part of the trap and one wire to the metal plate or screw holding it in place. When the mousetrap snaps, the circuit is automatically completed. Once closed, the functioning circuit can light a bulb, sound an alarm, drive a simple motor, or any other simple circuit driven activities you can think of or imagine. And of course, all of this can happen remotely.

Clothespins make great little clamps. One of our favorite uses of the clothespin, however, is as a switch. Drill holes in the ends of the pin where the two pieces of wood come together and insert a couple of small bolts attached to wires. Run those wires to a battery pack of several "C" or "D" cells and then on to a bell or light and you have a circuit. Of course with this particular setup, the bell will ring continuously unless you press the ends of the clothespin together, opening the jaws and breaking the circuit. In the description of the ADPM later in this chapter you will see how we use this system.

Another possibility is to mount those screws (or you could use thumbtacks) to the ends of the clothespin handles rather than the jaws. Whenever you press the handles together, the bolts or thumbtack heads will come together and complete the circuit. Pretty neat. Stretch a long enough piece of wire between the clothespin and the rest of the machine and you can operate the system from outside of the room.

It's your turn. What other items could be used in electrical circuits as switches? What things not already on the list, but which might be considered appropriately preposterous materials, could be used as switches? Did you think about lining opposite sides of paper tubes with aluminum foil so that a steel ball could roll through the tube completing the circuit? Oh, the possibilities!

Bases and Frames for Inventing Activities

All inventions need some place to be. This is not a particular problem if your students are working on practical inventions as described in the next chapter. A solar-powered flashlight won't take up much room. Even with the inventing we discuss in this chapter, you may want to allow students to spread out their work. Some students may want to use a lengthy and intricate pattern of dominos that act as a switch to complete a simple circuit. However, Rube Goldberg inventions easily take up large portions of your classroom if students are let loose with a hundred feet of clothesline.

For the sake of keeping the doorways accessible and the Fire Marshal happy, consider imposing some space limitations with bases or frames.

Bases

Plywood works well as a base for a number of reasons. First, it provides boundaries in two directions beyond which the invention should not go. Second, parts can be easily attached to the wooden base with nails, screws, glue, tape, thumbtacks, etc. Third, everything can be loaded onto the plywood base at the end of the period and moved to the back or side of the room. Inventions mounted on the plywood base can also be carried to an auditorium, library, or wherever for the big Invention Festival (or science fair), or, of course, carted off to someone's home as an enduring example of what a great time they had in your class.

Finally, you can easily determine the size limits that you want to use. The local homeowner's supply store will sell plywood (½-inch thick works well) in 4-x-8-foot sheets as well as in half and quarter sheets. They typically charge a bit more for the cut pieces (two half sheets will cost more than one full sheet), but you may be able to select the perfect sheet of plywood for your class and then have them cut it down for you. A 2-x-4-foot piece of plywood makes a nice base.

Frames

Recently, we have been working with another approach to bases. Rather than looking at the invention in terms of spreading out, we decided to go up. The result is an invention *frame* of PVC pipe. PVC is white plastic plumbing pipe we see so much of these days. It's tough, easy to cut, and can be assembled in many ways using T's, elbows, and crosses. The Automatic Door Prize Machine (ADPM) on page 136 is an example.

There are a number of advantages to using the frames. First, PVC is relatively inexpensive. Second, strangely enough, is that inventions don't have to have that "I'll keep it forever" feel. This is easier said from the teacher's perspective than the student's. The idea is that a group uses the frame to hold their invention, and afterward it (the invention and the frame) can be disassembled and the frames kept for the next class. You can even put most of those parts back into the Junk Box for reuse. How environmentally conscious!

The frames are reusable because they press-fit together and then have components clamped to the frame pieces. For example, take another look at the ADPM. All of the items on the frame are held there with what are called hose clamps. Hose clamps are made of a metal band that forms a circle and then passes through a small housing with a special screw. A screwdriver is used to tighten or loosen the clamp. If you take a look under the hood of a car you'll probably see hose clamps, for instance where the radiator hose connects to the radiator. A large hose clamp is usually used to attach that floppy plastic hose to the back of a clothes dryer. You can get them at the local hardware/homeowner supply store, or where automotive parts are sold.

Once you remove the items held to the frame with hose clamps, the frames can simply be pulled apart. There is a fitting, wherever two pipes come together. The fitting is glued to *one* of the pipes, but not the other. This way the two pieces can be press-fit together, but the fittings don't get lost when things are taken apart. Everything on the ADPM, yes *everything*, then fits into the big wooden box you see between the two frames in the picture. Whenever we demonstrate the machine, we wheel in the box (it has wheels on one side), set up the machine, run it, then put it all away and wheel it back to the car.

The frame approach is also space efficient during the inventing unit. The frames are light and easily moved. While your students work, the frames can be moved to a convenient spot. When the period is over, the frames can be moved against a wall. They are not very wide, and of course occupy space vertically rather than commandeering your table or desk space.

Also in the frame's favor is the notion of perspective. On the one hand, the frame mirrors the typical school experience of seeing things in terms of a blackboard or markerboard representation. That is, what the student draws on a blackboard does not have to be translated into a different plane. The frame is where you put what was drawn on the board. The familiar chalkboard becomes a useful analog for the design, *and redesign*, of the actual invention.

When it comes to building things, we tend to have a horizontal, table-top perspective, rather than a vertical perspective. In this regard, the frame provides the opportunity to work in a reference plane somewhat different than usual—a new perspective.

Building the Frames. There are two key considerations to building the frames. One is who will build them. The second is what size they should be. The first question is easiest to answer. You should prepare the frames, that is, prepare the frame "kits" that the students will assemble. Why? For one thing, the adhesive used is not the sort of thing for young students to use. It is probably not the sort of thing that you want some adolescents getting into either. You won't have trouble working with it, it just might be a potential parental concern that is better avoided. Cutting the PVC presents a similar concern. Power tools go through this stuff easily, but the PVC version of sawdust is not something you want all over your classroom. And that is not even mentioning the notion of power tools in the room! There are plier-like tools designed for cutting PVC; however, you can probably imagine how easily such a tool could cut through fingers. Finally, though you could use that short-cut saw mentioned earlier, along with a wooden mitre box, there would be a lot of down time while the whole class waited to get parts cut with one saw.

All of this is sounding scary. Don't let it be! Working with PVC is easy and straight-forward. You may even be able to tackle some home plumbing repairs by the time you're done. It is simply wise to take precautions since we are working with students.

The best bet is to either recruit a parent, colleague, other school employee, or friend who has the shop tools, or recruit a parent, colleague, other school employee, or friend who is willing to hold the pipe while you cut it. Once those questions are addressed and resolved, we can move to the second key consideration—size.

The ADPM uses two frames that are each six feet tall and six feet long. That has worked out well for a machine that is often used in front of audiences at schools and workshops. However, it may be more than you need. While the plans offered here are scaled down, keep in mind that you can design frames to fit your situation. Construction techniques remain the same, you will just need more or less of the materials.

For this particular frame you will need (2) 10-foot lengths of 1¼-inch PVC pipe (get the Schedule 40, 370 PSI variety, it has a wall thickness of about ³⁄₁₆ inch). Ten feet is the standard length. If you can persuade the folks at the store to cut it for you, you will be way ahead of the game. If you do have that kind of pull with the local hardware folks, ask that they cut each 10 footer into two 42-inch long sections and three 1-foot sections. You will also need (4) tee fittings, (2) 90-degree elbows, (4) end caps, and (1) can of PVC cement. One can will put together a bunch of these frames, **so don't buy a can for every frame you intend to assemble**. The PVC and glue for one frame should cost less than fifteen dollars.

Now that you have all the parts and have cut the pipes to length (or had them cut for you), it is time to glue the fittings onto the sections. Keep in mind that what you are doing is making frame "kits" rather than finished frames. **This reminder is provided to save you from gluing together an entire frame**. No doubt it would be a lovely frame, but storing it would be a chore. Gather together some newspaper, if you need to protect your work surface, some paper towels, the plan (Figure 5.4, p. 132), and let's assemble.

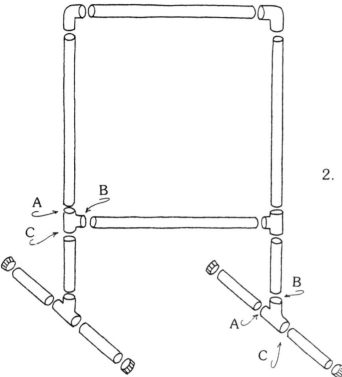

Figure 5.4. PVC Frame Plan for Rube Goldberg Inventions.

1. Locate (4) of the 1-foot-long pieces and the (4) end caps. Carefully open your can of PVC cement. You'll find that the cap has a metal wire attached with a fluffy ball at the end. Haven't seen one of those in awhile, have you? Get a bit of cement on the ball and wipe it around the inside wall of an end cap. Then run the ball around the last inch of the *outside* of one piece of pipe. Without wasting time, put the cap back on the can (you don't need to tighten it down) and press the end cap onto the end of the pipe with a twisting motion. Push it all the way down. Keep two things in mind: a) you can't take your time about this; you have to put the pieces together while the glue is wet, and b) once the two go together, that's the end of the story. You won't be able to put it on a little bit and then decide to take it off and try again. Proceed with confidence and push those pieces together. If you make a mistake, you won't be the first. Fortunately, the expense of making a new piece is minimal. And by the way, don't throw away the bad one; put it in the junk box!

2. Step one seems long, but if you got through it you have mastered PVC frame construction. Now cement *one* end cap to *each* of the three remaining 1-foot pieces. You should then have (4) 1-foot pieces, each with an end cap.

3. Next, you will need the four pieces you've just prepared and two tee fittings. Before gluing anything else together, notice that PVC has a line of printing along the pipe. Just for appearances sake, it is nice to try to orient all of this printing so that it is not seen when looking at the assembled frame. Keep that in mind as we continue with assembling the feet.

   To be clear, you will see that on the drawing we have labeled each of the three openings on the tee fitting. Refer to those labels as we continue. Take your PVC cement brush and put some cement on the inside wall of opening (A). Take one of your 1-foot lengths that has an end cap, and brush some cement around the last outside inch that does not have the end cap. Now wait just a second! As you twist these two pieces together, twist so that the lettering on the pipe faces in the opposite direction of opening (B) on the tee. That way the lettering will face the floor when the frame is assembled.

4. Take another of your 1-foot pieces with an end cap and cement it into opening (C) of the tee fitting you've been working with. Again, twist the two together so that the lettering faces the opposite direction from opening (B).

5. So far so good. Take a second tee fitting and the other two pieces with end caps and glue a second assembly just like the first.

6. Now that the feet are together, let's assemble the legs. Locate the two remaining 1-foot-long pieces and the two remaining tee fittings. The only tricky thing about this part is that we want to get that printing facing to the back. So, let's dry fit them first so you can see the orientation. Take one of the pipes and hold it vertically with the printing on the opposite side from the side you see. Take a tee fitting and slide opening (C) on to the top of the pipe so that the "stem" of the tee (opening B) points to the right. Repeat this procedure with the other pipe and fitting, except that the "stem" of the tee should point to the left. If you have this clear in your mind, take one apart, put on the cement, and twist them back together. Then do the other unit.

7. Hey, we're almost done with the gluing business! This last part is a lot like step (6). The difference is that we are using two of the 42-inch pipes and 90-degree elbows instead of tees. It might be worthwhile to proceed just as we did in step (6). Take one of the 42-inch pieces and hold it vertically in front of you so that the printing is on the opposite side from the side you see. Take one of the elbows and twist it on so that the re-

maining opening points to the right. Set it down, take another 42-inch piece and put an elbow on it so that the remaining opening points to the left. If all of this looks good, take one apart, apply the cement, and twist it back together. Then do the same for the other unit. That's it! You're finished gluing and the glue is already dry!

8. From now on this frame is assembled and disassembled by twisting together and apart the pieces you have prepared. To begin, take the two feet you assembled and the two legs. Twist the end of one leg into opening (B) of the tee in a foot assembly. Twist the other leg into the other foot in the same way. You should be able to do this so that the printing on the back of each leg is not visible from the front.

9. Take a 42-inch piece that has no fittings and fit it into opening (B) of one leg. Fit the other end into opening (B) on the other leg.

10. Take your 42-inch piece with the elbow facing right and twist it into opening (A) of the left end of the frame you've just assembled. The 42-inch piece with the left facing elbow goes on the right end.

11. Finally, take the remaining 42-inch piece and fit it in the openings of the two elbows. There you have a nice lightweight frame just waiting for some students to invent the first whatever it is!

As we have already mentioned, the frame construction techniques will be the same if you should decide that another shape fits your needs better. So feel free to adapt these plans to your situation.

PVC Accessories. With your new "inventor's easel" standing proudly in the classroom, there are at least two ways to proceed with assembling parts to the invention. The following page provides some ideas for frame "accessories" based on those we've used with the ADPM. These items can be used to support mousetraps, bells, or battery packs—whatever the need should happen to be. They can be attached with hose clamps as we have discussed. One potential problem is that it requires some tricky cutting of tee fittings. By cutting off the lower half of a tee, the resulting modified tee can be hose clamped very easily to the frame wherever you need. It can be attached on any frame member in any direction. Once attached, the possibilities for supporting other accessories is limited by your imagination. Take another look at the ADPM, and you will see a sampling of different uses. Look carefully and you will see the basic modified tee used seven times. A box full of these things will be used up in no time. We usually cut them out *very* carefully on a table saw with the blade just high enough to cut through one thickness of the wall at a time. If you have the equipment to make these, or know somebody who does, attaching items to the frame with these PVC accessories really lends a Rube Goldberg flair to the visual impact of the machine.

The Pegboard Approach. Another option is to use a pegboard panel lashed to the frame with wire, or better yet, plastic wire ties. You can get these ties in bags of 50 or more at auto parts stores or in the auto parts department of stores such as Kmart and Wal-Mart. Use three ties on each of the four sides, and your pegboard will be held firmly to the frame. When it is time to take things apart, cut the ties off with a pair of scissors.

For a frame constructed according to the plans in this book, buy a half sheet of ¼-inch pegboard. If you are building more than one frame, the cost of a full sheet of pegboard will be less than buying two half sheets. If you can

cut the pegboard (it does cut easily), great. If the supply store will cut it for you, even better. Depending on the car you drive, buying half sheets may be the way to go.

You could use twist-ties to lash items to the pegboard, or just wire. However, to put to use the advantages of the pegboard approach, buy a bag of assorted pegboard hangers. Slide a hook onto the board, hang your pulley from it, and you are ready to go. You can tape battery packs or mousetraps to the hangers that extend from the board. The best part is that by using these hangers, components can easily be moved around the pegboard as the invention evolves. If the item doesn't quite work here, move it over. Has the sound of a giant-sized circuit board, wouldn't you agree? Once the invention is "finalized" go to the back and put duct tape over the ends of the hangers to keep them from falling out accidentally. Keep in mind that the back of the pegboard is fair territory for the invention as well. A machine that sends a marble rolling across the front, around the back, and to the front again is a delight to watch!

Finally, whichever approach you decide to take, try not to let the idea of one frame per group limit your thinking. Perhaps you could have your students construct inventions that would tie into each other. That is, whatever happens on the frame from group A will end by initiating the action on the frame of group B, and so on. You could have four or five individual inventions that string together to make one invention 20 feet long! Wouldn't that be impressive to watch? So many possibilities!

The Automatic Door Prize Machine

Let's take a closer look at the Automatic Door Prize Machine (ADPM) as an example of what all of this is about. The ADPM was designed for use as a demonstration of Rube Goldberg inventing in the classroom. Because it would be necessary to transport it to and from various conferences, workshops, and classrooms, it had to be rugged, though constructed in a way that allowed easy assembly and break-down. However, an important consideration was that it retain its "home-grown" look and performance. The PVC frame fulfilled all of those demands. (See Figure 5.5, p. 136.) The machine has been able to survive years of use and works as well now as it ever did. It might be worthwhile to tell you what the philosophy of design is: process, not product. Sound familiar?

In practice, that perspective meant that our machine had to look and act like the machines that you and your students might invent in class. A key element of such machines is fallibility. Over the years we could have redesigned the ADPM so that it would work perfectly each time. After all, it is just a door prize machine. But it was important that people see that a machine that can work, does not always work. And so, you can see that the emphasis is on demonstrating and discussing the process of the invention, rather than on perfecting a product. Strangely enough, it was just after spending quite a bit of time pointing this out to an audience that the ADPM chose to assert its own character. The intention was to put our students at ease with the operation of their machines. Sure enough, in Murphy's Law fashion, the ADPM performed without a hitch from beginning to end!

Speaking of working, let's explain how the ADPM does what it is supposed to do. The intent is to "select" the lucky door prize winner from among the audience. We will tell you right off that the winning number, though selected by us at random, is in the machine before it begins to operate. Other than that little item, the rest is Rube Goldberg magic.

In a typical presentation we begin by distributing numbered clothespins, each with a plastic token bearing the same number to each of the audience members. We discuss the various attributes of the clothespin and its possible uses as presented in Chapter Four. Eventually we come to the notion of using the clothespin as a remote-control switch to activate an automatic door prize selector. Take a deep breath and follow along on the numbered drawing (see Figure 5.6, p. 137).

Here is how the whole thing is supposed to work (and sometimes does). Each audience member (or a representative of each class, if we are talking to several hundred students at once) comes to the ADPM and deposits a token in slot (1). After all tokens have been deposited, and with great fanfare, we close the slot and lock it with a tiny padlock (2). Next, by squeezing the clothespin handles (3) together an electrical connection to the electro-magnet (4) is broken. The magnet had been holding a steel ball at the top of track (5). The broken connection allows the ball to roll down the track. As it rolls it crosses aluminum foil switches (6), (7), and (8) each time causing the ADPM in Progress Bell (9) to ring. When the ball reaches the end of the track it drops into the detergent bottle cap (10) which pulls on rope (11) and springs the mousetrap (12). The swinging bar of the trap is attached to two other ropes, (13) and (14), attached to the bottle of yellow water (15) and attached to the bottle of blue water (16). When the trap is tripped the corks are pulled from beneath the bottles allowing the water to drain into waiting empty containers (17) and (18) on balance arm (19). When the containers are full, they lower the balance and thus raise the container (20) of green water (because blue and yellow make green, of course). Raising the green water starts a siphoning action through tube (21) which drains into the water receptacle (22) on the second frame. As the water level rises, the float (23) is raised, which in turn raises a piece of hanger wire (24) attached to a lever arm (25). When the float side of the arm is raised, the opposite end is lowered. This lowers the catch (26) on the end of the arm and releases the domino actuator wire (27), fabricated from a coat hanger, which is held under tension by a rubberband (28). The actuator wire springs to the right and knocks down the first of the dominos (29) on the

Figure 5.5. The Automatic Door Prize Machine (ADPM).

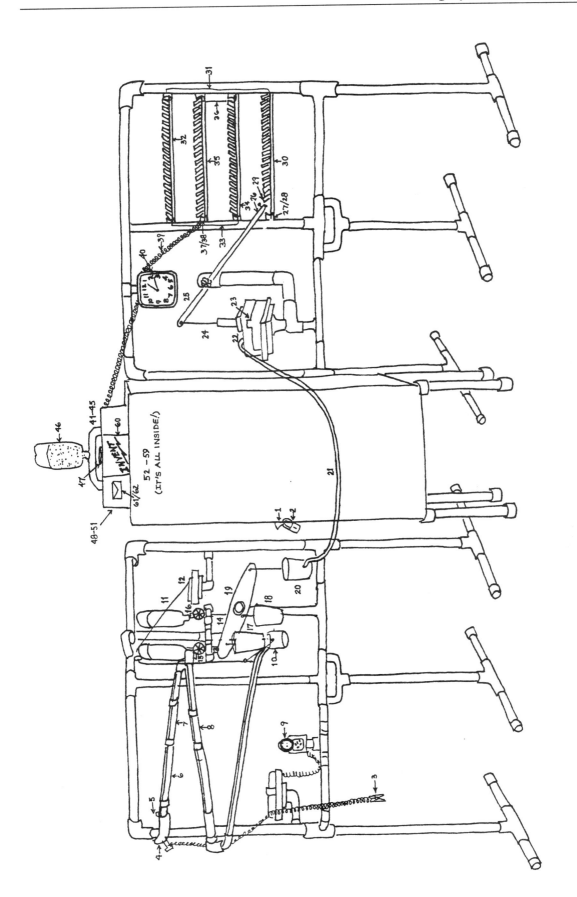

Figure 5.6. The ADPM by the Numbers.

lowest track (30). The last domino on the track falls against another actuator wire (31) which swings on its pivot and knocks over the top rack (32) of dominos. The last domino on this track falls against yet another actuator (33) and subsequently pushes over the first domino of this track (34). The final domino of this track is attached to the first domino of the remaining track (35) by a short piece of fishing line (36). When the one domino falls, it pulls the other domino down as well. The final domino of this whole series falls onto a small piece of aluminum foil (37) pushing it into contact with the head of a small bolt (38). Both the bolt and aluminum foil are connected by wires to the clock (39). When the domino forces the foil and bolt together, the circuit is completed and the clock begins to run. On the clock, at the position of the number two is a switch (40) made from two pieces of aluminum foil. When the minute hand reaches this position (we can set the clock to run for just a minute or for as long as an hour depending on what plans we have for the particular audience) it forces the two pieces of foil together and completes a circuit to the motor (41) atop the wooden box. When the motor runs, it pulls a short string (42) which is attached to another mousetrap (43) causing the trap to trip. As soon as the trap does trip, it breaks the circuit to the motor, thus turning the motor off. In addition, the strike bar of the mousetrap is connected by a string (44) to a plastic "key" (45) beneath the sand bottle (46) mounted on top of the box. The action of the mousetrap pulls out the key, allowing the sand to drain into a funnel (47) below the bottle. But this hard-working mousetrap still is not done. When the strike bar comes to rest after pulling out the key, it makes contact with a thumbtack (48) placed under the strike bar. Wires (49) and (50) from the strike bar and thumbtack connect to a cassette tape recorder (51). The completed circuit allows the recorder to play the theme music from *2001: A Space Odyssey* while the sand drains from the bottle. (We used *Pomp and Circumstance* for a group of

graduating seniors one time as a special surprise, but you could use whatever you like.) Though it cannot be seen, the sand is draining through a tube (52) inside the box into a bucket (53). The bucket is suspended by a rope (54) and attached to a signboard (55). When the bucket fills with sand, it lowers and so causes the sign to be raised up and out of the top of the box. As the top of the sign passes out of the box, it pushes a length of aluminum foil (56) out of contact with a thumbtack (57), both of which are connected by wires (58) and (59) to the aforementioned tape recorder (51), thus breaking its circuit to the batteries and shutting it off. The sign (60) reads "And the winner is . . ." and has an envelope (61) attached. Within the envelope is a plastic token (62) like the ones that had been distributed to the audience and then deposited in the machine. A number written on the token will match the number written on one of the clothespins distributed way back at the beginning of all of this. The holder of that clothespin is the lucky winner!

Sometimes the ADPM runs well and sometimes it does not. On more than one occasion we have forgotten to check a connection, or turn the tape recorder switch to the "on" position, and other things like that. All of that just goes to show what students can expect as they work on their own inventions. In any case, you can see that the ADPM does not use any items that are not readily available. Probably the most sophisticated component is the bell. You might have trouble finding a small electric bell. Even so, it uses an array of energy sources and simple science principles to do its work.

What of that big box where the actual "selection" occurs? Do you remember the pencil sharpener activity in Chapter Four? Well, we use that big mysterious box in the same way. Depending on the group that we are working with (workshop, one class, etc.) we will often hand out papers with just the outline of the box drawn on it, and ask that our participants draw what they think is going on inside the machine that selects the winner.

The drawings serve as a great way to initiate that creative thinking. And as was the case with Mr. Toriello's class in the scenario, it is very important to find merit in *every* idea offered.

When we do the "what's in the box?" activity, it is usually just after the dominos turn on the clock. We will have set the clock to run 30 minutes or so before actuating the mechanism to release the sand and turn on the recorder. In practice, the audience does not know that these things are going to happen. As a result, when the mousetrap suddenly snaps, the sand starts to drain out of the bottle, and the first strains of *Also Sprach Zarathustra* begin to blare, it comes as quite a surprise! Of course all the time in between at least one of these authors is watching, and *hoping*, that everything is going to happen on cue. It's all so exciting!

Taking Your Students Through an Inventing Experience

We've discussed the tools needed, the junk needed, looked at some alternative uses of items, and preparing the frames or bases. The discussion of the ADPM should have given you a good idea of the nature of these sorts of inventions. Now, let's take it all to the class.

Ideally, you will start out with the Discovery Inventing activities that we discussed in Chapter Four. Following with Rube Goldberg Inventing and moving to Practical Inventing, as discussed in Chapter Six, will provide you with an in-depth experience with creative thinking and science education. Whether you plan to begin with Discovery Inventing, the thought of jumping right into the design of these Rube Goldberg machines may seem a bit overwhelming. We recommend that you work your way up to it, just as this chapter has been laid out. Begin with the *Invent! Cards* to get things started. The *Invent! Cards* are not as neat as the real things, but

isn't it nice to know that there's a situation where the real thing is the next item in your lesson plan!

Now that you have introduced inventing with the cards, invite your students to begin bringing materials for the junk box. It may work well to announce this on a Monday with the intention of beginning work with the junk box the following Monday. As students see what other students bring in, it will stimulate their own thinking about what is expected and/or acceptable. Once you have some materials in the junk box, allow discussion time, as outlined earlier, to identify attributes and consider alternative uses.

A valuable aspect of the alternative uses discussion is providing the opportunity for students to build things like switches from clothespins, paperclips, aluminum foil, and so forth. Let them investigate the components that will eventually be combined into systems. Similarly, cutting up paper towel tubes to make marble tracks, and arranging dominos to activate foil switches provides some good background experience. Try to avoid, however, requiring a lot of planning and writing *before* they have the chance to work with materials. There will be many opportunities to ask for verbally based assignments, but if you ask for them now you will lose students who are not strong on traditional verbal tasks.

Next is the construction of the toolbox. Without a doubt when you come into class with a box full of tools, or allow students to bring tools to school, they will know that you are serious about this project *and* that this is going to be something very different from what they are used to. If at all possible, allow the opportunity to build a toolbox as described earlier in this chapter. For your students, the purpose will be constructing a box to hold the tools. For you, the purpose is development of students' manual and visual thinking skills as they see a project take shape. We have watched it happen and seen the excitement generated.

At this point you might want to give everybody the same simple challenge. Perhaps you could have them build a machine that raises a weight using at least five steps and two different energy sources. Energy sources might include simple battery-operated circuits, gravity, solar energy, or heat (for instance from a candle, not from a blowtorch). These easy assignments with an established goal should not occupy weeks of time, but will allow very important experience.

The big project comes next. Provide students with several options for machines to be invented. For example, you might give them the choice of inventing a machine that pops a balloon, raises a flag, or extinguishes a candle. Require a minimum number of steps (15?) and a minimum number of energy sources (5?). You could have each team submit a *preliminary* drawing of their design at least, so you can have some idea of what is coming down the pike. However, the name of the design game is redesign, and they must know that redesign is acceptable and encouraged. If you have a student who draws out a complex machine on the first try, puts it together according to the plan, and it works from the get go . . . get that student's name and offer to provide financial backing! Otherwise, be happy to see students make revisions, it means they recognize and solve problems. *Process, not product!*

All that is left is to set up the Invention Festival (Chapter Eight), unless you also want to integrate all of this with your other subject areas (Chapter Seven). There is also the idea of a Patent Office in your own classroom (Chapter Nine). Of course, before you know it the local TV crew is going to be there to see what your students have done, so you had better get ready for this as well!

Summary

You have probably noticed that this middle chapter is longer than the others. The reason is simple, Rube Goldberg Inventing, as we have conceptualized it here, embodies the heart and soul of creative thinking in the context of science education. Providing this opportunity to your students offers science content and basic science process skills in a truly creative problem-solving experience. You will find that the intrinsic humor of these activities lowers the anxiety level of your students as they work on their inventions providing an atmosphere more conducive to solving the problems at hand. That is not to say that it will eliminate frustration. Without a doubt, when that marble refuses to fall where it is supposed to fall, we have the makings for a frustrating experience. However, such frustration is the nature of investigation; that is, finding answers to questions that are not readily apparent. Such a lesson is why students come to school. Go ahead, have the most imaginative, creative, and enjoyable classroom in the school and foster creative problem-solving ability at the same time that students are learning science. Just go right ahead!

Chapter Six

Practical Inventing

In this chapter you will find:

    The need for a specified need;

    Unusual inventions from the past;

    and the steps in practical inventing!

A driving force in human affairs, and perhaps the foundation of civilization, inventing causes change, development, and evolution in world affairs. Inventive thinking, therefore, should be encouraged to solve problems for humanity. The knowledge of how to invent may well be the key to new products and inventions that will transform the environment and supply many of society's needs.

Practical inventing represents a shift in emphasis from what we have done thus far. The focus is still on process rather than product. However, the product does assume greater importance, since meeting an identified need is the aim of practical inventing.

If you have (or intend to) take your students through an entire program as we have shown you, then practical inventing is the logical next step. If you are planning to do only practical inventing, we strongly recommend that you orient practical inventing as a *creative problem-solving* approach to a particular situation. If you emphasize the verbally-based foundation steps discussed in this chapter, you could dim the creative light and lose students who tend to not perform well on verbal tasks. Inventing is a cognitive challenge for your students. *Your* challenge is to provide an environment that facilitates and fosters the creative search for patterns, perspectives, and relationships. As with other forms of inventing, such an environment is open-ended, and it's difficult to know where it will lead!

A Practical Scenario

It was Friday morning and much quieter at the breakfast table than usual; Christopher and his younger sister are there together.

"What will you be doing in school today?" asked Christopher Scofield's mother.

"We are inventing stuff," he answered while eating his cereal with one hand and flipping the metal catch of his lunchbox with the other.

"That certainly sounds interesting! Does everybody work together on this?" asked his mother.

"Nope. Miss Gordon says that everybody should invent something of their own."

"You can't invent anything," chimed in Emily from the other side of the breakfast table.

"Yeah, I can. And I know just what it will be."

"Really?" said his mother. "What will it be?"

"Well, someone has been taking stuff from my lunchbox, so I'm going to invent an alarm to catch them."

"Alarms aren't new," said Emily, "So how can you invent one?"

"Mine will be the first *lunchbox* alarm. Have you ever seen one of those? Of course you haven't, because you're too *little* to go to school *or* to have a lunchbox!"

Christopher's mother brought his lunch to the table and opened the lunchbox. "Be nice to your little sister, dear. Have you told Miss Gordon that someone has been taking things from your lunch?"

"No, but she'll find out today because we have to tell her what we've decided to invent."

"Perhaps I should give her a call. I make lunch for *you*, not for everybody else at the school."

"No!" Chris said. "I've got this all planned."

"Well you let me know if someone keeps taking things from your lunchbox. Now go brush your teeth and then you'd better get going."

Chris followed his mother's directions and then came back downstairs and put on his coat. Emily handed Chris his lunchbox as he left. He had been thinking about this alarm ever since Miss

Gordon mentioned that *everyone* had to invent something of their own. In fact, he had already looked at *every* inventing book she had in the classroom *and* had looked up burglar alarms in the library. It was the most reading Christopher had ever done without being told to, and he kind of enjoyed it.

But the real matter at hand was figuring out the best way to hook up this alarm so that he could catch the thief. He really had not been able to spot anyone taking things from his lunchbox, so it must be someone who comes in the classroom while he is in art class. Probably some first grader wandering around the halls. "Soon," he thought, "the little kid will be brought to justice!"

Miss Gordon was serious about letting students work on their inventions. Everybody had thought if the inventions weren't finished in one day, they would move on to something else. Instead, Miss Gordon let them work during science class that whole week and even let them stay in class during lunch to work on projects. Every day the dessert disappeared from Chris's lunchbox after art and before science. A working alarm was more important than *ever!* By the time Chris left for home on Friday he had almost completed his alarm system.

The lunchbox had turned out to be a good case for his invention. After all, he needed to hook up wires and batteries and a bell. As it turned out, putting together a circuit to ring the bell was no problem. In fact, the biggest problem had been getting the batteries stuck in one place so that they didn't roll around and smash whatever his mother had packed. The other problem, the tough problem, was devising a switch. He had not expected that to be so difficult, and he had spent all weekend going through three different design ideas. The switch had to be something that would turn on the alarm when the box was opened, but

also that he could turn off so that it didn't ring the bell when *he* opened the box. It also had to be something that was strong enough that he could turn the lunchbox over, like a clumsy first grader might do, without the switch getting knocked out of place by the stuff inside.

The switch problem had finally been solved by making a push tab from heavy cardboard. The base of the cardboard was taped to the inside of the top of the lunchbox. Its long tab could reach all the way to the bottom of the box, and when it did, it pushed a flexible piece of aluminum away from another piece of aluminum. Each piece was connected to a wire that ran to the batteries and the bell. When the top was opened, the flexible piece of aluminum would bend back against the other piece and complete the circuit. It worked every time.

He also found a way to disarm his alarm without opening the box. He had come up with the idea of cutting one of the wires from the batteries and then passing the two ends through the back of the box where it was hinged. He put a piece of duct tape on the bottom of the lunchbox so that the wires did not touch the metal case. Then he taped the wires onto the piece of tape with their bare ends about 1 cm apart. Finally, he put a piece of aluminum foil that was 2 cm long on the sticky side of another piece of duct tape. He folded the very end of the tape over on itself so that there was a little flap that would not stick to his lunchbox. He then taped this piece over the bare ends of the wires. As long as the tape was there, the foil completed the circuit. But whenever Chris wanted to open the box, he would first peel up the strip of tape by the flap and break the circuit. Really, he couldn't believe that he had figured out all of these things. But here was his lunchbox, the first one complete with an alarm, and he was as proud as could be. In fact, he enjoyed opening the box himself just to hear the bell ring exactly as he had designed it.

Chris was noticeably excited on Monday morning and insisted that his mother let him load up the lunchbox.

"So it's all ready, is it?" she asked. "How about showing me how it works?"

Chris did explain it all in detail. "Today I will find out who has been taking the dessert out of my lunch everyday, Mom. There's no way that he can open this without setting off the alarm."

"I'll be anxious to know how it works! But for now, get those teeth brushed and get going!" his mother said with a pleased smile.

Christopher headed upstairs and brushed his teeth. He could barely contain his excitement about using his new invention. There couldn't possibly be anyone else in class with an invention as good as this one!

As he went downstairs to get his coat a loud ringing sound filled the house. "My alarm!" he cried as he raced downstairs. By the time he got to the bottom of the stairs his mother was there as well. And so was . . . Emily. Emily was there with someone's lunch dessert in her hand and on the verge of tears.

"Emily, you!" said Chris's mother. Chris meanwhile did not know whether to be happy or sad. His invention worked, but he hadn't expected to catch his little sister! Of course this did explain why his dessert was always missing even before science class. The fact was, the dessert never made it to school!

"Christopher, your lunchbox alarm worked very well," said his mother. "You take it to school and explain to Miss Gordon that using the alarm you did find your dessert bandit. I will have a talk with Emily!"

■ ■ ■

Meeting a Specified Need

An invention is an answer to a problem. More than that, it meets a specific need with a new and original answer to a problem. The inventions that you and your students looked at in Chapter Four, Discovery Inventing, all represented a way of meeting a specific need identified by the inventor. The inventions that you and your students came up with in Chapter Five, Rube Goldberg Inventing, also represented machines that met a specific need. In that situation, the "need," or task was supplied by you. It may be the case that you supplied the students with the choice of several tasks. Now, as we move into the topic of practical inventing, it will be important to let your students identify the need. On the one hand, it is obvious that a need perceived by the student(s) will hold greater importance than an artificial one imposed by the teacher. On the other hand, identifying something in need of improvement or outright origination may be the most difficult part of this experience.

You probably found from the other exercises that once the creative floodgates are opened, thinking flows fast and furious. The same is true here. However, typically we do not teach our students to look for ways of improving things, so this initial task is particularly daunting. All that is necessary is a sufficient change of perspective to allow seeing things in different ways.

Nothing New Under the G-Type Star in Our Solar System

Unless you are standing around with something that desperately needs doing, or you simply happen to have flashes of insight because nowadays your creative thinking is working overtime, you might find it difficult to identify an interesting inventive idea. Yet virtually anything around you could be done differently, better (in the eyes of the beholder), or with some modification.

No doubt you are saying, "If it's not broken, don't fix it." We agree. Some things work fine just as they are. However, those things probably are working much differently than they did 50 or 100 years ago. Change happens! So, where there is possibility of worthwhile change, let's embrace it. Where change can wait another day or two, let's sit back and enjoy the lemonade. But possibilities are out there!

The series of drawings on page 146 represent a sampling of inventive work based on a very simple device—the pencil sharpener. How much can you change a pencil sharpener? Well, the claims for each of these drawings were significant enough to warrant the award of a patent. You can see that they do demonstrate a wide range of applications. For instance, did you know there is a hand-cranked pencil sharpener that puts a point on those flat carpenter pencils? The patent drawings shown below date from 1874 to 1988—more than 100 years of pencil point preparation improvements! Is there nothing new under the sun?

The pencil sharpener patented by John Hall in 1874 (Patent No. 154,982) requires that the pencil be held at an angle and then stroked across the V-shaped chisel. (See Figure 6.1, p. 146.) First the cutter slices off some of the wood, and then the file helps to form the point. The pencil is rotated with each stroke in order to surface it all the way around. Albert Buzby's improvement (March, 1876, Patent No. 171,777) does not deal with the actual sharpening, but rather with a mounting system so that the hands of the sharpener do not get soiled in the process.

Jones's pencil sharpener (April, 1881, Patent No. 240,520) looks quite a bit like the little sharpener that we've all come to know and love. (See Figure 6.2, p. 147.) It was designed for "sharpening pencils in as perfect a manner as is possible." Likely to

Jones's dismay, Archibald McKinnon apparently did not believe that Jones had taken pencil sharpening to its highest point, and so in 1887 received Patent No. 359,026 for his improvement of the process. Notice that McKinnon offers a two step procedure. First the pencil is roughly sharpened by the cutter mounted on the left side of the block. After that, it is sanded smooth by turning it against the sandpaper mounted in the right side.

Patent No. 819,104 shows the sort of pencil sharpener that we have seen in our classrooms for years and years. In fact, this particular patent was issued to John Webster in 1906 as an improvement to his own patented sharpener from 1900 (Patent No. 640,846)! (See Figure 6.3, p. 148.) Just when you thought it was safe to go buy a trusty old sharpener at the office supply store, along comes Arthur Frederick with his improvement in 1937 (Patent No. 2,146,890). Though the inside of this sharpener looks suspiciously like the inside of any other sharpener, take a close look at parts 22 and 23 at the left end of the drawing. Yes, this idea goes right back to Buzby's idea in 1876. Those parts you see are tiny brushes that clean the freshly sharpened pencil. Now that we think about it, is there really anything so satisfying as a clean and pointy pencil?

Admittedly, Anthony J. Alpha's sharpener (July, 1988, Patent No. 4,759,129) is in a different class than the previous models. (See Figure 6.4, p. 149.) However, the idea of attacking the problem of sharpening a flat pencil with a rotary motion is representative of creative thinking. What sort of perspective switching and pattern finding do you suppose Alpha had to do to come up with this device? Look closely, there is nothing new. There is nothing magical. There is simply the ability to "see" things in a different way. You and your students should be getting pretty good at that!

(Text continues on p. 150.)

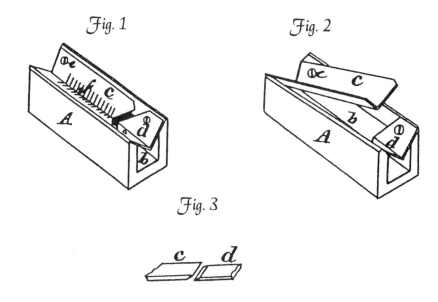

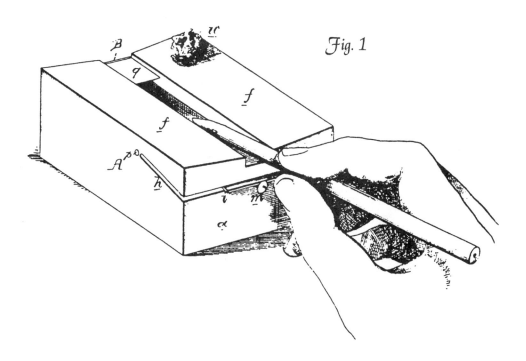

Figure 6.1. Hall's Patent (top) and Buzby's Patent (bottom).

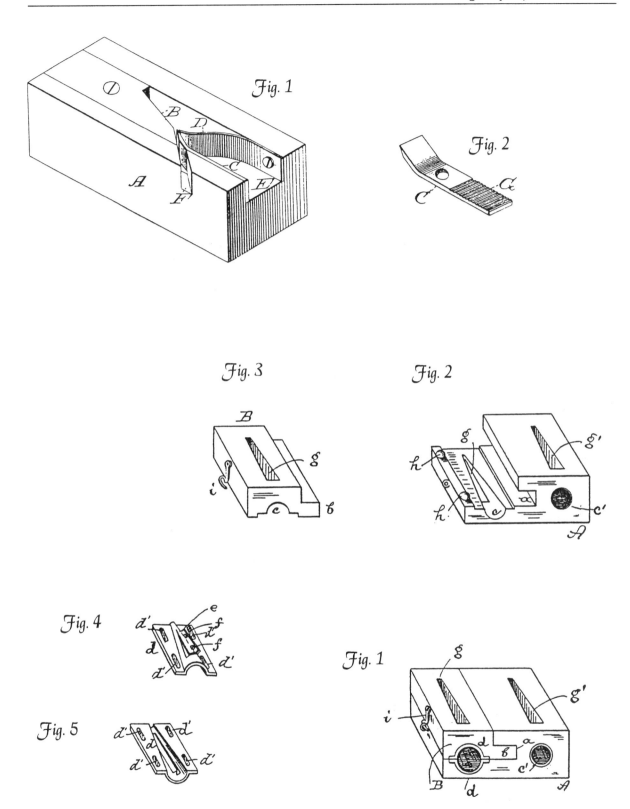

Figure 6.2. Jones's Patent (top) and McKinnon's Patent (bottom).

From *The Inventive Mind in Science: Creative Thinking Activities.* © 1998 Teacher Ideas Press. (800) 237-6124.

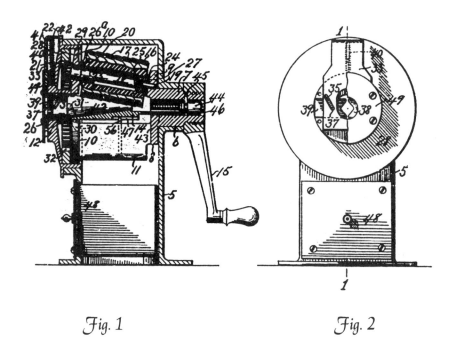

Fig. 1   *Fig.* 2

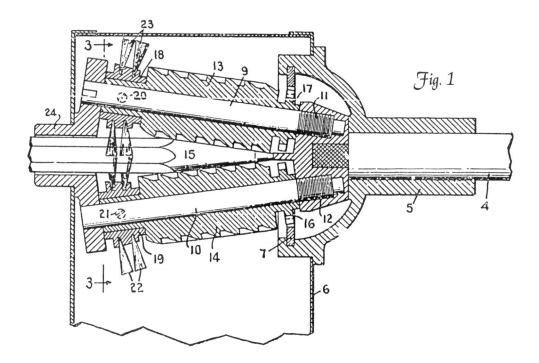

Fig. 1

Figure 6.3. Webster's Patent (top) and Frederick's Patent (bottom).

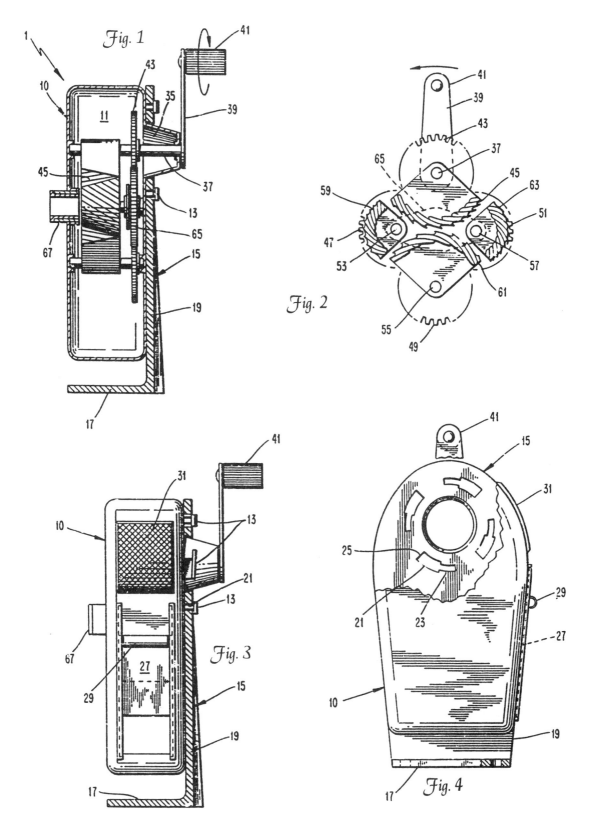

Figure 6.4. Alpha's Patent.

From *The Inventive Mind in Science: Creative Thinking Activities.* © 1998 Teacher Ideas Press. (800) 237-6124.

Unusual Inventions
from the Past

Here is a challenge to get those invention ideas going. Following is a "What could it be?" form, and the six pages following that show some nice, practical inventions spanning the years between 1898 and 1983. For your class you might want to copy the patent drawings or make transparencies. Allow students to use the "What could it be?" page to determine the purpose of each invention. We will even give you a hint on the one that looks like a baby crib—the lower section is actually a grapefruit! And no, the grapefruit is not the invention; it's what's attached to the grapefruit. Give it a try. Notice that we have given you a "What *could* it be?" page instead of a "What *is* it?" page. This emphasizes possibilities, rather than correctness. But here, if you are interested, are explanations for each drawing.

The first drawing represents a head-covering patented by Joseph Smyth in 1898 (Patent No. 606,982). (See Figure 6.5, p. 152.) We don't know how well the invention did at the turn of the century, but as this century prepares to turn, variations of this collapsible head-covering can often be seen at outdoor sporting events.

In 1966 Louis Bostick patented this improvement to the skateboard (Patent No. 3,235,282). (See Figure 6.6, p. 153.) The wheels are mounted to carriages, something most of your students probably already know. The improvement is that carriages are mounted to a track that runs the length of the skateboard. So, the carriages can be moved to different positions under the board. The position shown in Fig. 8 would be good for cruising. The position shown in Fig. 7 would be good for sharp turns. The other positions could accommodate all of those lovely tricks we like to do. This particular patent was not

issued for a skateboard, but rather for an improvement (so says the designer) to the skateboard.

The third drawing is a 1983 entry. (See Figure 6.7, p. 154.) Patent No. 4,325,178 went to Monya Scully for this Muffling Cup. What is a muffling cup? The next time you just want to scream at someone, take your muffling cup in hand and scream to your heart's content. You will be able to vent your anger without disturbing the people around you. Sounds like a great gift idea!

The well-known team of Mealey and Mealey (Elizabeth and George, that is) received Patent No. 696,070 for this little jewel in 1902. This neat device enables the operator to clean windows, "particularly windows at an elevation from street-level," both inside and out from the inside. And that short piece (4) at the bottom of the handle (3) allows extensions when going after those really elevated windows. (See Figure 6.8, p. 155.)

Alfred Clark was one of those visionaries who apparently felt that the best relaxation is work. And so in 1913 Patent No. 1,051,684 was awarded for this Rocking Chair Butter Churn. (See Figure 6.9, p. 156.) Just imagine the infomercials.

Finally, we offer the work of Joseph Fallek. (See Figure 6.10, p. 157.) It would seem that one morning around 1928 Joe was eating his breakfast when—splat—another case of grapefruit juice in the eye. Perhaps Joe had not slept well the night before, or was facing a difficult day at work, but whatever the case this was the last straw. The wheels started turning, and by the time it was over, the Grapefruit Shield (Patent No. 1,661,036) had become a reality. And the best news is versatility. You see, not only is this effective for grapefruit, but for other citrus fruits as well!

(Text continues on p. 158.)

What Could It Be?

For each of the unusual patents given, list at least one possible purpose for the device. Be sure to identify each with its patent number and inventor.

Patent Number: _____ Inventor(s) _____

Possible function: _____

_____

_____

Patent Number: _____ Inventor(s) _____

Possible function: _____

_____

_____

Patent Number: _____ Inventor(s) _____

Possible function: _____

_____

_____

Patent Number: _____ Inventor(s) _____

Possible function: _____

_____

_____

Patent Number: _____ Inventor(s) _____

Possible function: _____

_____

_____

Patent Number: _____ Inventor(s) _____

Possible function: _____

_____

_____

Fig. 1

Fig. 2

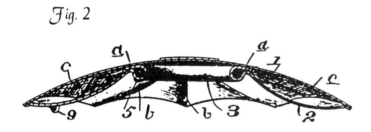

Fig. 3

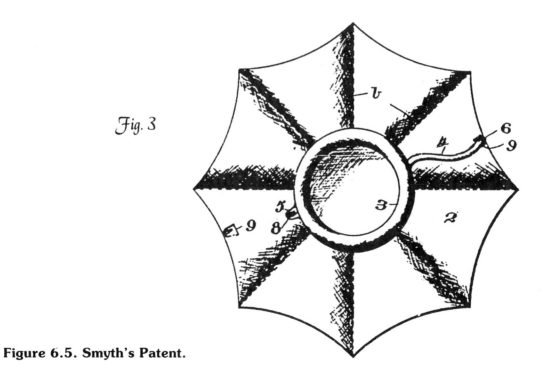

Figure 6.5. Smyth's Patent.

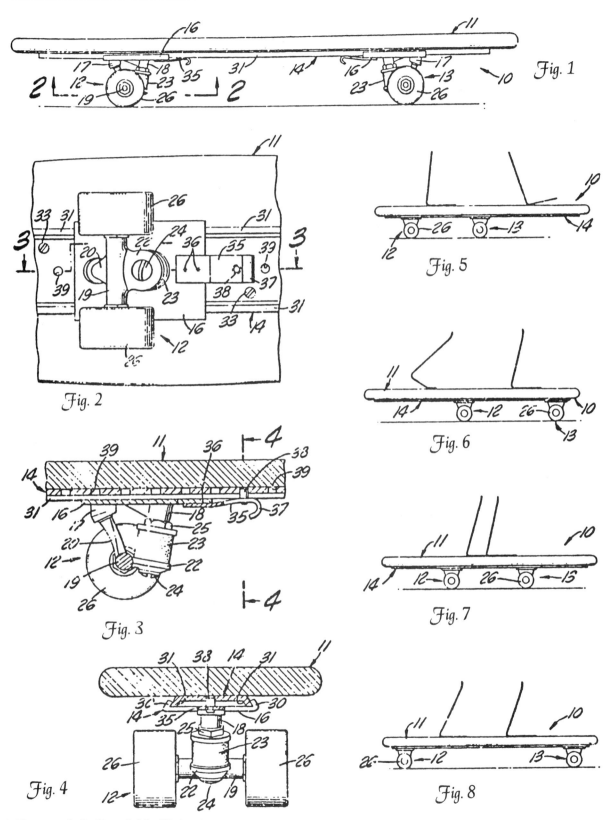

Figure 6.6. Bostick's Patent.

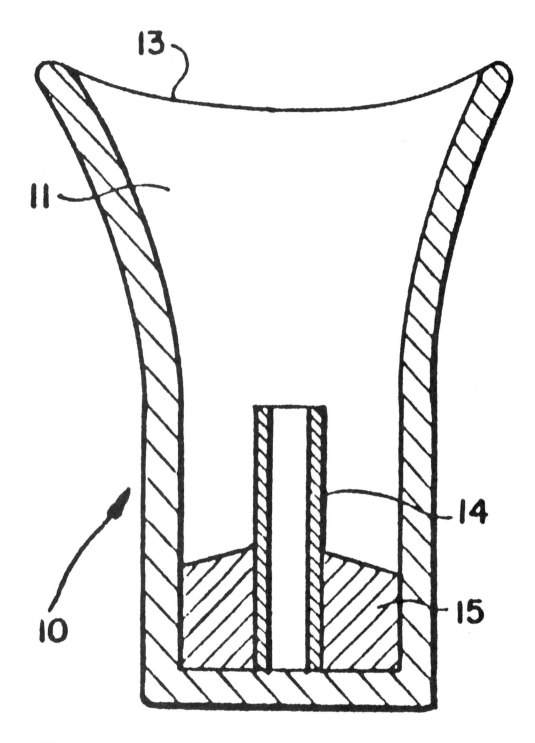

Figure 6.7. Scully's Patent.

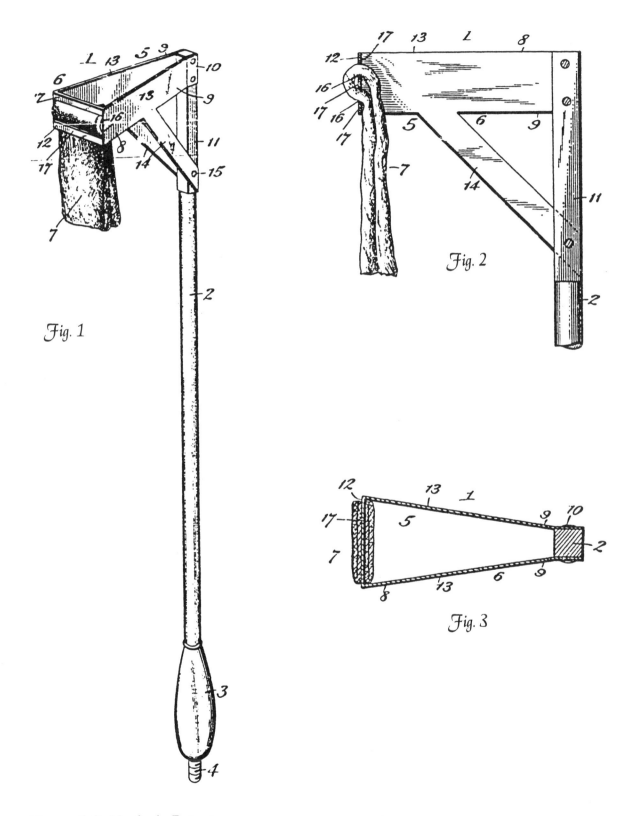

Figure 6.8. Mealey's Patent.

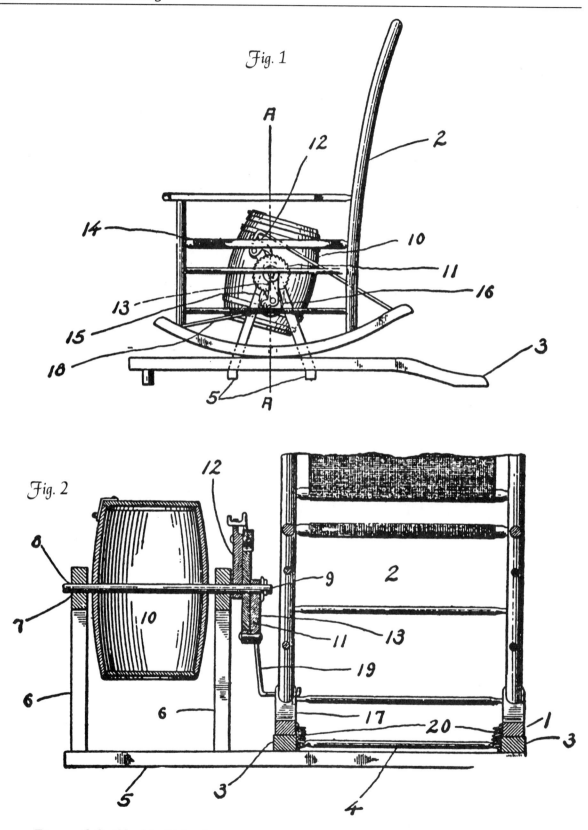

Figure 6.9. Clark's Patent.

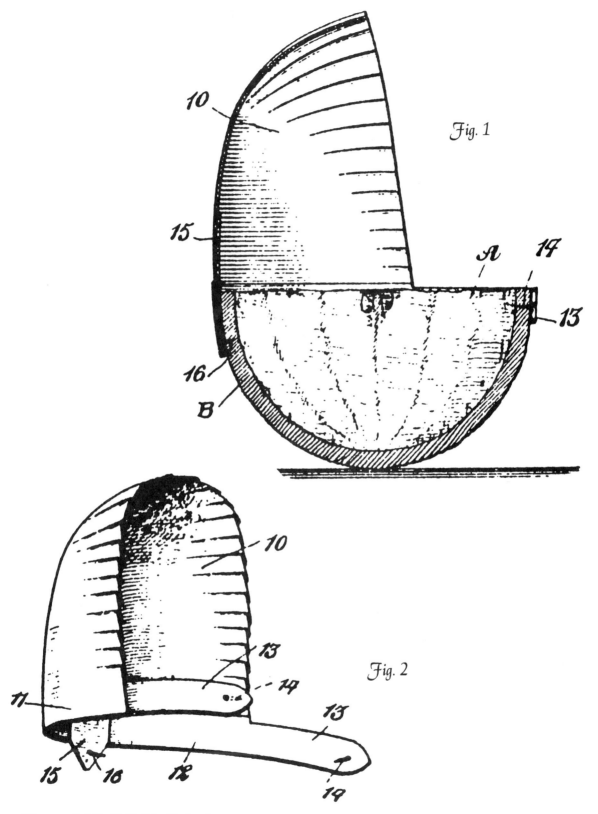

Figure 6.10. Fallek's Patent.

This brief look at just a few patents should indicate that when we talk about inventing things, it does not have to be the telephone or the LASER. Look for things in your life that could be done differently and then go to it. No doubt your students can identify all sorts of inventive opportunities. One more example? Okay. While we were researching this book, we came across a patent for a noisemaker to be attached to a bicycle. Rather than using a clothespin and a baseball card this invention is durable and more securely attached. That was all. It was just a "better" way of doing this very simple thing. Of most importance is that your students have the opportunity to think in this way.

The Five (or Six) Steps of Practical Inventing for Designing Particularly Practical Inventing Activities

We can conceptualize the practical inventing process as having three parts: Foundation Steps, Process Steps, and a Concluding Step. Each of these represents discrete components of the overall process, and so each has a different activity focus. The Foundation Steps are verbally oriented—expressing the need and researching former solutions. The Process Steps involve hands-on manipulation of materials. The Concluding Step refers to patenting. Though this is also a verbal task, students work with the special motivation of patenting *their own* invention.

It is not necessary to prepare frames or bases as for Rube Goldberg Inventing. Some inventions may require a base, others may fit into a shirt pocket. However, there are some things from Chapter Five that would be useful. One is the Inventor's Junkbox. The items in that box are not only raw material for inventions, but provide ideas of what to do and how to do some things. For instance, seeing how a can opener works might give your student just the information needed to arrange a set of gears.

The Inventor's Toolbox is also needed. That collection of tools is essential to the construction of projects. It isn't reasonable that students have access to all of the tools they might need, but having a few basic tools readily available is a boost to any project. In addition, some rolls of duct tape (or masking tape, if you prefer) along with clothespins (to use as clamps) and twist ties (to use for twist tieing) are items that should always be on hand.

The critical elements of a practical inventing lesson are a) providing the opportunity to work through each of the steps of inventing, and b) allowing the *students* to identify the need or problem that they will address. The following example of a practical invention lesson will address each of the first five steps of inventing. The sixth step, patenting the invention, is discussed at length in Chapter Nine, A Word About Patents. The activities provided there will help tie all of this inventiveness together in a form that can be shared (with the principal, parents, the PTA, your colleagues, etc.).

The Foundation Steps

There are two steps to be considered. The first is *identifying a problem or need*. The activities of the previous section, Meeting a Specified Need, were intended to help you and your students prepare for this step. Sometimes a need seems to be evident, but more often identifying the need provides a stumbling block. Be prepared by being able to demonstrate that everyday items are fair game for inventive improvement. How could pencils be made better? How could students organize papers more efficiently? How could you design an intruder alert alarm to be sure no one opens your lunch box? How could swing sets be made to not tip over?

As you can see, practical inventing is highly individual. Each person accesses a unique knowledge base and processes new ideas in a personal way. Teachers, however, can facilitate the process. While you should avoid overstructuring the thinking process, you can provide guidelines in the form of daily activity suggestions. For example, on the first day or two, you may have students spend time individually thinking about possible needs or problems, and some time discussing possibilities in small groups The goal is for each student to identify and state a personal need or problem to solve.

The activity sheet on page 161 is designed to help identify personal needs by establishing need categories. They might put together a list of categories, such as classroom, home, playground, cafeteria, bedroom, chores, pets, and vacations. Note that the categories do not always have to be places, but can be events or times. Challenge your students to list at least two inventions and two invention *possibilities* for each category. All are offered as a means to stimulate thinking in different perspectives, rather than suggestions for specific projects. Remember, with practical inventing it is important that the student identifies and selects the project. You might want to okay ideas to avoid having any thermo-nuclear devices glowing in your classroom, but student selection results in ownership.

The second of the Foundation Steps is *researching former solutions to the problem.* **We cannot caution you enough about this step.** As we established in Part I, creative and inventive thinking are what people (and that includes children) do. It is language convention that often gives children difficulty.

Inventing provides your verbally weak students the opportunity to demonstrate the depth of their thinking in a way you may never have seen. And, it provides your verbally strong students with a way to demonstrate and extend their thinking in a challenging way at their own level. Having identified problems to solve—needs to meet—your students will be anxious to move to Process

Steps. If the research step is overemphasized, requiring a lot of reading and writing, some students will be lost. If you have brought them to this point through the activities presented in this book, they will be prepared to do a research activity now. **If you are beginning here, without the earlier activities, test the waters carefully.**

Researching prior solutions can be a fascinating activity. In Chapter Nine, A Word About Patents, you will find information regarding what is available from the U.S. Patent and Trademark Office and how to access it. If you have Internet access, you will be able to go right to the Patent Office's web site. But that sort of electro-tech stuff is not necessary for what needs to be done. Encyclopedias and your school library can provide plenty of information to help your students find out if a) the problem has been recognized before, b) how it has been addressed, and c) has anybody used their same idea already.

If this is the first time students have attempted practical inventing, extra assistance for researching former solutions may be necessary. Availability of books and other resources focusing on how things work, science, invention references, and the historical development of technology is very helpful. Check the References and Resources section for suggestions regarding books for your classroom or library.

Even more important the first time is showing students how to look for information in a book and to briefly record it. If you model the process of researching former solutions rather than merely telling students what to do, they will be better prepared to conduct their own research. Modeling the process involves searching for relevant resources, locating pertinent information, and recording helpful information, accompanied all the while by verbalization of thinking that occurs.

In addition, the Inventor's Journals can be used to help students become more systematic during the inventing process. The journals are an excellent means of recording the inventing process. Students can record any pertinent information collected from resources as well as their own ideas. Those records can be reviewed anytime and are especially useful when it becomes necessary to redesign the invention or pursue an alternative.

Asking questions is one of the most helpful strategies that teachers can use to encourage students' thinking. The questions listed on the Researching Prior Solutions page (see p. 162), and other similar questions, help to focus and guide the students' work.

Researching prior solutions, though indispensable in the work of inventors, is an "on the one hand . . . on the other hand" situation for students in your classroom. On the one hand, if the student finds that an idea is untested, enthusiasm increases tremendously. On the other hand, finding out that someone else has already done what you propose is fairly frustrating. That frustration needs to be seen from the perspective of *information*, rather than defeat. The student will either know not to pursue a particular approach, and so make adjustments, or to identify another problem to establish ownership. In either case, researching prior solutions to a problem provides ideas and perspectives that the student likely had not considered previously.

The Process Steps

With the idea identified, researched, and documented in the student's Inventor's Journal, it is time for the Process Steps. There are three sub-steps at this level. All three rely on students' own thinking. Interestingly enough, the science textbook and books like it can become *tools* toward the construction of knowledge during these three steps. Students use them to see how this or that could be done as part of their work, rather than seeing them as just books with information that they have to learn (memorize).

The first step is *generating ideas toward a new solution*. Whether working in groups or individually, this step gives the inventor a list of possibilities. A popular term for this activity is brainstorming. When doing this, ideas are offered and listed (yes, actually committed to paper), in a *non-judgmental* fashion. The purpose is to list ideas that may eventually work into a solution without being accepted or rejected along the way. One person's strange idea can stimulate someone else's great idea. Cognitive psychology calls it spread of activation. What happens is that when you think of one idea, that leads *your* thinking to another idea, then to another, and so on. In brainstorming it is important to not impose criteria that would narrow its course. And when more than one person is involved in brainstorming, it is obvious that the spread of activation can go in many, many directions! We are not telling you to tolerate anything that steps over the bounds of decorum and good taste. However, there will be ideas that might seem silly or just not feasible, but those should not be ignored. Again, brainstorming is not a discussion session. Rather, it is a fast paced opportunity to open up the range of possibilities. Providing a day (a class period) for this idea generation, and then waiting overnight or a weekend to let ideas incubate is a good approach. If the Foundation steps occupy the first few days of the week, Friday may be a good time for some enjoyable brainstorming.

The next of the Process Steps is *designing the invention*. Keep in mind that designing an invention is not like drafting a set of blueprints—the design evolves. You probably have heard the expression that writing is a matter of rewriting. Think of inventive design in the same way: design is a matter of *redesign*. With Inventor's Journals handy, or perhaps an Inventor's Sketch Pad (notebook?), it is time to draw out a possible solution.

Invention Ideas

To help you identify a personal need, start by thinking about the places where you spend a lot of time and the types of things you do. Write down some of these places and things where it says **category.** *These categories might include "playing in the back yard" or "cleaning my room." Next, list at least 2 inventions which already exist that relate to each category. Finally, list 2* **invention possibilities** *for each category.*

Category: _____

Existing inventions: _____

_____

New possibilities: _____

_____

Category: _____

Existing inventions: _____

_____

New possibilities: _____

_____

Category: _____

Existing inventions: _____

_____

New possibilities: _____

_____

Category: _____

Existing inventions: _____

_____

New possibilities: _____

_____

Category: _____

Existing inventions: _____

_____

New possibilities: _____

_____

Researching Prior Solutions

What is MY idea at this time? _____

_____

What has been invented before that is similar to my idea?

Idea 1. _____

_____

What are the advantages to this idea? _____

What are the disadvantages to this idea? _____

_____

Idea 2. _____

_____

What are the advantages to this idea? _____

What are the disadvantages to this idea? _____

_____

Idea 3. _____

_____

What are the advantages to this idea? _____

What are the disadvantages to this idea? _____

_____

Idea 4. _____

_____

What are the advantages to this idea? _____

What are the disadvantages to this idea? _____

_____

NOTE! NOTE! NOTE! An inventor's design drawing need not make sense to anybody but the inventor! Don't put the unnecessary requirement on your students that their artwork be understandable to anyone else. You might want to require *some* drawings as items for their portfolios, if your school is a portfolio kind of place, but otherwise allow the students the freedom to design in ways that speak to them.

In all honesty, it will be difficult to keep students who have identified a need at bay while you have them design their inventions. The bottom line is that one or two days in a straight design mode would probably be sufficient. Simply get them thinking ahead about constructing their inventions. By drawing things they can anticipate problems, but by no means all of the problems. There likely is not a lab in the land that designed an invention and proceeded to build it without glitches getting in the way.

We typically require a drawing, to be initialed by the Invention Inspector, before construction can commence. Again, the drawing need not be a work of art by any means. The student must, however, be able to explain what the drawing represents. You might want to let the students use the Chapter Nine drawings page (p. 211) at this point. The page is intended for a representation of the finished product for use in the patenting process, but it has a slightly more official activity look than just plain paper. The Inventor's Journal or a notepad, however, may be a better use of paper at a time when drawings are likely to be revised regularly.

The third of the Process Steps is *to construct the invention*! Remember, building an invention is a matter of rebuilding. If you and your students did the Rube Goldberg Inventing from Chapter Five, then you understand this quite well. Be aware that even building well-designed inventions will likely take longer than you expected. If you want verification, give NASA a call. Taking longer than anticipated is not a problem as long as you have done some planning. That additional time represents *thinking*, and on-task thinking at that!

Our description thus far has included about one week for the Foundation Steps, with the first of the Process Steps on a Friday. Monday and Tuesday of the second week are allocated to design activities. That leaves Wednesday through Friday for construction, with an all important weekend before the final one or two days to get the inventions together. That second weekend gives your students time to think over what they are doing, how things are going, and how to resolve particular problems they may be encountering. You won't need to tell them to go home and do this reflective thinking. Chances are great there is little you can do to keep them from thinking about their projects!

Your role during the construction stage becomes much more of a one-on-one situation. Students will need your help, but usually do not expect you to solve the problems for them. Carefully worded guidance and hints will direct them to techniques for solving their own problems. As with Rube Goldberg Inventing, be prepared for a high activity level, some noise, some frustration, and some proud moments when inventions do what is expected! Encourage sharing ideas and cooperation between groups and individuals. For yourself, find time to stand back and watch your students thinking. It is a rewarding experience.

The Concluding Step

We have now discussed five steps in the inventing process. Those five steps take an inventor from identification of a problem through construction of the invention. Because we are concerning ourselves with practical inventing, we are going to figure that a practical invention is the result of all this applied brain power. In such a case, the final step is to patent the invention and enjoy the Constitutional benefits of being a patent holder. It's true, the United States Constitution confers these benefits upon inventors. Chapter Nine, A Word About Patents, will provide you with the information you need to pursue your own patent for a project. If you decide that you and your students really do not want to spend the time and expense of a U.S. patent, then Chapter Nine will provide a wealth of information for establishing your own in-classroom patenting process. In either case, it is a valuable lesson for students to learn that creative, inventive thinking was valued by the drafters of our Constitution. What possibility for integrating curricula!

Summary

Practical Inventing allows students to bring inventions to the world, as well as allowing them to see the things that surround them each day from different perspectives. Something as simple as a lawn rake can be appreciated in terms of its design elements, and as an answer to a problem. They may not go out and rake the lawn with smiles on their faces, but it can mean that they have an improved inquisitive and problem-solving nature.

One trouble with Practical Inventing compared to Rube Goldberg Inventing is that practicality is subjective. What one person sees as the perfect answer to a problem, someone else sees as interesting but not particularly useful. Inventors, writers, and pioneers, among others, prepare for this situation. You can expect your students to take pride in what they have created, and should do all you can to demonstrate that the thinking that went into that product is highly valued. Perhaps you have no need for a machine that automatically sorts marbles by size, but the inventor saw it as a need and met that challenge. That creative, inventive, and problem-solving ability is what we want to develop in those who will become the problem solvers in our society.

We come to the close of Part II. The last three chapters have outlined a thoroughly hands-on approach to the world. Along the way, we have tried to find ways to understand that world better, to become informed and active participants in that world. The series of chapters in Part III offers ways to integrate your science and inventing activities with other subject areas, display your students' work to the delight of others, and allow students to explore the place of inventing within the framework of our country!

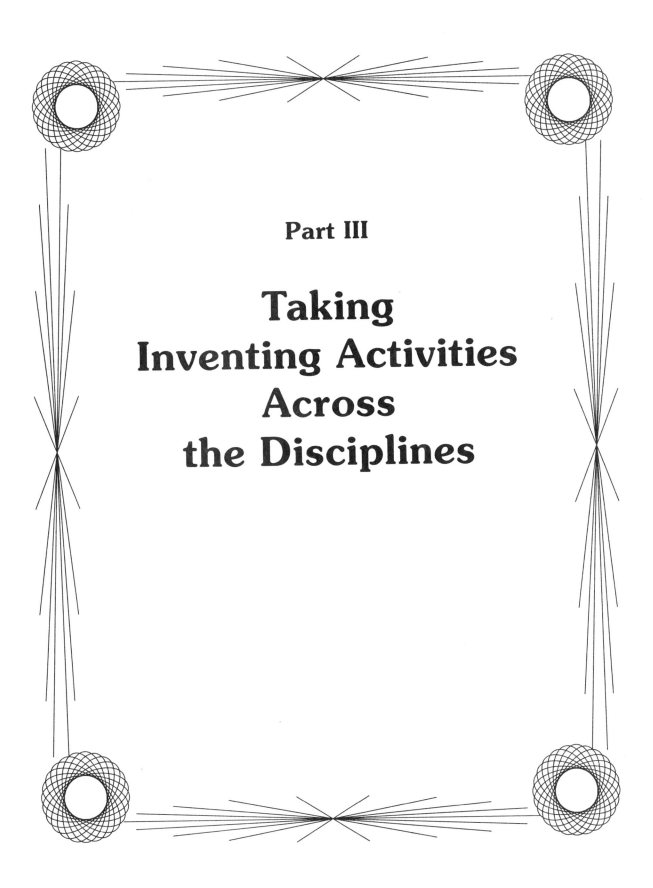

Part III

Taking Inventing Activities Across the Disciplines

Chapter Seven

The Janus Approach

Inventing
Across the Disciplines

In this chapter you will find:

> *The mystique of technology revealed;*
>
> *Retrogression;*
>
> *Historical developments of technology;*
>
> *Macro-Learning activities;*
>
> *and the Nuclear Powered Pinwheel!*

The Mystique of Technology

There is a mystical and magical aura to the world of technology and technologists. Some of the processes and machines emerging from their "workshops" are nothing short of amazing. To an increasing degree, the gap between using and understanding that amazing technology becomes difficult to bridge. Is it difficult because technological endeavor is incomprehensible for most people? Or is it a matter of not being familiar with the jargon, principles, and activities of those who routinely work with technology? More likely, most of us are simply unfamiliar with the work of technologists. And that's to be expected. After all, we can't know all there is about everything.

So what's the problem? Well, did you feel uneasy the first time you put your hard-earned money into an envelope and deposited it in an ATM? Are you uncomfortable about the number of people with access to your personal information from credit card numbers? If so, you can appreciate the need to be more than just a user of technology. This chapter is about demystifying technology and using it as a means for integrating curricula. A historical appreciation of technological development, and its social ramifications are timely topics for educators and their students.

Using Technology vs. Understanding Technology

The mutually beneficial relationship between science and technology discussed in Chapter Three provides an ideal foundation for the integration of subject areas. Keep in mind that *using* technology in the classroom does not necessarily mean the same thing as *understanding* technology. Many of us use computers and the gadgets that go with them regularly. But learning how computers work is a daunting prospect at the least. Therein lies the mystical nature of technology—the products of which we use, but have decided is beyond understanding.

The educational system's approach of ushering young students into the future using sophisticated technological advancements creates doubts with some educators. Youngsters quickly learn to use the products of technology and apply them in contrived problem solving situations—typically, however, without an understanding of the technology.

Do you remember any of those computer science classes that began to pop up in the early 1980s? There were pictures of the insides of computers, and perhaps even a cut-away version to peek into. This was still a long way from understanding how it all worked, but it was an attempt. How rapidly did that give way to an emphasis on the *use* of software programs, as computers and their software quickly increased in both sophistication and popularity? The emphasis now is on learning to use software packages, which in themselves can constitute entire courses.

However, solving the problems of the future, with technological and social ramifications, requires an experiential-based knowledge of the past—something that technologists appreciate, but is missing for young people. The technologist is aware of the intervening steps of development between the previous model and the new and improved version. For those outside of technological development, we simply experience the increased capabilities that the newest machine provides. This acquiescence to becoming uninformed users of technology is precisely the stuff from which science fiction is made. And science fiction is the seed that so often blossoms into future reality.

Demystifying Technology

The good news is that making the process and progress of technology more understandable is entirely within our capabilities as educators. Our key is the Janus perspective.

Janus, a Roman god, had two faces and thus was able to see in two directions at once. Metaphorically, Janus could see both the past and future. Since technology is the combining of existing information, it is necessarily dependent on what has already been developed. Therefore, what is "high tech" today will be the step that leads to "higher tech" tomorrow. Appreciating this notion exposes technology as a traceable progression.

Of course, as would Janus, we can also look at this from the opposite perspective. The "high tech" that we have difficulty understanding today is also *based* on something at a lower level (a level that we may be able to understand) from the past. There is nothing mystical or magical about technology. In essence the mystique is simply a function of the number of steps that exist between the familiar level and the level at which the cutting-edge technologist works.

For example, with the word processing program that we are using, a few keystrokes can change fonts, add headings, check spelling. Well, you are familiar with the power of

these programs. Yet all of this, which now comes on CD-ROM, takes up many megabytes of disk space, and carries a mega-price tag, is just a fancier version of that $12 program we bought back when PCs were just becoming popular. The typewriter was history! The point is that the super programs we use today are just extensions of the simpler programs that preceded them and typewriters!

While on a teaching assignment in Shanghai, People's Republic of China, we noticed that on the sales counter of each roadside stall was an abacus for tallying a customer's purchase. The same was true, however, for fine department stores in downtown Shanghai. Though a modern electronic cash register sat at one end of the counter, there would be an abacus within easy reach of a sales clerk. In one glimpse we saw the ancient and the state-of-the-art computer. The Janus approach demystifies technology by looking for the "abacus level" of any given technology. Admittedly, even the abacus does not work without learning how to use it. However, the way it works is easily observable.

From the abacus we might move to simple calculating devices, and then on to Babbage's calculating machine, which many (apparently oblivious to the abacus) consider to be the first computer. Perhaps you recall that red and white plastic Digi-Comp machine that your math teacher brought out about 30 years ago. It looked impressive with all its rubber bands and levers, but the only explanation given was that it showed binary calculations. Oh, okay. It was an opportunity to explain something that was lost. Items such as the Digi-Comp were seen as tools for demonstrating the principle of binary calculations, and so the *answer* to the problem was seen as important. However, an inside look (obvious since the Digi-Comp was an open framework) would have *explained* the logic of such calculations. Little did our math teachers know at the time that by century's end digital computers with their billions of binary computations would change the world.

Long distance communications offers a similarly striking example. There was a time when a message could be sent orally or in writing by means of a messenger on foot. If you did not particularly trust the messenger, you could go along with him. You may have wanted to keep in mind that the shoes of a messenger bearing bad news were not always the ones in which you wanted to be found, but that is another matter. Eventually, various modes of transportation facilitated faster delivery of messages, whether it was by horseback, boat, truck, or plane. The entire process could be witnessed if one chose to do so. It was entirely possible to observe the handling of written messages and the movement of those messages from one form of transportation to another. With the advent of the telegraph and eventually the telephone, wires were used to electrically send messages. The process had become more complicated and it was much more difficult to understand how a verbal message could be coded into an electrical form and carried by wires. But there were still the wires heading out into the sunset, and if you had a mind to, you could follow those wires all the way to the destination of your message. There was something to "hold on to" in terms of understanding what was going on.

With the advent of computers, electronics, and satellites, people trust devices which are highly sophisticated and accompanied by only abstract explanations. How *do* those messages get from our computer to some satellite and then down to a *specific* computer on the other side of the world? How can it happen so fast? And how many *other* computers might also be receiving my message?

For many of us, the result of these technological advancements is scientific and technological illiteracy. Again, it is not necessary for everyone to know everything. The problem arises when these products or processes assume a mystical quality that makes people think they cannot and should not attempt to

understand it. Your students need to understand that *the products of technology are not magic.*

Retrogression

Though technologists have an appreciation of the developmental nature of their work, they sometimes use a Janus approach in another way. We prefer to call it *retrogression* because the endeavor yields something "new," but is based solidly on something "old." We have already mentioned the space shuttle landing as a super-sophisticated sailplane. Other examples abound. For instance, it is likely you have seen someone cruising around on roller blades, a type of roller skate with the wheels lined up one behind the other. Actually, this is how roller skates were *originally* made! The change to pairing the wheels was made to increase stability. The differences that have made roller blades so successful are the new materials used for wheels and the boot to which they are attached. Retrogression is updating solutions from the past to solve problems in the present.

All of those single-use cameras on the market today exemplify this. When your students do the next activity, you will find that cameras for the amateur photo-bug began as single users. When all the film was exposed, the whole contraption went to the film processor. A key difference is that the camera was then reloaded and returned, along with the pictures of course. Today we seem to prefer to throw it away. We didn't say the new idea was better, just that it borrows heavily from the past. Ask your local film developer if you could have some of those used cameras for your class. Chances are great they will be happy to unload them on you.

Those cameras can become your students' first in-depth look at the world of camera optics (try getting one of those "panorama" versions for comparison). From there, you can move on to more sophisticated cameras, like those you don't throw away. And depending upon your particular class and goals, you may wind up going as far as demystifying those $250,000 electronic cameras that they use in TV studios. (Are you already thinking about camcorders and that old VCR you saw in the bookroom holding up used textbooks? Great!) Do you think your students could understand this technological progression? Certainly! The activity page (see p. 172) lists several examples of retrogression.

Integrating Inventing Activities with Other Subjects

The retrogression activity demonstrates an inventing theme that lends itself to integrating the disciplines. The reason is obvious—inventions represent solutions to problems that people have faced in all aspects of life. Some inventions addressed leisure time, others health needs, still others the tools scientists need to pursue their work. Rarely does an invention arise without some need identified by someone. Researching inventions by the *need* they filled, is another way to integrate language arts and social studies with the science behind the invention. The next section, The Historical Development of Technology, focuses on the sometimes strange, sometimes serendipitous circumstances behind inventions. Following that, Macro-Learning will discuss two more sophisticated models for addressing inventing as an interdisciplinary problem-solving project. Tracking the Traceable Technology explains how to take an item as simple as a pinwheel and trace its relationship to a high-tech application. Topic Integration for Macro-Learning Experiences (T.I.M.E.) offers an idea for a thorough examination of a pressing social problem, and how an invention could appropriately address that need.

Finding the Past Alive and Well in the Present

Retrogression refers to updating past technologies to solve problems in the present. Many examples exist. Choose one of the items from the list and research its development. In particular, look to see why the old version went out of style, and what brought the new version to popularity.

Choose one of these products: Rollerblades   Ceiling Fans
Cotton Fabric   Single-Use Cameras

Product: _____

It was originally developed in: _____ by: _____

Brief description of the original product (explain how it was made, what it did):

_____

_____

Why did it go out of fashion? (For example, was it difficult to use, was it expensive, what came along that was "better"?)

_____

_____

_____

In what ways are the old and new versions the same?

_____

_____

_____

In what ways is the new version better than the old version?

_____

_____

_____

What do *you* think will happen next in the development of this item?

_____

_____

_____

Historical Developments of Technology

Most inventions have some unexpected story behind their development. Why did the part-time scientists at Eastman Kodak sing in the dark back in the 1930s? What does a broken heart have to do with the soft drink, Dr. Pepper? The stories are sometimes wild and sometimes descriptive of plain luck. Next time you sit in front of bowl of cornflakes, ask yourself what lucky accident brought this tasty treat to your table. Investigating the unusual origins of inventions provides a good chance for your students to understand that coming up with a fantastic new idea is something that they could do. Most important in the process is the prepared and open mind.

Researching the origins of inventions is a history lesson that you will not have to force on your students. For instance, stimulate interest by telling your students that Listerine is named in honor of someone. Who is it named for, and why? Band-Aids virtually revolutionized home health care. However, it was not invented by a highly paid research scientist at a pharmaceutical company. Instead, it was invented for very practical reasons by another employee of the company. The rest . . . is history.

You might want to establish an extra-credit project for your students involving invention research. The following is a sample format for an entry in the Invention History Notebook (see p. 174). As students complete the forms, add them to a binder. This way you can establish your own inventing resource materials for subsequent classes. A number of excellent books discuss the strange origins of inventions. See the list in the References and Resources section. While having these books available is a good idea, the Invention History Notebook contributes to the sense of ownership when materials are developed with one's own hands. In addition, the entries in the Invention History Notebook will tend to be reflective of your students' interest, rather than spanning the range of the books in the References and Resources list.

Just so we don't leave you in unbearable suspense, here is the lowdown on the above examples:

1. Leopold Godowsky and Leopold Mannes were full-time musicians with a part-time interest in photography. They worked together for years trying to develop a process for making color photographs. Eventually they were invited to work at the facilities of the Eastman Kodak laboratories. They would sing musical passages while they developed film in the dark room as a way of timing the process!

2. While working at the Old Corner Drug Store in Waco, Texas, Wade Morrison would often talk of how his girlfriend's father had come between them in Virginia. Charles Alderton, the pharmacist at the store mixed up a concoction of flavors as a beverage for his customers, and in hopes of helping out Morrison's romance, named it after the girl's father. Whether it helped the romance we don't know, but Dr. Pepper is still a favorite soft drink!

3. As it turns out, in the late 1870s two of the Kellogg brothers were working on developing new foods for the folks at their health sanitarium. While working with wheat one evening, both of the men were called away for business matters. It was two days before they returned to find a pot of soggy mush. Surprisingly, when the mush was flattened through rollers, it formed into flakes! When toasted to dry them out, a ready to eat food had been invented. Subsequent work was done with rice and corn. So you see, that bowl of flakes is a result of an "unintended" step in the development process.

Invention History

Notebook Entry No: _____

Material compiled by: _____ Date: _____

The Invention: _____

Invented by: _____ Date: _____

Patent No: (if applicable) _____

Briefly describe what the invention does:

_____

_____

_____

_____

_____

Briefly describe how the invention was invented:

_____

_____

_____

_____

_____

How do you think the invention could be improved?

_____

_____

_____

_____

_____

_____

_____

4. This antibacterial mouthwash was introduced in 1880. The name honors Sir Joseph Lister, who in the 1860s campaigned for "antiseptic surgery." The notion was not well received at the time, but Joseph Lawrence was impressed by Lister's plea. So what may well have been named Lawrencerine is now known the world over as Listerine. Lawrencerine certainly would have been a mouthful!

5. The fledgling Johnson and Johnson company was very much involved with the development and manufacture of sterile bandages in the early 1900s. But it was an employee in the purchasing department that had the greater need to address. His young wife was constantly cutting or burning herself in the kitchen. Rather than preparing a dressing each time, Earle Dickson prepared some bandages in advance that could be easily applied. He placed a sterile pad on an adhesive strip. To keep the bandages ready, he placed crinoline fabric over the sticky portions. When Dickson demonstrated his bandage to the big shots at Johnson and Johnson, a product that we have all used at one time or another, was born. An instant success? No, but an advertising campaign that distributed Band-Aids free of charge to Boy Scout troops countrywide put the product on the road to injury healing immortality.

Macro-Learning

Children, in their day-to-day lives, do not tend to categorize their experiences by academic context. Neither do adults for that matter. That is to say, we don't take an experience, such as paying for an item at the store, and code it away as another pleasant mathematical experience. If you accept a Piagetian explanation, our memories are more holistically represented as *schemas*. Schemas are generalized representations of expectations, such as what to expect when purchasing an item at the store, and so include experiences from many contexts. Such an experience includes math, but also language and social interaction. We modify our schemas with details to represent specific situations.

School, on the other hand, tends to be highly contextualized—science at one time, mathematics at another, English, art, music at yet other times. However, making the connections between subjects, something we might call *macro-learning*, makes all that information meaningful and valuable for the individual. Without instruction that provides for those connections, is it any wonder that students often fail to see how learning in one context (the classroom) can be transferred to another (life experiences outside of the classroom)? Doesn't it seem strange that we tend to expect this last crucial learning to take place on its own? Likely it *would* take place on its own, given enough time and analogous experiences. *Education*, however, is supposed to keep everybody from reinventing the wheel.

Tracking the Traceable Technology: The Nuclear Powered Pinwheel

Tracking technology is an approach to the creative-thinking integration of subject areas. This approach combines creative thinking, Discovery Inventing, and the Janus perspective. The following activity provides one example.

A nuclear powered pinwheel would be awesome, wouldn't it? Why do you suppose? Is it because nuclear energy is so powerful? Is it because anything that can drive submarines under the polar icecap or provide power to huge cities must be capable of blowing your little pinwheel up and down the halls and right *through* the door of the principal's office? If you think so, then the nuclear powered pinwheel may provide a good example of demystifying technology while integrating curricula!

The nuclear pinwheel lesson demonstrates the relationship between a pinwheel and the vague concept many of us have of nuclear energy plants. Since we do not know whether you are teaching lessons on nuclear energy, electricity, or pinwheels for that matter, we have provided the structure for a Janus approach lesson, rather than detailed lesson plans and activity pages. Use this example as a model for developing lessons you need. Our presentation of the Nuclear Pinwheel has three lessons: the pinwheel and its motion, generation of electricity and the motion of pinwheels, and matching nuclear energy to the motion of pinwheels.

The Pinwheel and Its Motion

What does a pinwheel have in common with a nuclear power plant? Let's begin with the pinwheel and see if we can eventually find the relationship. We have provided a pinwheel pattern if you don't happen to have one handy. (See Figure 7.1, p. 177.) Simply cut out the square, and then cut down to the cross marks on the diagonal lines. Next, put a bit of rubber cement on the corner marked (1), and then pull it down so that the point touches the hashmark labeled (A). Similarly, put some cement on (2) and then press it down at line (B). Continue this way. Is it starting to look like a pinwheel? When all four corners are cemented, push a pin through the center and then into the eraser of a pencil. Presto!

Most of your students will know how to make the pinwheel rotate. Once the initial flurry of wheel spinning has occurred, have students analyze the pinwheel. What can be said about it? They should notice that it has four "blades," and that it rotates around the axis (pin). They should also be able to see that it rotates best when air is blown across the blades in a particular direction.

You can investigate the action of the pinwheel if some variables are manipulated. For instance, they can construct pinwheels with more blades, with larger or smaller blades. Additional investigation increases understanding of the pinwheel's action and how that action can be influenced.

When you are satisfied that they understand basic pinwheel design and construction, the next question addresses getting the pinwheel to spin. Is blowing on the pinwheel the only way to get it to turn? It is possible to spin the wheel by moving it rapidly through the air by waving an arm or running. Using wind to turn the pinwheel is the same principle used with centuries-old windmills and cutting-edge-technology wind turbines. What

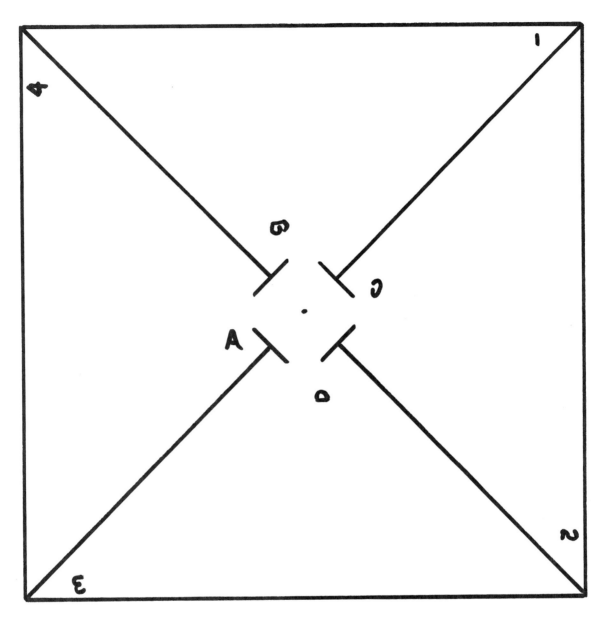

Figure 7.1. Pinwheel Pattern.

other ways are there to move the wheel? Most obvious is the waterwheel. Using pictures of those quaint riverside waterwheels, have your students identify similarities and differences between the pinwheel and waterwheel design. A key difference is that the waterwheel typically has the blade mounted perpendicular to the flow of the water. Notice that the student pinwheels have more of a propeller shape. Of course, the greatest amount of pressure is generated when the water hits the waterwheel blade head on. And, since the course of the river doesn't change all that often, once the blades are set at 90 degrees they pretty much stay there. The propeller style allows for more variation in wind direction. If time permits, let students build some waterwheels from aluminum pie plates. Just cut tabs on the pie plate and turn them perpendicular to the axis. Use a pencil for the axle. This could get a little messy, but it is a good demonstration!

The next step is more difficult to make. What if there were no wind to turn the pinwheel, and no local river to use. How else could the pinwheel be turned? Having trouble? Well, how were the wheels of locomotives turned in the days before petroleum-powered engines? Steam? Sure! Water in any suitable container could be heated wherever it happened to be, and the generated steam channeled over the pinwheel to turn it. In a more sophisticated application, it could even turn the wheels of a locomotive. Certainly be careful using steam in your classroom, particularly around young students. However, with proper precautions, a steam kettle on a hot plate can generate enough steam for you to run pinwheels. You might want to make new ones out of a heavier grade of paper, or perhaps aluminum foil. If you use the foil, it is a good idea to fold a strip into two layers and then cut the pattern. One layer of foil might be too flimsy for the pinwheel.

At this point the students have constructed pinwheels, waterwheels,

and steam-driven pinwheels. They should understand that there are a number of ways to get the pinwheel to spin. Depending on the level of integration with other disciplines, you may have discussed windmills in the Netherlands and the development of manufacturing throughout the U.S. with power supplied from waterwheels.

It is time to move on to the last key concept. The students need to switch perspective from a wheel spinning on an axle to a wheel which *turns* an axle. This issue is what differentiates a child's toy and a tool that changes the world. Here's how to set up such a demonstration (see Figure 7.2).

From the local store, get a couple of ¼-inch eye screws. You will also need a ¼-inch dowel and about a 12-inch length of wood (a 1x4 or 2x4 would do just fine). Screw the two eye screws into the board as shown below. The dowel (about 12-inches long) should be able to sit in the eyes.

Now make another pinwheel assembly from some fairly heavy paper. *Carefully* attach the pinwheel to the end of the dowel. Put a bit of white glue on the end of the dowel first, and use a thumbtack rather than a pin. Here's the tough part. You must set the assembly aside and let the glue dry. Do this as the last activity of the period or day, and let the glue dry overnight. Things will work much better if you do. You can go high-tech and use a fast drying epoxy in this step, but be forewarned, the only way to get epoxy out of hair is to cut it out.

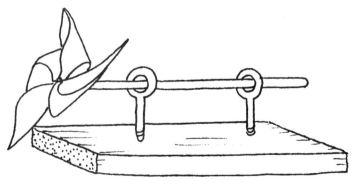

Figure 7.2. The Pinwheel on Axle Model.

Once the glue has dried, place the pinwheel into the eyes on the wooden stand and let them blow the wheel. If possible, use your steam kettle again to drive the wheel. The question now is, "What work could this turning axle do?" It could power a saw by hooking it up with a belt. It could raise a weight by attaching a rope. Let them come up with a list, and then tell them they have done a good job. So have you.

Generating Electricity and the Motion of the Pinwheel

Your students now have a thorough understanding of pinwheelology, and probably have no idea that it will end up in nuclear power plants. Boldly proceed! Next is the idea of generating electricity.

You might ask, "Where do we get electricity?" What did they say—power plants? Then ask, "Where does the power plant get energy from?" Eventually, you will arrive at the basic question, "How is electricity generated?"

This is your call. The degree to which you want to pursue this topic is dependent on many things. However, for our purposes, you can explain the principle as follows.

Electricity is generated when a coil of wires is rotated quickly between two magnets. The change of magnetic fields causes a flow of electrons in the coil of wire. We call that flow an electrical current. You could wrap some wire around an old 35mm film container, poke holes in each end of the container, and slide an axle through. Two stands of aluminum foil on each side of the coil could *represent* magnets. We emphasize that because the generator does not have two pieces of aluminum in it. You might be able to set up something that looks more like a magnet. With your model adapted in this way, the students could see that by spinning the pinwheel the axle turns, and so the coil of wire spins between the magnets. If you are working with older students it may be worthwhile to ask a mechanic friend for an old car

generator. Have the friend take it apart to view the inside.

The obvious question is, "How can we get the axle to turn so that the electricity could be generated?" A handle could be attached to the end of the axle and someone could turn it. If you have access to one of those small, hand-cranked generators that can light a small bulb, now is the time to bring it out. Usually the plastic case on those classroom generators is clear, students can see inside. Unfortunately, all they can see are the gears between the handle and the self-contained generator. No matter, we don't want to dwell on the hand cranking idea anyway. Rather, we want to ask how the generator could be turned if there were no one available to crank it all the time.

The pinwheel! Yes, the pinwheel turns the generator. And what if there were no wind readily available to turn the generator? The steam! Make those connections. We have come from a fairground toy to a tool for the generation of electricity, even when there is no constant wind and no handy river. All that is needed is a water *supply*, and some way to heat it.

Nuclear Power Plants and the Motion of the Pinwheel

Some of your students may already be able to answer our initial question. However, this is the final step, the one that makes the connection between earlier technology and advanced technology. We must admit, we don't have any special nuclear power demonstrations to recommend. Rather, it is guest speaker time, or time to call the power company and find out what brochures and charts they can send you about nuclear power. Your students are at the point of understanding what the speaker tells them, or what is represented on the glossy classroom posters the power company sends.

You see, there is nothing "nuclear" about the electricity generated at a nuclear power station. The power station has generators. The generators are attached to turbines, fancy pinwheels, that when turned also turn the generator. How is the turbine turned at a nuclear power station? It is turned with steam. Rather than using coal or oil or some other fuel to provide heat to boil the water into steam, a nuclear power plant uses the heat generated from a controlled nuclear reaction (a tremendous amount of heat from a small amount of fuel). That's all. Nuclear energy is just another way of generating steam to run a turbine—a nuclear pinwheel. From that pinwheel motion comes the spinning generator and the flow of electricity.

Making the connections from one level of technology to the next for the *first time* is something that we often refer to as inventive genius. But as you can see, there is nothing mystical or magical. And with practice, *given the opportunities to see relationships and consider patterns and perspectives*, it may be your students who demonstrate inventive genius on a scale that affects us all someday. Exciting to think about, wouldn't you agree?

Topic Integration for Macro-Learning Experiences

To regularly integrate our subject areas perhaps we need a special class period in the day: Topic Integration for Macro-Learning Experiences (Let's call it T.I.M.E.). The class addresses the same issue, but from three perspectives: the historical basis of a particular problem/issue and prior attempts at a solution, problems/issues as they effect the present, and problems/issues as they affect the future. Each of these is enough to occupy heads of state throughout the world, so focus by allowing a group to concentrate on one perspective at a time.

Divide students into three groups, though at some time each student should be a member of each group. One group would be the *T.I.M.E. Travellers,* whose work focuses on the topic from a historical perspective.

T.I.M.E. Keepers concentrate on the application of interdisciplinary information to solve current individual or social problems. *T.I.M.E. Changers* look to the future. These students focus on the dynamics of social systems and/or scientific endeavors that will change the world. The culminating activity brings the three groups together to see how a solution suitable for the present can be accomplished with an eye toward the future. Draw from all of the subject areas to formulate solutions.

What do you think? Do judges and juries deliberate *after* hearing evidence *before* they render a verdict? Likewise, part of an educational curriculum should be devoted to making learning meaningful across disciplines *before* the formal educational experience ends. Admittedly, T.I.M.E. is a concept best adapted for the middle school through high school years (and beyond). The inventing theme offers a macro-learning opportunity integrating subject areas around a concrete item. To top it off, it serves as an exercise that develops the ability to deal with the three perspectives discussed in T.I.M.E. on global issues your students will face.

The next pages (181–83) offer a sample format for a T.I.M.E. activity. Notice that there are three pages. One page is labeled for the *T.I.M.E. Travellers,* another for *T.I.M.E. Keepers,* and a third for *T.I.M.E. Changers.* When each group is finished, it is time for the "summit" meeting. At this meeting the three groups try to synthesize a plan based on the work of each group.

First compile a list of possible topics to pursue with this activity. To make the lists easier to compile, establish categories to consider. For example, if *transportation* were a category, students might list air pollution from the burning of fossil fuels as a problem, space taken up for parking lots, the noise given off by airplanes, and the difficulty in repairing a flat bicycle tire. Let's switch to a different category and use food packaging as our topic.

(Text continues on p. 184.)

T.I.M.E. Document

T.I.M.E. Travellers

Group Members: _____

_____

T.I.M.E. Topic: _____

It is the task of the T.I.M.E. Travellers to research the topic regarding its development. Your group is concerned with what has **caused** *the current problem and what* **prior solutions** *have been recommended or tried. The T.I.M.E. Travellers need not solve the problem, but instead must be able to provide a clear explanation of the problem's history. The work of the T.I.M.E. Travellers is crucial to the success of the T.I.M.E. Summit.*

Consider the following questions, among others, that your group identifies:
+ Is there an identifiable cause of the problem?
+ How far back does the problem date?
+ Have there been prior attempts to solve the problem?
+ What factors have caused prior attempts to fail?
+ How has our society and/or environment changed since the problem began?

Consider the following approaches to gathering information for your report:
+ Where would information about this problem be kept?
+ What disciplines should be consulted when gathering information?
  For example:

Legal	Educational	Environmental	Social Services
Medical	Military	Economic	Mathematical
Scientific	Agricultural	Political	Artistic

+ Who in the school or community could shed light on the topic?
+ Should we use interviews, newspaper reports, letters, or a combination of all to locate information?

Your final report should include at least three components:
+ The original cause or identification of the problem.
+ An account of solutions offered and/or tried.
+ An explanation, from a historical perspective, of why the problem still exists.

T.I.M.E. Document

T.I.M.E. Keepers

Group Members: _____

_____

T.I.M.E. Topic: _____

It is the task of the T.I.M.E. Keepers to research the topic regarding its affect on the present. Your group is concerned with what **effect** *the problem has on peoples' lives. The T.I.M.E. Keepers need not solve the problem, but instead must be able to provide a clear explanation of what makes the problem a problem. Your time frame includes as long as five years ago up to the present. The work of the T.I.M.E. Keepers is of critical importance to the success of the T.I.M.E. Summit.*

Consider the following questions among others that your group identifies:
+ What are the identifiable consequences of the problem?
+ How are peoples lives affected by the problem *at this time*?
+ What efforts are currently underway to address and/or solve the problem?
+ What factors lead you to believe that current efforts are insufficient?
+ How has the problem changed our society and/or environment?

Consider the following approaches to gathering information for your report:
+ Where would information about this problem be kept?
+ What disciplines should be consulted when gathering information?
  For example:

Legal	Educational	Environmental	Social Services
Medical	Military	Economic	Mathematical
Scientific	Agricultural	Political	Artistic

+ Who in the school or community could shed light on the topic?
+ Should we use interviews, newspaper reports, letters, or a combination of all to locate information?

Your final report should include at least three components:
+ The immediate effect of the problem on daily life.
+ An account of what organizations are working on the problem at this time.
+ An explanation of why you believe that current efforts will or will not be successful in solving the problem.

T.I.M.E. Document

T.I.M.E. Changers

Group Members: _____

_____

T.I.M.E. Topic: _____

T.I.M.E. Topic: *It is the task of the T.I.M.E. Changers to consider the topic regarding its impact on the* **future***. Your group is concerned with what* **effect** *the problem will have if left unsolved. The T.I.M.E. Changers need not solve the problem, but instead must be able to provide a clear explanation of the consequences that might result if the problem persists. Your time frame may extend as far into the future as your information sources take you. The work of the T.I.M.E. Changers is imperative for the success of the T.I.M.E. Summit.*

Consider the following questions among others that your group identifies:
+ If left unsolved, will the problem become worse?
+ What new problems might arise as a consequence of this problem?
+ How would the continuation of this problem change the lives of people in the future?
+ In what ways will the problem change society in general and/or the environment?
+ Is it possible that what we consider a problem might become a normal part of life in the future?

Consider the following approaches to gathering information for your report:
+ Who or what organizations would have a long term view toward the problem?
+ What disciplines should be consulted when gathering information?
  For example:

Legal	Educational	Environmental	Social Services
Medical	Military	Economic	Mathematical
Scientific	Agricultural	Political	Artistic

+ Who in the school or community could shed light on the topic?
+ Should we use interviews, newspaper reports, letters, or a combination of all to locate information?

Your final report should include at least three components:
+ The consequences that could clearly be expected in the immediate future.
+ A prediction of what other problems could result from failing to solve this problem.
+ An explanation of why you believe or do not believe that new technologies will first have to be invented in order to solve the problem.

A preliminary discussion with all three groups would indicate that we are faced with a problem regarding the types of packages used for prepared foods. That is, whether we go to the local fast food restaurant or heat up a frozen dinner in the microwave, a plastic container of some sort remains. With people getting these containers with *every* meal purchased, the amount of waste is overwhelming. Yet food must be packaged, and packaged in a manner that protects the consumer. It is the students' job to address this problem. Note that there is not a lot of background provided. The T.I.M.E. Travellers will have the responsibility of finding the background. We present the challenge.

The particular focus that the T.I.M.E. Travellers must adopt is addressing, "What has been done in the past?" In answering, they should look to social situations that surrounded previous packaging systems (Were particular materials available or unavailable due to wars, labor problems, business practices?); scientific aspects of the situation (Are there synthetic materials that were not yet developed? Were there health problems with previous solutions?); and the impetus for changing from one type of package to another (scientific, economic, social consciousness?). As part of their work, the T.I.M.E. Travellers should locate or reproduce examples of previous packaging systems. These reproductions could be models or photographs, etc. The T.I.M.E. Travellers rely on research across subject areas to explain how this problem has been addressed in the past.

The T.I.M.E. Keepers have a different focus. For them, the question is "How is this problem affecting people's lives today?" What are the social, legal, economic, and practical issues? What do people think about these issues? Rather than relying on the same research methods adopted by the T.I.M.E. Travellers, the T.I.M.E. Keepers must talk to people. They may want to conduct surveys within the school or community. They should interview local business owners as well as

consumers. They may enlist the PTA as representative of the adult population for gathering information. The T.I.M.E. Keepers must be able to tell what the current perspective on the problem is, and why people believe the problem could affect the future. Certainly, a collection of contemporary food containers would be a part of their presentation.

The T.I.M.E. Changers look to the future. Specifically, they try to answer, "How could this be done differently?" Ideally, they will identify the social factions that would have to be satisfied with the solution. For instance, the packaging must be suitable to the consumer, and also must be economically feasible for the vendor. But it goes beyond that. The packaging must not be an obvious start for a new problem. The work of the T.I.M.E. Changers will be to come up with four or five possible solutions. Don't make the T.I.M.E. Changers wait for information from the T.I.M.E. Travellers and T.I.M.E. Keepers. Since their focus is the future, allow them to consider possibilities without imposing present criteria or the familiar "we've already tried that" of the past.

After the three groups have completed their work, a T.I.M.E. Summit is held. At this point groups share their information, and it is from *this* sharing that a new solution is synthesized. From the Janus perspective, the problem is being attacked from three distinct perspectives, yet is being solved by the considered combination of all. In terms of creative thinking, the three groups are able to seek patterns, perspectives, and relationships regarding one topic, though from three distinctly different vantage points.

Ideas will not necessarily jump right off of the page, but the thorough background provided by each group will begin to expose *patterns* and *relationships*. The range of resources that your students use when working in groups provides varied and valuable perspectives. Even so, the summit may decide that more information is needed. If that is the case, there should be enough information available to direct the search for more information. Whether that additional search is undertaken is up to you.

Let there be no mistake, a viable answer to the problem is not the goal of this activity. It would be nice, but our emphasis is on developing problem-solving ability. This exercise represents creative thinking and creative problem solving at its highest level, *despite the age or level of your students.* Your students should discover that problems have many parts, that resources are necessary to find solutions, that not all problems can be solved with given technology, and that every *attempt* at an answer *contributes* to an eventual answer.

Though the underlying purpose is the integration of subject areas, what you are building is an *interdisciplinary creative problem-solving consortium.* This consortium could be grade-level specific or across grades. You could establish a district-wide consortium that assigns one school as T.I.M.E. Traveller for a particular problem, while another school serves as T.I.M.E. Keeper, and yet another as T.I.M.E. Changer. If you and your students have e-mail access, we could establish a *global* creative problem-solving consortium with students around the world collaborating with your students. Imagine bringing a global perspective to creative problem solving in your own classroom!

Summary

In this chapter we have tried to find an approach that demystifies technology and demonstrates that inventing is a function of the world around us.

We have seen that technology is not magical. It proceeds in a traceable, step-by-step fashion. We simply need to find an understandable level, and then move forward. A key element is to keep an eye toward where we have been, and where we are going. That notion is the Janus approach.

There are two aspects to the Janus approach that appeal to a student's interests. One is finding that much of what we consider new is evident in inventions developed long ago, "improved upon," and eventually becoming even more like their original versions. Another is that many inventions come into being for strange reasons or unintended situations. All of this demonstrates that inventing is within student capability.

Retrogression and historical development activities provide an easy approach to understanding technological development. Combining these activities with the Discovery Inventing activities of Chapter Four (in particular Invention Investigation on page 82) will enable the integration of language arts and social studies along with hands-on science.

Tracking the Traceable Technology and Topic Integration for Macro-Learning Experiences (T.I.M.E.) are both intended as sophisticated models of creative problem solving that can be organized within your class, school, district, or the world. These activities offer exciting possibilities for making all subject areas meaningful to the arena in which students are supposed to apply that knowledge: *life!*

Chapter Eight

Invention Festivals

In this chapter you will find:

> *How to have an Invention Festival with the Science Fair;*
>
> *Why it would be nice to have an Invention Festival as a separate event;*
>
> *An invention evaluation system;*
>
> *and recognition of inventive achievement!*

Now that you have all of those marvelous inventions in your classroom, you and your students will want to share them with the rest of the world. Such displays are occurring more often as part of school-wide science fairs. An alternative is to let your inventors demonstrate their work in its own right at an Invention Festival. Be warned, it won't be long before other teachers are asking whether their science fair can tag along as part of your annual, media-attended Invention Festival!

Invention Festivals vs. Science Fairs

Inventing as presented with its *process, not product* philosophy, tends to run somewhat contrary to the product-oriented tradition of science fairs. Science fair students typically prepare a display of the "experiment" they conducted (they are investigations, but not always experiments) and supply the public with some example of the materials involved. With rare exception, the projects are replications of textbook activities, sometimes with minor revisions. The student follows the steps of the experiment and follows the steps for preparing a display. The result is an experiment that somebody else designed, and a display format that another somebody else provided. Without doubt the inventions we have been discussing, in particular Rube Goldberg inventing, blow this mold wide open.

The invention is not a static display. It brings that same hands-on active approach from the classroom right into the science fair. Just wait until the first time you hear one of your students explain his or her invention. You will see a new level of involvement, understanding, and pride. We are sure you will want to find a way to let students share that with those outside of your classroom. An Invention Festival, either as a part of the science fair or on its own, provides an opportunity for the school population to experience and value the creative nature of science and interdisciplinary activity. Be sure to have a video camera handy. Photographs are great, but inventions *do* things, so capturing that on video tape is a great addition to a portfolio, a way of sharing a student's work with parents, or simply a prized memento. A video tape of your Invention Festival is also an excellent item to take to a professional conference or workshop.

An Invention Festival as Part of the Science Fair

One way of getting around the "us vs. them" situation is to make your Invention Festival a part of the science fair. Obviously, the guidelines for inventions need to be different than expectations applied to other projects. This is only a problem when we get to awards (which seems to be something that folks are set on doing). It would not make sense to judge an original invention with the same criteria applied to a replicated experiment. And, if your Invention Festival is featuring Rube Goldberg inventions (as we hope it will), there is going to be a distinct lack of little cards with "Hypothesis" and "Procedure" printed on them. Rather, you will have an excited student pointing out the myriad of steps involved and waiting to "run" the invention again. (Sometimes these inventions take a while to set up, and so running it may have to be scheduled.)

We have seen cases where the powers that be did not consider inventions to be representative of science, and so the inventions were relegated to a corner of the room away from the "real" science projects. Fear not! Accept that corner graciously. People will be fascinated by the workings of the machines and their ingenuity. Next time around, you will have a more prominent display area. Better yet, consider an Invention Festival independent of the Science Fair.

The Invention Festival

Should you decide to sponsor your own Invention Festival, there are at least two approaches. The one you choose will depend upon the scope of the inventing activities you decided to conduct. For instance, if you have decided to extend the inventing theme across the school year and address each of the three types of inventing, then your festival plans may differ from a focus on one of the three types. Characteristic of either approach is the same philosophy we have been emphasizing. That is, put your emphasis on recognizing the thinking involved in these projects.

Recognize all efforts. If you simply *must* give awards, base them on previously announced criteria, such as the number of steps involved or the number of different energy sources used. We often figure in the number of times an invention needs inventor assistance to even the chance that a previously working machine should prove recalcitrant at the big moment. We will describe a possible format in the Recognizing Achievement section of this chapter.

There are more possible circumstances leading up to the Invention Festival than we could possibly account for here. So, our comments about arranging your festival are made with the idea that we are speaking only about your class. Next year, when you have the entire school, or perhaps the entire district, involved, then you will know what adjustments to make.

If Your Students Have Run the Gamut

If students have been through all three types of inventing over the course of the year, saving those Discovery Inventing activities from October and November, and the Rube Goldberg machines from the winter, would put too much of a strain on available storage space. An option? Schedule three mini-festivals throughout the year. As students' enthusiasm increases from one type of inventing to the next, expect the same to happen for the parents.

If Your Emphasis Is on One Type of Inventing

It may be the case that your students will do all three types of inventing, but three festivals is not an option. Work with that. Select the type of inventing that you want to highlight with a festival. Since this is your one chance to impress your audience, try to avoid the "drop-in" approach, and instead arrange your festival so that *each* invention can be demonstrated for attendees. If the scheduling is just not possible, arrange your festival to have a display period before and after the demonstration period.

Recognizing Achievement

Sure, students will be proud. Sure, they will continue to think about how to improve their machines or debug that one pesky step that won't cooperate. No doubt they will remember their inventing experience long after they have left your classroom. But even so, people like to be recognized for their achievement. To that end we supply you with four documents. (They are all in the Appendix.) One is a suggested Invention Evaluation Form. Another is the Recognition of Inventive Achievement. You will also find a certificate representing the Spirit of Rube Goldberg Award (we always make this award when working with a group of students), and the Recognition of Special Achievement in Inventing certificate.

The Invention Evaluation Form

Whether we like it or not, things that go on in school must be evaluated. With Discovery Inventing and Practical Inventing it is easy enough for you to establish specific criteria for students to address in their projects. The Rube Goldberg inventing poses more difficult problems. For that reason, we have provided a sample evaluation form for such inventions (in the Appendix). A key component of evaluation is that students know the evaluation criteria.

We have divided the form into three parts: Complexity, Performance, and Appearance. Each of these categories rates one or more attributes of the invention and assigns points. The form is not intended to find the best invention. We have no idea of a question that could possibly be written to allow you to accomplish this. Do you remember what we told you about Band-Aids back in Chapter Seven? Difficult as it is to believe it was initially met by little more than a yawn from the public.

Complexity. This category is worth 40 points in two questions. As you notice, the more steps involved, the more points received. Since there is a separate category for Performance, a student can receive credit in this category even if the component fails to work. This doesn't mean that someone can just hang a bunch of pulleys all over the room and say they have 90 or so steps. *Steps* is the operative word. To be counted as a step, the component must contribute to performing the task for which the machine was designed.

The second question asks about the number of energy sources. The form allows credit for more energy sources, rather than fewer. In a way, that might sound strange since a machine working with just one source of energy *might* be considered more efficient. However, in our work we are usually trying to demonstrate to teachers that *many* sources of energy can be used in inventing. If multiple energy sources are inappropriate for the project your students are working on, eliminate the question. We recommend adding another question that recognizes the complexity of the machine without considering performance.

Performance. There is only one basic question here: How well does the invention perform? While most points go to a machine

that works without assistance, even those that do not work get points, with several levels in between. We award points for non-working machines because often a sound design does not work for reasons beyond the inventor's control. Think of it as a bad hair day for machines. We also want to recognize that machines rarely run perfectly. You will see that the point spread between a machine that works with minimal help and one that works just fine is not very great. If we were to award bunches of points because the machine happened to work just then, the focus again moves to product over process. Do you see how easily that can happen? The most points available here is twenty, and those of you who are quick with numbers already see that this means performance is worth 20 percent of the total.

Appearance. When was the last time you had an "appearance" requirement. Okay, those science fair projects usually have to be neatly lettered to get the blue ribbon. In our situation, the two questions regarding appearance do not even remotely address penmanship. The first question asks specifically about humor. The intention is not that the machine do a little stand-up comedy routine, but to incorporate humor in the design or decoration to give students the message that humor is okay. For instance, encourage them to use humorous labels for the machine components. A machine that rings a bell when students are falling asleep in class might be named, "Mrs. Skolnick's Student Attention Device." That message is the one that will transform your classroom from a collection of frazzled, under pressure students to one of laughter and on-task behavior.

The final question looks for originality. This is included for a number of reasons. There is bound to be a considerable amount of diversity among the inventing groups in the class. Some people will also come up with an idea that others will want to use as well. This requirement encourages even more diversity among machines. Opportunities for students to get points for originality in school are rare, particularly in the academic disciplines (creative writing excepted). So encourage students to include objects which reflect personal interest and are not likely to be found in other inventions. Originality points can also be earned for using common objects in ways other than intended use. For instance, when the clapper on an electric bell vibrates, it could tug a string that sets off a mousetrap. In any case, the opportunity for originality is not only provided, but is valued.

A student or group of students receiving the maximum points for each item receive a score of 100—for your convenience. You can weight that score, make it a part of another score that your students receive, add more questions specific to your class, and so on. Take this as a guide. If you are going to have a distinguished panel of judges review the inventions using these forms, be sure they understand the emphasis on students' *thinking*.

The Certificates of Recognition

We highly recommend that you recognize *each* student for work done on the inventions. We have provided the Recognition of Inventive Achievement certificate as a sample. You can fill in the student's name, and the name of the invention. In addition, we buy a pack of 2-inch gold foil notarial seals at an office supply store—a pack of a hundred costs a few dollars. We put a seal on each certificate and emboss it. Chapter Nine, A Word About Patents, discusses the embosser and shows you our seal. It adds a great touch to awards.

The Recognition of Special Achievement in Inventing certificate is one we use if we want to encourage certain aspects of the inventing process. For instance, we might announce an award for the invention with the most steps and the least inventor assistance. We might also announce an award for the

most humor, or the most sources of energy. In any of these cases, there is never a "best" category. (We must admit that one time we gave out the "Best Use of Slime" award.) If you had been there, you would understand.

Finally, an award worth giving is the Spirit of Rube Goldberg Award. You can customize guidelines for this prize so that it fits best. Sometimes it might go to the person who worked hard through a very frustrating problem with the machine. Another time it might be used to give a pat on the back to the student most willing to share ideas and skills with other groups. And certainly, look for that student finally finding a way to express him or herself. It is very likely that a student who has never succeeded in more traditional school assignments will emerge from this unit with new found self-esteem. The Spirit of Rube Goldberg Award was meant for such students.

Summary

Students in the band perform at the big Spring Concert. Football or basketball team members perform at championships. Students in science, on the other hand, stand quietly next to displays and report what happened with their experiments. The Invention Festival, however, is a *performance*. It is enthusiasm and excitement about academic work turned into a working machine. Capitalize on that excitement by recognizing student achievement with your awards, and showcasing their accomplishments at your own Invention Festival. Don't be shy about calling the local TV station and newspaper. They love to come out and see, photograph, and write about such events. Don't be surprised when one of the students' parents sees you at the supermarket and says, "Mark just *loved* the inventing stuff you did in class! He has a little brother *just like him* who can hardly wait to be in your class!" Of course we don't know your Mark, but welcome the compliment!

Chapter Nine

A Word About Patents

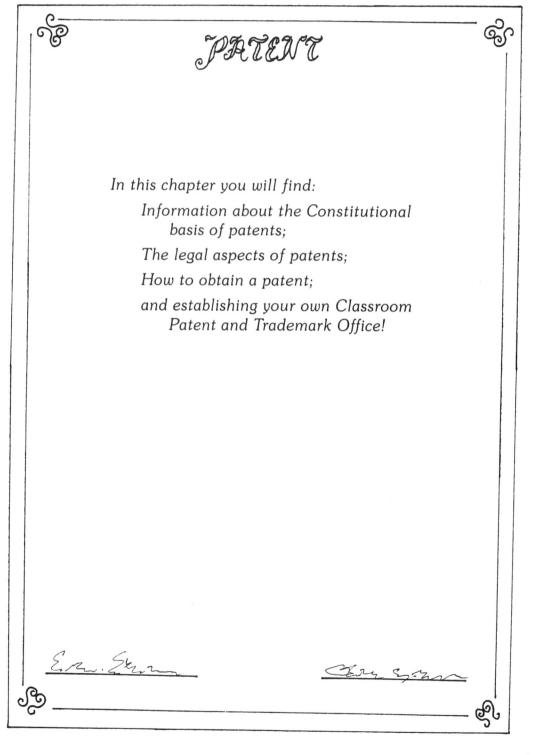

PATENT

In this chapter you will find:

Information about the Constitutional basis of patents;

The legal aspects of patents;

How to obtain a patent;

and establishing your own Classroom Patent and Trademark Office!

For many the idea of patents conjures thoughts of people in government offices, wearing those old visors. It brings to mind batteries of attorneys eager to gobble the financial resources of the garage-shop inventor. We think of masses of red tape and bureaucracy—a real downside to the excitement of inventing.

Yet the concept of patents and the process of obtaining one are not mysterious. Talk about integrating the curriculum—patents are a provision of the Constitution! So while it is likely that you will not need to go through the patent process with a student invention, an excursion into patent protection can be fascinating. In addition to making our Constitution relevant to students, copies of issued patents provide a documentary glimpse of history as it was made. What does the patent issued to the Wright brothers look like? What claims do you think they made? Is the Coca-Cola recipe patented to prevent others from copying it? Let students look for the patent number on common products to see how our laws reach right into their classroom.

The Legal Aspect of Patents

A key to effective teaching is first finding out what the student already knows. So let's take a moment to see what we know about patents. To be fair, the upcoming quiz on page 195 will only deal with U.S. patent law. And, to ensure that everybody gets at least one correct answer, it will include a question about whether patents are a provision of the U.S. Constitution.

No. 821,393. PATENTED MAY 22, 1906.

O. & W. WRIGHT.

FLYING MACHINE.

APPLICATION FILED MAR. 23, 1903.

3 SHEETS—SHEET 1.

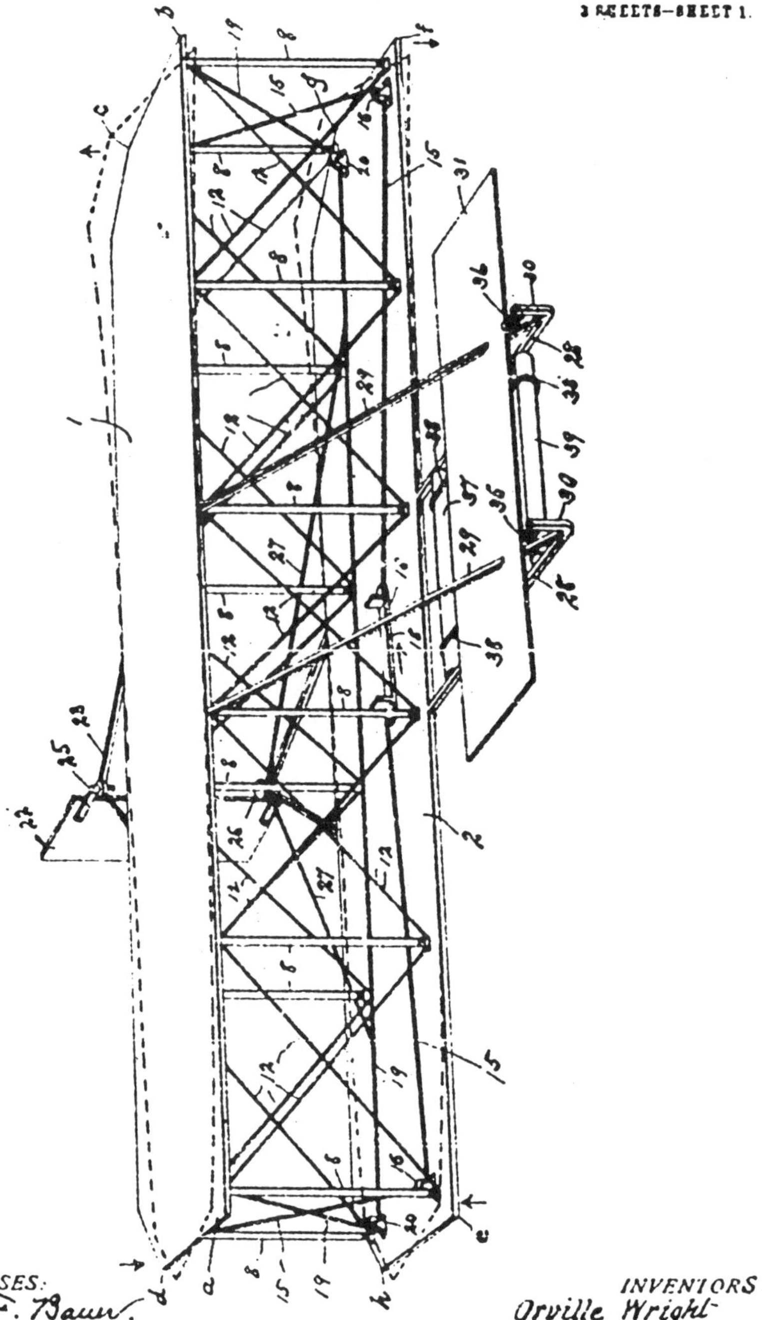

WITNESSES:
William F. Bauer.
Irvine Miller

INVENTORS.
Orville Wright
Wilbur Wright
BY H. A. Toulmin

Figure 9.1. Wright Brother's Patent Drawing.

What Do You Know
About Patents?

1. By what right may individuals claim ownership of their inventions?

2. A patent grants the right to make, use, or sell an invention.

    True   or   False

3. A patent is granted for what length of time?

4. How many people can be named as inventor on a single patent?

5. The United States government may use a patented invention with or without obtaining the permission of the patent holder.

    True   or   False

6. To whom was U.S. Patent No. 1 issued?

Let's see how you did. Article 1, Section 8, Paragraph 8 of the Constitution states "Congress shall have power . . . to promote the progress of science and useful arts, by securing for limited times to authors and inventors the exclusive right to their respective writings and discoveries." Sounds like a Constitutional basis for the use of inventing in the science curriculum. There's a powerful argument to take to the principal when you want some funds for your inventing project!

It might seem strange that such a clause would be included in the body of the Constitution; promoting the progress of science through the assignment of patents would seem more like an amendment or law. Somehow watching out for science and the useful arts seems removed from questions of government paramount at that time. For whatever reason, placing value on original thinking was seen as fundamental to a free society.

The answer to question two is False. A patent does not grant the right to make, use, or sell an invention. We'll talk about that later in the chapter, but for now we should know that all people in the U.S. are essentially free to make, use, and sell inventions.

How long is a patent valid? It is valid for 20 years, and that's it. In very rare cases is a patent renewable. And, there is no limit to the number of people who can be named as a joint inventor on a patent. Each individual named simply must be a contributor to the actual inventing process. A financial backer, for example, cannot be included as a joint inventor.

The answer to question five is True. A patented invention may be used by and for the government without obtaining the permission of the patent holder. The patent holder is, however, entitled to compensation for the use of the invention. Interestingly enough, a patent can be issued for an invention even though use of that invention would be in violation of the law or the rights of others. One exception is the strict law governing the use of special nuclear material for use in atomic weapons. Patents are not granted for such devices.

Admittedly, the final question is trivia. We included it so that you may dazzle your friends, colleagues, and students with your knowledge of U.S. patents. If you already knew the answer, take a bow. Patent No. 1 was issued to John Ruggles in 1836. The patent was awarded for traction wheels that would enable locomotives to climb inclines more easily. However, his patent does not represent the first patent *ever* issued. The first one was actually issued to Samuel Hopkins in 1790 and was signed by George Washington. Unfortunately, a great fire destroyed all of those early patent records. Ruggles's Patent No. 1 represents the first patent since the fire. Try that in your next trivia challenge!

What a Patent Does

A patent may be granted for a useful, novel, and nonobvious process, machine, manufactured product, composition of matter, improvement, asexually reproduced plant, or ornamental or decorative design. Ideas and newly discovered laws of nature are not patentable. For our purposes, let's concentrate on the invention of machines.

A novel machine accomplishes its task in a way that has not been demonstrated before. "If the invention has been described in a printed publication anywhere in the world, or if it has been in public use or on sale in this country before the date that the applicant made his invention, a patent cannot be obtained" (Schepp, 1980, p. 10). An inventor must apply for a patent within one year of describing the invention in published form, making it available for public use, or placing it for sale. Apparently, after that time the novelty wears off. The characteristic of nonobvious indicates that someone familiar with the field to which the machine is related would not have been able to draw the same conclusion as a matter of course. So changing the color of your food processor does not constitute qualification for a patent.

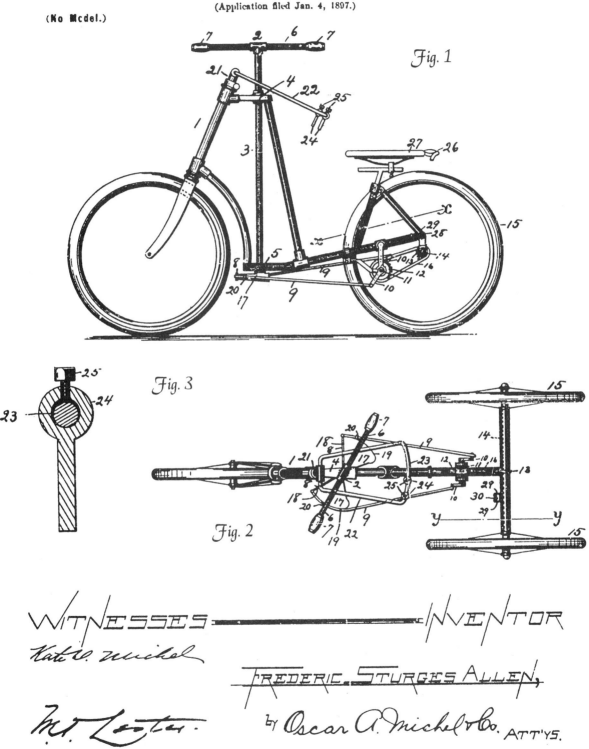

No. 606,952.

F. S. ALLEN.

TRICYCLE FOR PROPULSION BY HAND POWER.

(Application filed Jan. 4, 1897.)

Patented July 5, 1898.

(No Model.)

Fig. 1

Fig. 3

Fig. 2

WITNESSES

INVENTOR

FREDERIC STURGES ALLEN,

by Oscar A. Michel & Co. ATT'YS.

Figure 9.2. A Hand-Powered Bike (1898).

The notion of *useful* must also be addressed. It is probably safe to say that usefulness is in the *eye* of the user. With regard to getting a patent, the bottom line is that the machine must do whatever the inventor claims it can do. As already mentioned, ideas cannot be patented. And, at the Patent and Trademark Office a great machine idea begins with a machine that works.

Assuming that the invention in question meets this criteria, a patent is awarded for 20 years. Generally speaking it is not renewable. So, for 20 years after the date of issue, the inventor(s) named have the right to exclude all others from producing, using, or selling a machine that does those things for which the patent was granted. We say "those things" because the inventor must state their claims to the Patent and Trademark Office as part of the application. If granted, the patent applies only to those claims that were submitted and approved.

What the patent actually grants is the right to *exclude* others from using the invention without first obtaining permission of the inventor, or that person to whom the patent has been assigned, for that 20 year period. So if you want to invent something and use it, even sell it, go ahead (and just to make life easier, let's agree that when we refer to inventing and inventions it is something original). We are all allowed to do that within the confines of the law. It's when it comes to questions of infringement that the holder of a patent will have the stronger position.

What a Patent Does Not Do

We now know that a patent does not grant the right to produce, use, or market something. Even more to the point, obtaining a patent does not grant the right to produce, market, or use something that would violate the law or infringe upon the rights of others. So it is conceivable that you might invent an electric motor that will push your station wagon along at 200 mph, but don't try waving your patent in front of the trooper when (if?) you are pulled over for speeding. It's a nice thought really; the inventive process is not shackled by the limits of the law, just the sensible application of those efforts.

The Patent and Trademark Office and the patent, in and of itself, do not offer the inventor legal protection. Rather, in the event of litigation, the patent is a recognized document attesting to an original claim to the invention. That's not to say that they are infallible, but it's a nice piece of evidence to offer.

One other item would be worth mentioning since inventing activities in your classroom may often occur in groups. In the case of joint inventors named on a patent, the award does not protect them from each other. The patent addresses the originality of the invention, and matters of one person against another are outside of its concern. So, when a patent is granted to several inventors, each of them is accorded the same rights.

What does this mean? It means that if inventor A wants to market the invention, it is not necessary to have the permission of inventor B. Interesting? This is where legal agreements outside of patenting come into play—and they are not the domain of the Patent and Trademark Office. Here is yet another extension of this activity we call inventing, having your students draw up agreements among themselves regarding the handling of their patented work. Time to ask whose mom or dad is an attorney willing to talk to the class.

Seeing Issued Patents

Just in case the principal won't okay your field trip from Minnesota to Washington, D.C. to visit the Patent and Trademark Office, there are other options available for bringing authentic patents into your classroom. If you happen to know the patent number(s) for the patents you'd like to see, you can order them from the Patent and

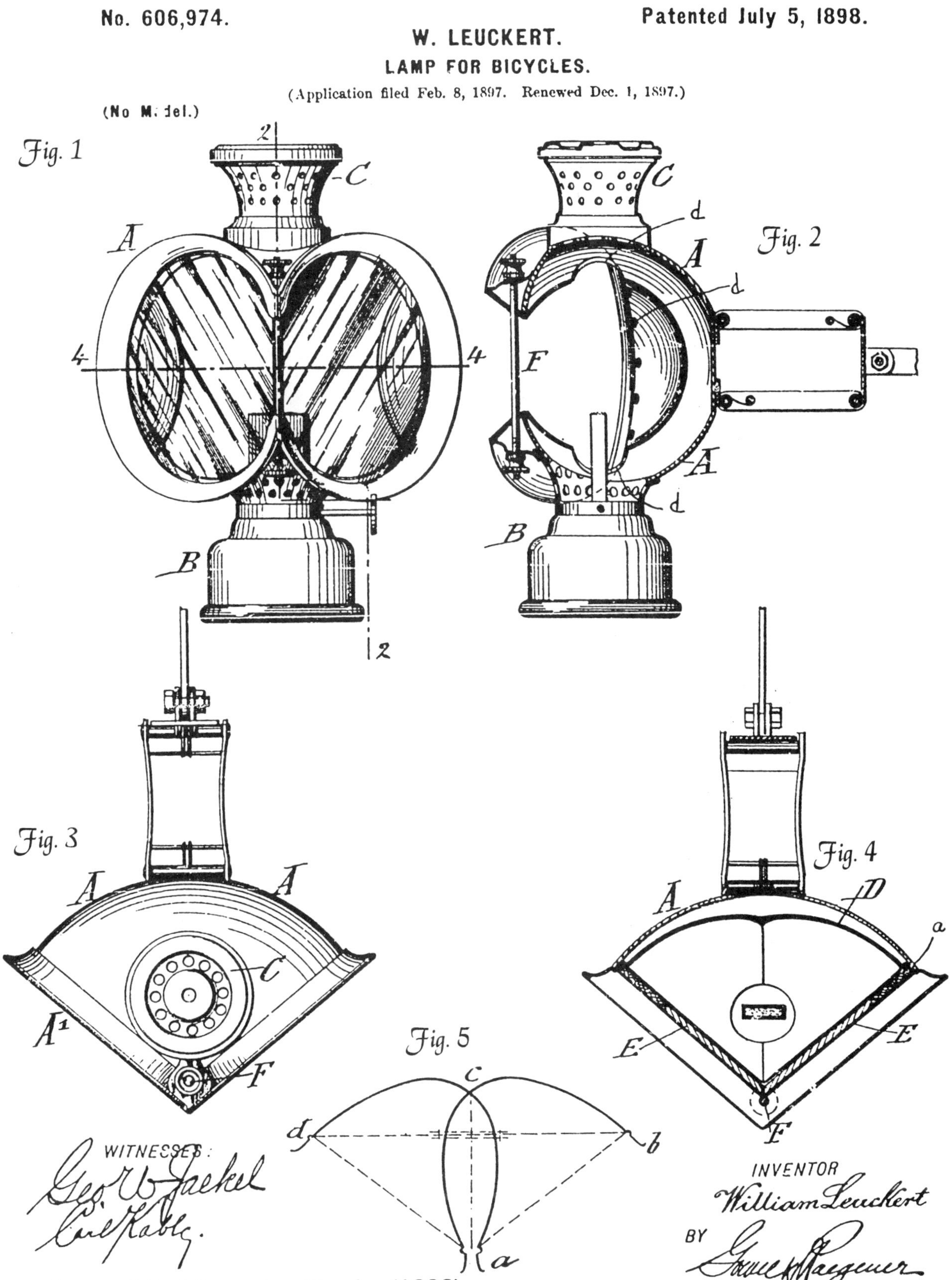

No. 606,974.

W. LEUCKERT.
LAMP FOR BICYCLES.
(Application filed Feb. 8, 1897. Renewed Dec. 1, 1897.)

Patented July 5, 1898.

(No Model.)

Fig. 1

Fig. 2

Fig. 3

Fig. 4

Fig. 5

WITNESSES:
Geo. W. Jaekel
Carl Kable.

INVENTOR
William Leuckert
BY
Gavel Wagener
ATTORNEYS.

Figure 9.3. A Lamp for Bicycles (1898).

Trademark Office. If you don't need particular patents, the *Official Gazette of the United States Patent and Trademark Office* is interesting. The *Gazette* is printed weekly and can be obtained from the Superintendent of Documents, U.S. Government Printing Office, Washington, DC 20402. (Check the major metropolitan cities in your area; some have GPO bookstores.) The subscription price for the *Gazette* might be a bit steep for your budget ($617), and really, a copy every week may be more than you need. Individual copies can be ordered ($41), and it would be nice to have one or two of those for students to use.

There are two more exciting options for patent research. Copies of patents may be reviewed at any of the 80 libraries around the country named as Patent and Trademark Depository Libraries (PTDL). The libraries serving as PTDLs maintain a numerically arranged set of patents. See the Appendix (p. 230) for the locations of these libraries. Some libraries offer more services than others.

Finally, if you have Internet access, type in *http://www.uspto.gov/* to get to the Patent and Trademark Office Web site. You can do various searches on-line, though at this time patent drawings are not available, just text. If you just want some general information about the services offered by the Patent and Trademark Office, call them at 1-800-PTO-9199.

Obtaining a Patent

Preparing an application and pursuing a patent is arduous and involved. However, it is not set up to preclude the average citizen from completing the task. While expensive, in terms of Patent and Trademark Office fees it is something an individual with a *serious* application can pursue. There is an application fee, and another fee for the successful patent issue, which add up to just over a thousand dollars. (It depends on the number of claims and the number of pages involved.) In addition, there are maintenance fees over the life of the patent. These fees are paid at 3.5, 7.5, and 11.5 years and total about $3000. The biggest expense is having someone else, an attorney or agent, do the work for you. That shouldn't sound new; such is the case with most undertakings. If an attorney or agent handles the processing of your application, the most expensive aspect will be the patent search.

The Patent Search

It is likely that by the time your students do a patent search it will be on their PC with a Patent and Trademark Office CD-ROM. For now, it is a matter of searching records. The records are categorized and cross-referenced, so you need not search from the first patent and read everything since. However, the thoroughness of the search relates directly to the success or failure of the application. Keep in mind that whether you do this yourself or turn it over to someone else it occurs *prior* to submitting an application and is referred to as a *preliminary* search. You conduct a careful examination of records to find out whether your invention and the claims you make for it have already been recognized by a previous patent. There's no way to avoid a lot of work.

Two things to know about having someone else search this for you are, a) this preliminary search incurs the bulk of expense for preparing an application, and b) no matter who does the search, the Patent and Trademark Office does not accept it as the official search. Once the application is submitted, the examiners do their own search.

Searches can be conducted at the Patent and Trademark Office, in the Public Search Room, at Crystal Plaza, 2021 Jefferson Davis Highway, Arlington, Virginia 22202. Lists of original patents and cross-referenced lists of patents for subclasses can also be ordered from the office. As previously mentioned, there are 80 libraries around the country named as Patent and Trademark Depository Libraries (PTDL), as well as Internet access. Keep in mind that Internet access is a text only service at this time.

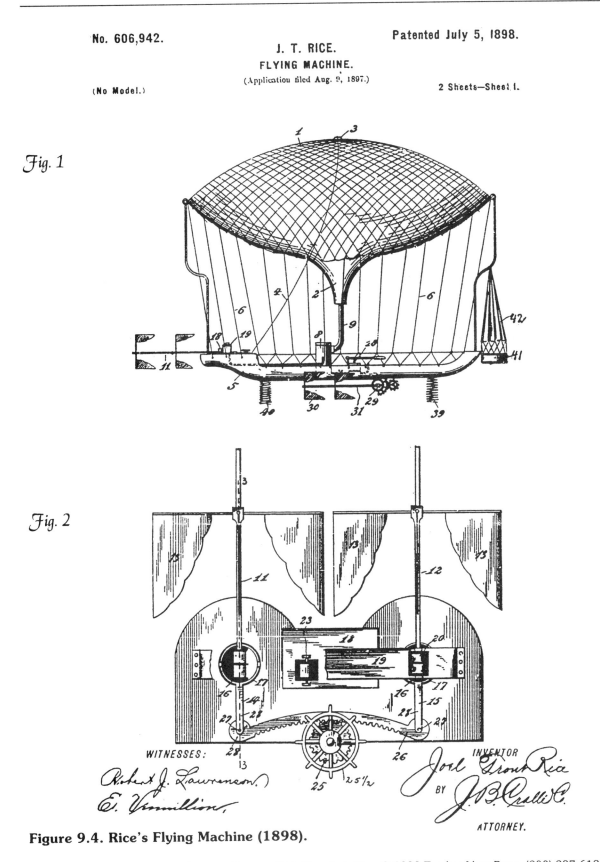

No. 606,942.

(No Model.)

J. T. RICE.
FLYING MACHINE.
(Application filed Aug. 9, 1897.)

Patented July 5, 1898.

2 Sheets—Sheet 1.

Fig. 1

Fig. 2

WITNESSES:

INVENTOR

BY

ATTORNEY.

Figure 9.4. Rice's Flying Machine (1898).

From *The Inventive Mind in Science: Creative Thinking Activities.* © 1998 Teacher Ideas Press. (800) 237-6124.

The Application

With a completed search and intact hopes for a patent, it is time to file an official application. A complete application has three components and is submitted to the U.S. Department of Commerce, Patent and Trademark Office, Assistant Secretary and Commissioner of Patents and Trademarks, Washington, DC 20231. Pretty exciting!

The Oath and Declaration

The first part of the application is a written document containing an oath or declaration and the invention specifications. The declaration identifies the inventor(s) and their citizenship, the invention, and acknowledges that to the best of their knowledge the invention is original and of their own making. Specifications include a written description of the invention and the claims the inventor(s) makes about what the invention accomplishes.

The Drawings

Second are the drawings of the invention. These must be done carefully and be fully representative of the invention with regard to claims the inventor wishes to patent. Any aspect of the machine that contributes to the claims made must be illustrated. Telling the examiner that it's too difficult to draw or explain is never a good idea. The Patent and Trademark Office also has specific requirements for the preparation of these documents. Those considered unacceptable will be returned to the applicant. *A Guide to Filing a Patent Application* has a complete explanation of the procedures and specifications. It is available from the Patent and Trademark Office (for free).

The Fees

Of course, no application is complete without the filing fee. In the case of patents there are three categories, each with its own fee schedule. The categories are: utility, design, and plant. A *utility* patent applies to machines and such. *Design* patents do not apply to the machine, but rather to a particular artistic aspect. For example, a design patent was issued for the Statue of Liberty. The patent did not cover "statues," but rather the design of this particular statue. Finally, *plant* patents deal with the invention and asexual reproduction of new and distinct varieties of plants. The inventing in this book falls under utility patents, which, by the way, happen to have the highest fees. For those who are not corporate big wigs, the 1996 basic application fee is $385. Fees are added if the applicant is presenting more than three claims. In event of a successful patent application, there will also be a patent fee of $645. Fees are also added depending on the number of pages of description and the number of sheets of drawings which must be printed when the patent is awarded.

There is one other element in this process: time. Though patent applications are handled in a timely manner, there is no doubt that this is a time-consuming project. Patent applications are not prepared in a weekend, express-mailed, and acted on by Friday. There are well over 90,000 applications submitted annually. Eighteen months for application review is a good guide to use; two years might be better. Obviously *waiting* to submit a patent does not increase one's chances of being successful.

Your Own Patent and Trademark Office

No doubt you've seen this coming. This sketch of the patenting process provides a fantastic amount of material for classroom use. Everything *we've* discussed from the Constitution to the *Gazette* could be used to design a multi-disciplinary experience that could run throughout your school year and into subsequent years. We caution, however, not to fall into the "information trap." That is, allow your students to get involved in inventing first, then let them work with all of this patents information. It is *easy* when copies of the *Gazette* are sitting there to begin with "Let's read these and be sure our invention does not copy somebody else's."

Most of what your students invent, with the possible exception of Rube Goldberg inventing, are things that are not new to us. *But they are new to your students.* The opportunity to practice generating new ideas is what this is about. If we limit their thinking before they begin, the creative moment is lost.

A Personal Patent for Your Particular People

What we have here is the basis for a fantastic inventing program in your classroom or school. With a few binders and copies of some pages provided here, you can establish your own Patent Office.

Patent Searches

Of course, the first students who invent will be the ones that establish everything. For future students to do patent searches, establish at least two sources: Patent Listings, and your own version of the *Gazette*. Here is one way to proceed.

The Listings. Beginning with your first inventing excursion, set up your own listing of patents. As students complete inventions, have them apply for a patent from you or your school (as we will discuss in the next section). Those patents, all in the particular format you adopt, can be added to your Patent Notebook in chronological order. You have a ready-made division of categories: Discovery Inventing Patents, Rube Goldberg Patents, and Practical Patents. Set up a notebook for each category. If you would like to establish subcategories, simply include a page at the beginning of each notebook that subclassifies each patent according to its number. That is, all Subcategory A patents will have numbers listed on the Subcategory A page. After one semester or school year of inventing, you'll have established a legitimate patent record for student searches in succeeding years.

What a record of student achievement this provides! Is your school working with the portfolio assessments? If so, here you have it. Imagine laying out these notebooks for Parents' Night, the PTA, or the Science Fair (English Fair, History Fair, Art Fair).

(Text continues on p. 208.)

Patents Issued

School _____

Note: Categories are limited to Discovery Inventions (DI), Rube Goldberg Inventions (RG), and Practical Inventions (PI).

Year	Inventor	Invention	Patent No.	Category
___	_____	_____	_____	_____
___	_____	_____	_____	_____
___	_____	_____	_____	_____
___	_____	_____	_____	_____
___	_____	_____	_____	_____
___	_____	_____	_____	_____
___	_____	_____	_____	_____
___	_____	_____	_____	_____
___	_____	_____	_____	_____
___	_____	_____	_____	_____
___	_____	_____	_____	_____
___	_____	_____	_____	_____
___	_____	_____	_____	_____
___	_____	_____	_____	_____
___	_____	_____	_____	_____
___	_____	_____	_____	_____
___	_____	_____	_____	_____

Patents Issued
for Discovery Inventions

School _____

Inventor(s)	Name of Invention	Patent No.

Patents Issued
for Rube Goldberg Inventions

School _____

Inventor(s)	Name of Invention	Patent No.
_____	_____	_____
_____	_____	_____
_____	_____	_____
_____	_____	_____
_____	_____	_____
_____	_____	_____
_____	_____	_____
_____	_____	_____
_____	_____	_____
_____	_____	_____
_____	_____	_____
_____	_____	_____
_____	_____	_____
_____	_____	_____
_____	_____	_____
_____	_____	_____
_____	_____	_____
_____	_____	_____

Patents Issued
for Practical Inventions

School _____

Inventor(s)	Name of Invention	Patent No.
_____	_____	_____
_____	_____	_____
_____	_____	_____
_____	_____	_____
_____	_____	_____
_____	_____	_____
_____	_____	_____
_____	_____	_____
_____	_____	_____
_____	_____	_____
_____	_____	_____
_____	_____	_____
_____	_____	_____
_____	_____	_____
_____	_____	_____
_____	_____	_____
_____	_____	_____
_____	_____	_____
_____	_____	_____

The Gazette. As a culminating activity students could publish their own version of the *Gazette*. You might include articles describing the theme of your inventing unit (the environment, communication, etc.), something from each teacher whose discipline you have touched (or your own explanation if you are teaching all of those subjects!), a word from the principal, and of course, all of those patent applications with drawings! You may start something prestigious for your school as volumes of the *Gazette* increase. Perhaps you could take this district-wide. Just imagine one student writing back to you saying he or she has just received his or her first U.S. Patent.

The Application

Students should submit a patent application after inventions have been constructed. Let's waive the fees, but require the declaration, specifications, and drawings. A sample declaration follows (p. 209). Make as many copies as you wish. The specifications page and drawing page (pp. 210–11) are generic as well. In all cases, we have minimized required writing. If the student who typically struggles with written tasks excels (or at least responds well) to the inventing activity, you may want to use care about written task requirements. Seize the motivation gains from the activity, but use your judgment to determine how much to ask.

Examining the Applications

It is understandable that you wish to retain the title of Commissioner of Patents at your school. However, that does not mean that you must examine all the patents. Select several students to serve as patent examiners. Provide the record of patents issued to your students and the submitted applications. The final word must come from the Commissioner, but the examiners make recommendations.

When examining applications, it is important to know that one invention can accomplish the same task as another invention, but must do it differently. As we've said before, that almost happens by default with Rube Goldberg inventing, which is one of the reasons it applies to the classroom so well. Be sure your examiners are aware that, for example, a new paint brush should not be denied a patent simply because paint brushes already exist. The question is whether this version applies paint in a new way. Foam brushes apply paint, but they are easier and less expensive to produce; and they do not leave bristle marks.

(Text continues on p. 212.)

Patent Application Declaration

To the designated Commissioner of Patents:

Your petitioner(s), _____

_____ ,

citizen(s) of the United States and student(s) at _____

_____ ,

requests that a patent be issued for the invention described in these pages.

I (we) state that to the best of my (our) knowledge I am (we are) the original and first inventor(s) of the invention described in these pages.

_____
Inventor's signature

_____

_____
Additional Inventors

Specifications Page

Name of Inventor(s): _____

Name of Invention: _____

In the space below describe the invention and how it works.

Patent Drawing Page

Name of Inventor(s): _____

Name of Invention: _____

In the space below draw the invention. Make sure the drawings represent all claims made by the inventor. (Be sure to illustrate everything it can do.)

The Patent Award

Just in case you're wondering, it is illegal to mark "Patented" on something that is not. None of the forms we have provided have the words "U.S. Patent" on them. Similarly, our patent certificate follows suit. In the Appendix you will find a blank version of the certificate. You can copy it as is and fill in appropriate information. If you have the means for customizing your certificate, you can do so by simply making a copy of the certificate from the Appendix. On your word processor, set the page to "portrait." Set the left and right margins to 1.5 inches and your bottom margin to 1 inch. *Set the top margin to 5.5 inches.* Type your text using a 24 pt. font. Center the text from left to right. If you use no more than four or five lines of 24 pt. type, it should print onto your page just fine.

You may do something like the following:

Official Pontiac Elementary School Patent
Awarded to Christopher Scofield
Inventor of the Automatic Balloon Popper

May it be known to all that this patent is issued to the inventor named below for the invention as named herein.

Pontiac Elementary School
Christopher Scofield
Inventor of the Automatic Balloon Popper

Awarded this **3rd** day of *February*, *1998*.

Dr. Christine Ebert
Commissioner of Patents

515
Patent Number

Then fill in the date, the patent number, and the signature of the duly designated Commissioner of Patents! A gold seal (available from office supply stores) is a nice touch. To be even more official, you can emboss the seal. Stores that make and sell rubber stamps also make embossers—those seals that Notary Publics (among others) use to make an impression in the paper. Tell them what you want to imprint, and they can make it for you. They are not expensive and last for years. It looks very impressive! Our imprint appears at the end of this chapter.

Summary

Activities with patents, U.S. and our "official" school versions, are exercises in American government. Patent laws are an official recognition of the value placed on creative thinking. Patent applications do not ask for age, gender, ethnicity, economic status, or educational background. They ask for a clear description of your invention.

There is no doubt that the patent process should keep frivolous applications from swamping examiners. Careful research, attention to detail, and time are required to do this correctly. Hmm, sounds like a real and worthwhile enterprise for students to experience. Procedures you establish in your class can be accurate representations of this process.

What of Coca-Cola? That's a product recognized around the world. Could we just cruise into the patent office, copy down the formula, and start a new company? Well no because of the time limit on patents. If Coca-Cola and products like it were patented, after 20 years the formula would be available to anyone who cared to have it. So formulas such as Coke, believe it or not, are just closely guarded secrets. Patents are not intended to hide knowledge, but rather to provide people with due recognition of creative efforts—then to share knowledge. That sharing is what enables the "progress of science and the useful arts" as described in the Constitution of the United States.

Appendix

In this section you will find:

> *Pages for assembling an Inventor's Journal;*
>
> *A set of the Invent! Cards;*
>
> *A Rube Goldberg Invention Evaluation Form;*
>
> *A listing of the Patent and Trademark Depository Libraries across the country;*
>
> *A collection of certificates ranging from a classroom patent to the Spirit of Rube Goldberg Award!*

The Inventor's Journal

You can assemble some Inventor's Journals for your students using the following two pages (pp. 217–18). Follow this procedure:

1. Begin by making a copy of the page that has "Inventor's Journal" on it. You may want to use a card stock paper if your copier can handle it. Alternatively, you may want to use a colored paper for the cover. Make one copy for each journal you wish to assemble.

2. Now reload those pages into the copier so that you can copy on the back. Use the second journal page for the back. The second page has two headings which represent one set of pages. The headings are "Inventive Ideas" and "Inventor's Sketch Pad." You might do a test run or two to find out how to load the paper. When you are done, "Inventive Ideas" and "Inventor's Sketch Pad" should be on the **back** and at the **top** of the cover page.

3. You need to decide how many pages you want to have in the journal. Each full sheet of paper that you use will account for two *sets* of pages. The book we do here will have 11 of these sets of pages.

4. Make 5 copies of the "Inventive Ideas" and "Inventor's Sketch Pad" page for each journal you want to assemble. Now, reload those copies into your copier so that you can print on the back of the pages as well. When completed, you should have pages that read "Inventive Ideas" and "Inventor's Sketch Pad" on the top of both sides of the page.

5. Place a journal cover page face down on the table so that you are reading "Inventive Ideas" and "Inventor's Sketch Pad." Place five of the copies you made in the last step on top of that page (all pages should read the same as you do this—"Inventive Ideas" on the left, "Inventor's Sketch Pad" on the right).

6. Fold the pages in half and put a couple of staples along the folded edge. There you have it! Your colleagues will be thoroughly impressed.

The *Invent! Cards*

The following six pages contain all of the 36 cards that comprise a deck of *Invent! Cards*. (See pp. 219–24.) Make as many sets as you need for your students. Though regular paper will be most economical, it is nice to run the cards on card stock. They will last considerably longer than the plain paper version. Also, keep in mind making one set of cards to use as transparencies. They can be used with an overhead projector so that everyone can see a particular combination at one time. Following the card masters is an *Invent! Cards* award certificate (p. 225), if you think it may be of use in your situation.

Inventing Award Certificates and Evaluation Form

The next three pages (226–28) offer Inventing Awards that were described in Chapter Eight. They look best when copied onto colored paper. If you want to make an impression, use one of those "parchment" types of paper. Following the certificates is an Invention Evaluation Form designed to address some of the non-traditional aspects of Rube Goldberg Inventing. (See p. 229.)

(Text continues on p. 230.)

Inventor's Sketch Pad

Inventive Ideas

From *The Inventive Mind in Science: Creative Thinking Activities.* © 1998 Teacher Ideas Press. (800) 237-6124.

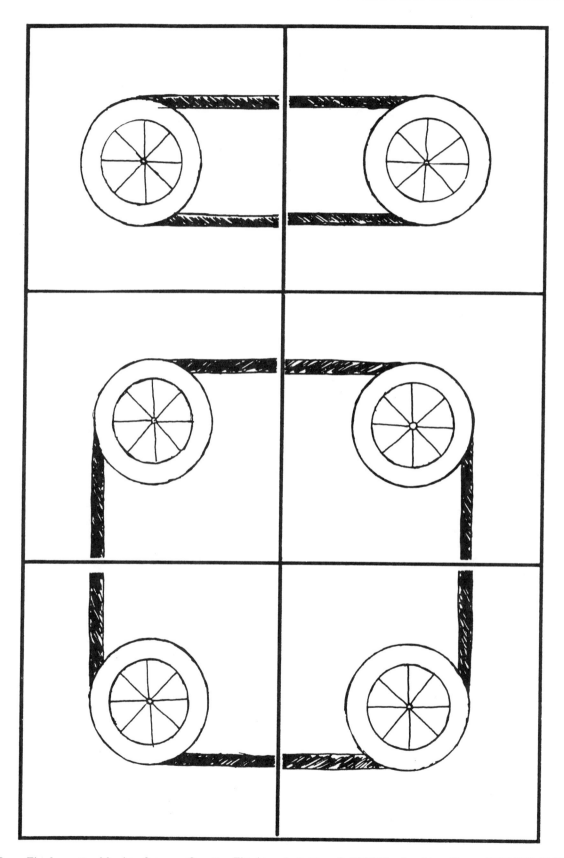

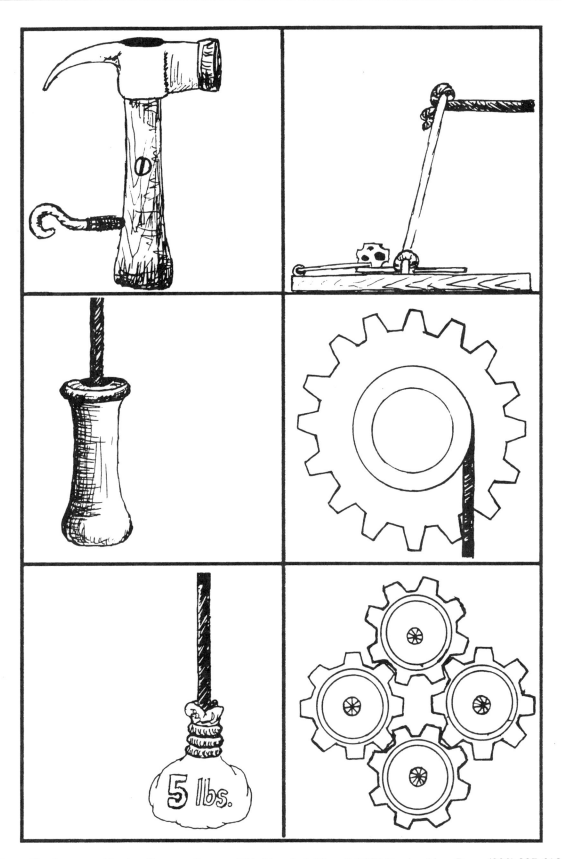

From *The Inventive Mind in Science: Creative Thinking Activities.* © 1998 Teacher Ideas Press. (800) 237-6124.

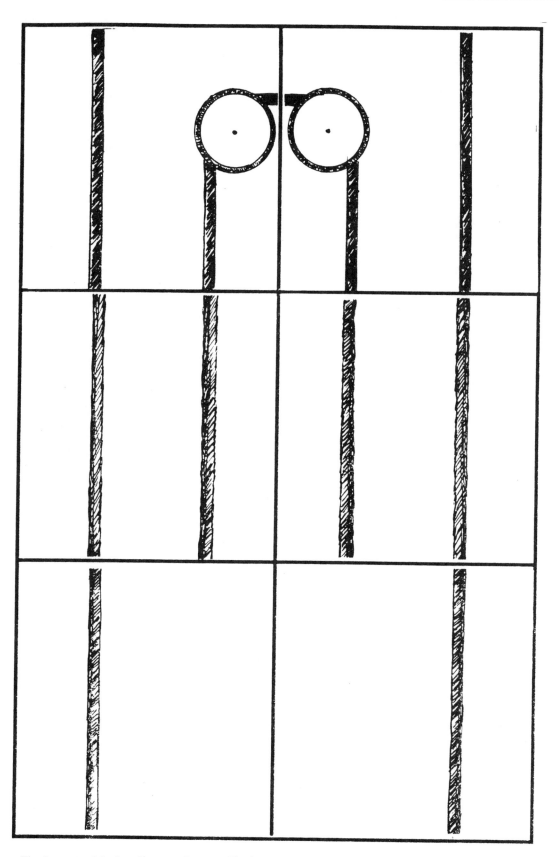

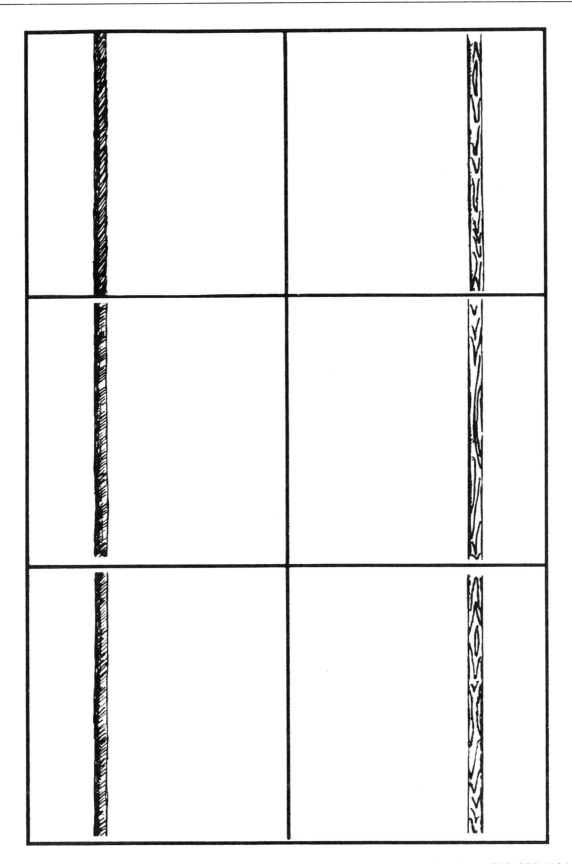

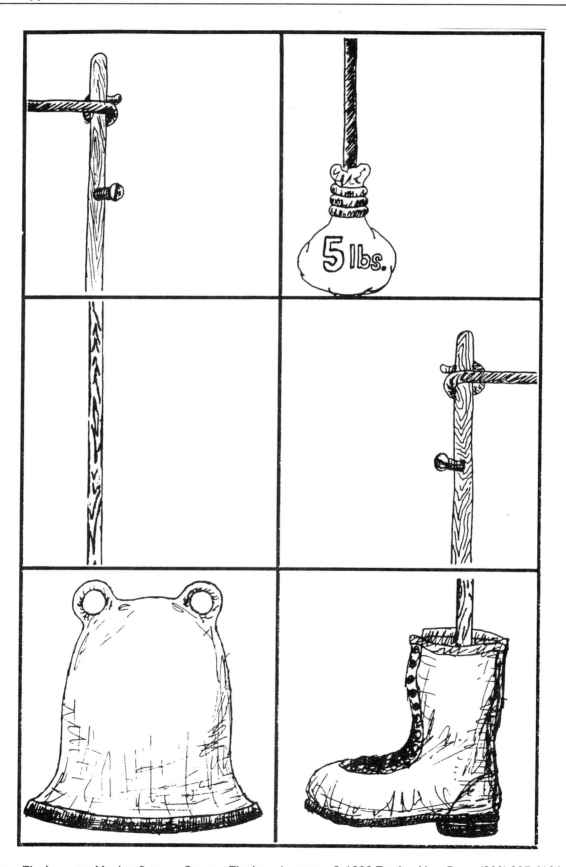

CERTIFICATE

of

INVENTION

Be it known to all that

_____

invented the

_____

_____

Awarded the   day of   , in the year

_____

The Inventive Mind in Science: Creative Thinking Activities

Recognition of Inventive Achievement

Let it be known to all that

_____

is duly recognized as the one and only inventor of the

_____

_____
Invention Commissioner

_____
Date

Recognition of Special Inventive Achievement

Know one, know all, that

_____

is hereby recognized for an invention demonstrating

_____

and so deserves our respect and admiration.

Awarded this _____ day of _____, _____.

_____
Invention Commissioner

Spirit of Rube Goldberg Award

Be it known to all that

_____

is hereby recognized for outstanding achievement
in the true spirit of Rube Goldberg

Awarded this _____ day of _____ ,
_____ .

_____
Invention Commissioner

Invention Evaluation Form

Complexity

How many steps are involved in the invention?   (circle one)

A) 1-2 (4 pts)   B) 3-4 (8 pts)   C) 5-6 (12 pts)   D) 7-8 (16 pts)   E) 9 or more (20 pts)

How many different sources of energy are involved in the invention?   (circle one)

A) 1 (4 pts)   B) 2 (8 pts)   C) 3 (12 pts)   D) 4 (16 pts)   E) 5 or more (20 pts)

Performance

How well does the invention perform   (circle one)

A) Does not work (5 pts)   B) Works with more than 2 assists (10 pts)   C) Works well with 1-2 assists (15 pts)   D) No assistance required (20 pts)

Appearance

How much humor is there in the appearance of the invention?   (circle one)

A) None (5 pts)   B) Brings a smile to your face (10 pts)   C) Makes you chuckle (15 pts)   D) Hilarious (20 pts)

How much originality is there in the appearance of the invention?   (circle one)

A) Totally traditional (5 pts)   B) One unusual use of materials/actions (10 pts)   C) Several unusual aspects (15 pts)   D) Mostly unique combinations (20 pts)

Total score: _____ + _____ + _____ + _____ + _____ = _____

Patent Information

The following pages list the 80 Patent and Trademark Depository Libraries located across the United States. The phone numbers were current when this book was written. Not all libraries offer the same range of services, so call before you line up the school bus for a field trip across the state. Following the list of PTDLs is our own version of a patent to use with your students (p. 234). Directions for formatting your word processor to customize the form are found in Chapter Nine. Don't forget those little gold seals, they lend a nice touch!

Patent and Trademark Depository Libraries

Alabama	Auburn University: Ralph Brown Draughon Library	334 844-1747
	Birmingham Public Library	205 226-3620
Alaska	(Anchorage): Z. J. Loussac Public Library	907 562-7323
Arizona	(Tempe): Daniel E. Noble Science and Engineering Library, Arizona State University	602 965-7010
Arkansas	(Little Rock): Arkansas State Library	501 682-2053
California	Los Angeles Public Library	213 228-7220
	(Sacramento): California State Library	916 654-0069
	San Diego Public Library	619 236-5813
	San Francisco Public Library	415 557-4500
	Sunnyvale Center for Innovation, Invention and Ideas	408 730-7290
Colorado	Denver Public Library	303 640-6220
Connecticut	(New Haven): Science Park Patent Library	203 786-5447
Delaware	(Newark): University of Delaware Library	302 831-2965
District of Columbia	Founders Library, Howard University	202 806-7252
Florida	(Fort Lauderdale): Broward County Main Library	954 357-7444
	Miami-Dade Public Library	305 375-2665
	Orlando: University of Central Florida Libraries	407 823-2562
	Tampa Campus Library, University of South Florida	813 974-2726

Georgia	(Atlanta): Library and Information Center, Georgia Institute of Technology	404 894-4508
Hawaii	(Honolulu): Hawaii State Public Library System	808 586-3477
Idaho	(Moscow): University of Idaho Library	208 885-6235
Illinois	Chicago Public Library	312 747-4450
	(Springfield): Illinois State Library	217 782-5659
Indiana	Indianapolis-Marion County Public Library	317 269-1741
	(West Lafayette): Siegesmund Engineering Library, Purdue University	317 494-2872
Iowa	(Des Moines): State Library of Iowa	515 281-4118
Kansas	(Wichita): Ablah Library, Wichita State Library	316 978-3155
Kentucky	Louisville Free Public Library	502 574-1611
Louisiana	(Baton Rouge): Troy H. Middleton Library, Louisiana State University	504 388-5652
Maine	(Orono): Raymond H. Fogler Library, University of Maine	207 581-1678
Maryland	(College Park): Engineering and Physical Sciences Library, University of Maryland	301 405-9157
Massachusetts	(Amherst): Physical Sciences Library, University of Massachusetts/Amherst	413 545-1370
	Boston Public Library	617 536-5400 Ext. 265
Michigan	Ann Arbor Engineering Library, University of Michigan	313 647-5735
	(Big Rapids): Abigail S. Timme Library, Ferris State University	616 592-3602
	(Detroit): Great Lakes Patent and Trademark Center, Detroit Public Library	313 833-3379
Minnesota	Minneapolis Public Library and Information Center	612 372-6570
Mississippi	(Jackson): Mississippi Library Commission	601 359-1036
Missouri	(Kansas City): Linda Hall Library	816 363-4600
	St. Louis Public Library	314 241-2288 Ext. 390

Montana	(Butte): Montana Tech of the University of Montana Library	406 496-4281
Nebraska	(Lincoln): Engineering Library, University of Nebraska-Lincoln	402 472-3411
Nevada	(Reno): University of Nevada-Reno Library	702 784-6500 Ext. 257
New Hampshire	(Concord): New Hampshire State Library	603 271-2239
New Jersey	Newark Public Library	201 733-7782
	(Piscataway): Library of Science and Medicine, Rutgers University	908 445-2895
New Mexico	(Albuquerque): Centennial Science and Engineering Library, University of New Mexico	505 277-4412
New York	(Albany): New York State Library	518 474-5355
	Buffalo and Erie County Public Library	716 858-7101
	New York Public Library, Science, Industry and Business Library	212 592-7000
North Carolina	(Raleigh): D. H. Hill Library, North Carolina State University	919 515-3280
North Dakota	(Grand Forks): Chester Fritz Library, University of North Dakota	701 777-4888
Ohio	Akron-Summit County Public Library	330 643-9075
	The Public Library of Cincinnati and Hamilton County	513 369-6936
	Cleveland Public Library	216 623-2870
	(Columbus): Ohio State University Libraries	614 292-6175
	Toledo/Lucas County Public Library	419 259-5212
Oklahoma	(Stillwater): Center for International Trade Development, Oklahoma State University	405 744-7086
Oregon	(Portland): Paul L. Boley Law Library, Lewis & Clark College	503 768-6786
Pennsylvania	The Free Library of Philadelphia	215 686-5331
	The Carnegie Library of Pittsburgh	412 622-3138
	(University Park): Pattee Library, Pennsylvania State University	814 865-4861

Puerto Rico	(Mayagüez): General Library University of Puerto Rico-Mayagüez	787 832-4040 Ext. 3459
Rhode Island	Providence Public Library	401 455-8027
South Carolina	(Clemson): R. M. Cooper Library, Clemson University	864 656-3024
South Dakota	(Rapid City): Devereaux Library, South Dakota School of Mines and Technology	605 394-6822
Tennessee	Memphis & Shelby County Public Library and Information Center	901 725-8877
	(Nashville): Stevenson Science and Engineering Library, Vanderbilt University	615 322-2717
Texas	(Austin): McKinney Engineering Library, University of Texas at Austin	512 495-4500
	(College Station): Sterling C. Evans Library, Texas A&M University	409 845-3826
	Dallas Public Library	214 670-1468
	(Houston): The Fondren Library, Rice University	713 527-8101 Ext. 2587
	(Lubbock): Texas Tech University Library (not yet operational)	
Utah	(Salt Lake City): Marriott Library, University of Utah	801 581-8394
Virginia	(Richmond): James Branch Cabell Library, Virginia Commonwealth University	804 828-1104
Washington	(Seattle): Engineering Library, University of Washington	206 543-0740
West Virginia	(Morgantown): Evansdale Library, West Virginia University	304 293-2510 Ext. 113
Wisconsin	(Madison): Kurt F. Wendt Library University of Wisconsin-Madison	608 262-6845
	Milwaukee Public Library	414 286-3051
Wyoming	(Casper): Natrona County Public Library	307 237-4935

Patent

May it be known to all that this patent is issued to the inventor named below for the invention as named herein.

Awarded this _____ day of _____ , _____.

_____   _____

Commissioner of Patents   Patent Number

References and Resources

Adams, James L. *Conceptual Blockbusting.* New York: W. W. Norton, 1979.

Bentley, Michael, and Christine Ebert. The World of Science. Belmont, CA: Wadsworth, 1996.

Bloom, Benjamin S., ed. *Taxonomy of Educational Objectives—The Classification of Educational Goals, Handbook 1: Cognitive Domain.* New York: David McKay, 1956.

Bragdon, Allen D. *Ingenious Inventions of Domestic Utility.* New York: Harper & Row, 1989.

Calandra, A. "The Barometer Story," *Current Science Teacher* (January 6, 1964): 14.

Caney, Steven. *Steven Caney's Invention Book.* New York: Workman, 1985.

Costa, A. L., ed. *Developing Minds—A Resource Book for Teaching Thinking.* Alexandria, VA: Association for Supervision and Curriculum Development, 1985.

DeVito, Alfred. *Creative Wellsprings for Science Teaching.* West Lafayette, IN: Creative Ventures, 1989.

Dunn, Susan, and Rob Larson. *Design Technology: Children's Engineering.* New York: The Falmer Press, 1990.

Ebert, Christine, and Edward Ebert. *The Invent! Cards: A Teacher's Guide.* Riverview, FL: Idea Factory, 1989.

Ebert, Edward S. "The Cognitive Spiral: Creative Thinking and Cognitive Processing," *The Journal of Creative Behavior* 28, no. 4 (1994): 275–90.

Edwards, Betty. *Drawing on the Right Side of the Brain.* Los Angeles: J. P. Tarcher, 1979.

Flack, Jerry D. *Inventing, Inventions, and Inventors.* Englewood, CO: Teacher Ideas Press, 1989.

Guilford, J. P. "The Three Faces of Intellect," *American Psychologist* 14 (1959): 469–79.

Kuehn, Christine. "Inventing: Creative Sciencing," *Childhood Education* 65 (1988): 5–7.

Macaulay, David. *The Way Things Work.* Boston: Houghton Mifflin, 1988.

Magic Eye—A New Way of Looking at the World. Kansas City, MO: Andrews and McMeel, 1994.

Marzio, Peter C. *Rube Goldberg: His Life and Work.* New York: Harper & Row, 1973.

Mayer, Richard E. *Thinking, Problem Solving, Cognition*. New York: W. H. Freeman, 1983.

McCormack, Alan J. *Inventors Workshop*. Belmont, CA: David S. Lake, 1981.

Mednick, S. A. "The Associative Basis of the Creative Process," *Psychological Review* 69 (1962): 220–32.

Panati, Charles. *Extraordinary Origins of Everyday Things*. New York: Harper & Row, 1987.

———. *Browser's Book of Beginnings: Origins of Everything Under, and Including, the Sun*. Boston: Houghton Mifflin, 1984.

Papallo, George. *What Makes It Work*. New York: Arco, 1976.

Petroski, Henry. *The Evolution of Useful Things*. New York: Alfred A. Knopf, 1993.

Schepp, Solomon J., ed. *The Concise Guide to Patents, Trademarks and Copyrights*. New York: Bell, 1980.

Short, Robert L. *The Gospel According to Peanuts*. Richmond, VA: John Knox, 1966.

Stanish, Bob. *The Unconventional Invention Book*. Carthage, IL: Good Apple, 1981.

Torrance, E. Paul. *The Torrance Tests of Creative Thinking: Technica—norms Manual* (research ed.). Princeton, NJ: Personnel Press, 1966.

Weiss, Harvey. *How to Be an Inventor*. New York: Thomas Y. Crowell, 1980.

Whitehead, Alfred North. *Science and the Modern World*. New York: Macmillan, 1967.

Index

About the Authors

Dr. Christine Ebert is an Associate Professor of Science Education at the University of South Carolina. Her work in science education focuses on conceptual change and development in students' understanding of science principles. In addition, she teaches courses in thinking and reasoning, and is extensively involved with collaboration between elementary schools and the university. Dr. Ebert has presented her work on science and creative thinking at conferences across the country and around the world.

Dr. Edward S. Ebert II is an Associate Professor of Education at Coker College in South Carolina. With a degree in Psychological Foundations of Education, Dr. Ebert teaches courses in educational psychology, child development, educational philosophy, elementary science methods, and creative problem solving.

From **Teacher Ideas Press**

CRITICAL SQUARES: Games of Critical Thinking and Understanding
Shari Tishman and Albert Andrade

Developed through Project Zero at the Harvard School of Education, these simple but powerful games are designed to develop students' critical-thinking skills and deepen their understanding of topics they are already studying. AND students love them! **Grades 3–12.**
xv, 123p. 8½x11 paper ISBN 1-56308-490-2

THE BEANSTALK AND BEYOND: Developing Critical Thinking Through Fairy Tales
Joan M. Wolf

Turn fairy tales and fairy-tale characters into a springboard for learning with this enchanting book! A multitude of activities challenge students to move beyond the simplistic study of fairy tales to develop problem-solving, critical-thinking, and creative-writing skills. **Grades 4–8.**
xiii, 133p. 8½x11 paper ISBN 1-56308-482-1

CREATIVE TEACHING: Ideas to Boost Student Interest
James P. Downing

Learn how to tap into your hidden creativity, engage students in the learning process, and foster creative thinking and expression with 75 activities, sample lessons, and numerous tips to get you started. **Grades K–12.**
xiii, 225p. 8½x11 paper ISBN 1-56308-476-7

INVENTING, INVENTIONS, AND INVENTORS
Jerry D. Flack

Flack's exciting, mind-stretching activities illuminate a rich, interdisciplinary field of study. Investigating inventions of the past and the present, funny inventions, and inventions we may see in the future provides a natural springboard to creative thinking. **Grades 7–9.** *(Adaptable for many grades.)*
xi, 148p. 8½x11 paper ISBN 0-87287-747-7

SIMPLE MACHINES MADE SIMPLE
Ralph E. St. Andre

Help students learn scientific principles and simple mechanics through hands-on cooperative learning activities that use inexpensive materials (e.g. tape, paper clips, coat hangers) to build levers, windmills, pulleys, and more! **Grades 3–8.**
xix, 150p. 8½x11 paper ISBN 1-56308-104-0

BLAST OFF! Rocketry for Elementary and Middle School Students
Leona Brattland Nielsen

You'll launch excitement in the classroom with this complete teaching package on rocketry. It's packed with fascinating facts and motivational activities! **Grades 4–8.**
viii, 109p. 8½x11 paper ISBN 1-56308-438-4

For a FREE catalog or to place an order, please contact:

Teacher Ideas Press
Dept. B63 · P.O. Box 6633 · Englewood, CO 80155-6633
1-800-237-6124, ext. 1 · Fax: 303-220-8843 · E-mail: lu-books@lu.com

 Check out the TIP Web site!
www.lu.com/tip